THE

# LOCH FISHER'

Stan Headley was born in Fife, but his family moved to
Orkney when he was seven. His youth was spent hunting
rabbits and fishing off the village pier. He was introduced
to trout fishing at the age of eight and, although his first
love in those days was sea fishing, he made almost all of his
pocket money tying trout flies. After wandering about the
UK and the Continent for a few years, he returned to
Orkney in 1975 and devoted every spare minute to learning
all he could about loch fishing for wild trout. His search for
knowledge has taken him to most of the best wild trout
fishing in Scotland and Ireland. He started writing articles
for the national angling press in the early 1980s, and the
high spot of his fishing career was winning the Scottish
National Fly Fishing Championship in 1990. Stan Headley
is the author of the highly successful *Trout & Salmon Flies of
Scotland*.

# THE
# LOCH FISHER'S BIBLE

STAN HEADLEY

ROBERT HALE · LONDON

ISBN-10: 0-7090-8142-1
ISBN-13: 978-0-7090-8142-5

Robert Hale Limited
Clerkenwell House
Clerkenwell Green
London EC1R 0HT

*A catalogue record for this book is available from the British Library*

2 4 6 8 10 9 7 5 3

Typeset in 10/14pt Palatino
Printed in Great Britain by
St Edmundsbury Press Limited,
Bury St Edmunds, Suffolk
and bound by
Woolnough Bookbinding Limited

# CONTENTS

# Acknowledgements

To try to thank each and every individual who has, perhaps unwittingly, aided and abetted me in the production of this book would be impossible. So, I would like to start by thanking, and apologising to, all those who feel they deserve a mention but fail to find their name listed below.

As this work has been the product of a lifetime's experience, I would like to thank the people who have provided me life-long support along the wet and wonderful road that is Scottish loch fishing. My undying thanks go to:

My beloved daughters, Catriona, Nadine and Marina, who put up with my summer-long absences with fortitude and forbearance, and learnt not to talk when the weather forecasts were on the 'telly';

'Stormin'' Norman Irvine, the best boat partner any loch fisher could hope to have, and someone who has stimulated my thinking on matters piscatorial more times than he will ever know;

My old man, Ed Headley, who got me started along that same road and who I hoped would read this book in his twilight years. Unfortunately, this cannot now happen as he sadly passed away in May 2004.

And, Billy 'Bumble Bill' Sinclair, a curmudgeonly old bastard, but a great friend and loyal supporter.

Now, on to those who turned up, unexpected and unlooked-for, to supply invaluable aid, succour and friendship (in alphabetical order):

George Barron, Brian Bingham, Mark Bowler, Davie 'Chaff' Chalmers, Jeremy Clark, Gordon and Katherine Crawford,

Keith Dunbar, Sandy Leventon, Eddie Maudling, Eddie McCarthy, Sandy McConnachie, Iain Muir, Neil Patterson, Andy Wren, Louise Williams, Paul Young.

All those kind souls who gave of their unrivalled skills and valuable time to help see this work to fruition (again, in alphabetical order):

Ian 'Coop' Cooper, for his photographic expertise; Katherine Crawford for all her help with my abominable punctuation; Colin 'Puck' Kirkpatrick, for his exquisite and artistic outdoor photography; Terry Lambert, for his stunning artwork; Gerry MacDonald, for his help with the flies; all those at Robert Hale (Publishing) Ltd., and Martin Kendall in particular.

And lastly, my respect and admiration must go to anyone out there who works tirelessly, and for little reward, to ensure that our wild fish heritage does not die but will continue to delight us all for generations to come.

May the gods of fishing bless you all!

Stan Headley
*November 2004*

# Illustrations

**Colour**

**Text diagrams**

**Illustration credits**

*Colour illustrations*
Ian Cooper: 1–6. Colin 'Puck' Kirkpatrick: 7–23.

*Text diagrams*
Figs 1–14: Terry Lambert.

# Introduction

This book has been lying, fermenting, in my brain for nearly twenty years now. The first synopsis was put together in 1985, and it has been taken out, rewritten, hashed about, pored over and put back more times than I care to remember.

I feel this is a book that needed to be written – if not by me, then by someone who knows and loves the lochs and wild trout of Scotland as much as I do. A detailed, comprehensive and authoritative commentary on the lochs and loch fishing of Scotland hasn't been successfully attempted since R.C. Bridgett passed over to that perfect drift in the sky. And now, more than ever, when much of what we know and love is threatened by the eroding effects of civilisation and urbanisation, Scottish loch fishing requires a book all of its own. I sincerely hope that this work addresses that lack, although whether it is comprehensive or not is, ultimately, for the reader to decide.

Whenever I have written of Scotland and its fishing I have felt deeply privileged to have done so. It is a wonderful subject, full of infinite variety and immeasurable beauty and splendour. Whether the matter under discussion – massive Western Isles sea-run fish, the wondrous trophy brown trout of the far north, the fast and furious scrappers of the Highland lochs, the characters that lend humour, gravitas and colour to the sport, or simply the tactics, techniques and fly patterns that are synonymous with loch fishing – there is always a distinct flavour of time, tradition and durability that is uniquely Scottish.

I hope my deep love of the subject matter comes through these poorly crafted words. All I can say in my defence, if one is needed, is that I am a fisherman who needs to write, and not a writer in search of a subject.

I hope we can meet by the side of some loch, sit in the heather, share a dram, admire each other's fly boxes and simply bask in the joy of just being there. Until that day, fish well and fare well!

---

### TIPS AND TOOLS

To look out the window or at a weather forecast and decide it is hopeless to go fishing is a self-fulfilling prophecy. It is impossible to prove the weather and the forecasters wrong by staying at home. The old adage that 'as long as your flies are in the water there's always hope' should be tattooed on some exposed part of every fisherman's body!

# Abbreviations

AFTM/ A form of fly rod rating system devised by the American
aftm Fishing Tackle Manufacturers. The system defines the
amount of weight required to make the fly rod flex to a
specific measure and then allocates a number, e.g. AFTM 7.
Fly lines also are awarded AFTM numbers, defined by the
amount of weight within a specific length, which then allows
them to be matched with rods which share a similar rating.
The system was devised to be used with DT (see below) lines.
To match a WF (see below) line to a rod, add 1 to the line
rating, e.g. a rod with a rating of 7 generally requires a DT7
line, or a WF8.

b.s. Breaking strain. A means by which the strength of monofilament material is gauged.

DT Double taper. A line configuration. The simplest explanation
is that the profile of the line has the thickest part (the belly) in
the middle of the line and the extreme forward and rear parts
of the line taper down to fine points.

H-H Half-hog. A very versatile style of fly with a deer-hair wing.

pH A scientific term used to define the relevant acidity or alka-
linity of a solution. The lower the number, i.e. <pH7 the more
acidic the solution, the greater, i.e. >pH7, the more alkaline.

r/l Reflected light. Light which enters the eye after bouncing of
any non-translucent surface or object. Almost everything we
see is a product of reflected light. (See t/l, below).

SNH Scottish Natural Heritage. The Scottish equivalent of English
Nature and the governmental body charged with the protection of the natural environment North of the Border.

sp. Species, as in Caenis sp.

| | |
|---|---|
| SSSI | Site of special scientific interest. A designation given by SNH to an area of great environmental importance. |
| t/l | Transmitted light. Light which enters the eye after passing through a translucent object or surface. Much of what a fish sees is a product of transmitted light. (see r/l, above) |
| UV | Ultra-violet. A naturally occurring component of sunlight which is invisible to the human eye, but which makes fluorescent materials glow with enlivened brightness. |
| WF | Weight forward. A line configuration. The simplest explanation is that the line profile has the heaviest, bulkiest part (the belly) immediately behind the forward tapered section, i.e. the weight of the line is forward of the middle. The longest part of a WF line lies behind the belly and is 'running line' and allows maximisation of casting potential. A WF line is like a dart whilst a DT line is like a javelin. |
| < | less than |
| > | more than |

# 1 Scottish Wild Brown Trout: A Biological, Geographical and Historical Setting

## And in the beginning …

Many thousands of years ago, as the glaciers of the last Ice Age receded from the British Isles, fish inched out of the saline waters and into the rushing, tumbling meltwater that scoured the semi-frozen land. There was nowhere else for them to have come from but the sea; almost all of Britain, and certainly all of Scotland, had been under a world of ice for hundreds of years, and all life on land and in water was eradicated when the ice came and stayed. But when the ice gave up and left, those questing fish found an ecological vacuum, and they explored every wet inch of it.

We would have recognised almost all those fish – barring perhaps arctic char, fresh from the sea, which not many of us are familiar with. Salmon and sea trout, sticklebacks and eels, sturgeons and shads, anything with a tolerance of salt, would have pushed up the virgin water, looking for a place that suited them. But what would these first brave explorers have found? A barren land, almost devoid of life and growing things: a land of boulders, terminal moraines with deep waters behind them, screes, glaciers stranded like whales on a beach, and rushing waters. And just as migratory salmonids flourish today in Scotland's bleakest environments, such as the western and northern coasts, back then they would have considered the geology and climate of the immediate post-glacial period of Scottish history as ideal.

The vital aspect of this colonisation is that few, if any, explorers would have had any desire to stay on. Salmon and sea trout would have deposited their eggs in suitable gravels and returned to the sea. The juvenile fish would have found enough sustenance in the nutrient-poor waters to reach maturity before making a headlong rush back to the welcoming waters of the sea. Most fish trapped in lochs and tarns would have perished, due to a variety of factors that would have included lack of nutrition, inability to complete their life cycles, winter freeze-up and lack of *lebensraum*.

But, against the trend, a few isolated populations of trout and char would establish themselves, living on plankton in deep, cold lakes far from their natural marine environment. Their very presence in these oligotrophic (nutrient-poor but oxygen-rich) waters would begin to alter the water chemistry and the fauna and flora of their environment. Lower and higher life forms could now establish themselves because fish swam the waters – phytoplankton and higher plants would benefit from the waste products of fish life and the carcasses of the dead. Insect life would likewise gain from the interaction of other life forms. The processing and reprocessing of nutrients would then develop its own momentum and, just as the snowball gathers more snow to itself as it rolls down the slope, so life, by its very presence and impetus would pile species upon species, the consequences of life being inevitable and irresistible.

It wouldn't have taken long, but soon every accessible piece of water in Scotland would have had its complement of fish – fish that came originally from the sea but eventually stayed to prosper. Char in the high tarns and trout on the slopes and in the glens. Salmon and sea trout would still come and go, but now the land had brown trout that were the colour of the sky, the rocks and the heather, and they gradually adapted to fit, neatly and snugly, into the gigantic jigsaw that is Scotland and the dynamic process that we call Nature.

Initially, then, trout would have been migratory, because the instinct would have been strong. Also, the land and its ground water would have been incapable of sustaining large quantities of adult fish and bringing them on to maturity. But, as the climate and the fertility of the land improved, and these benefits were transmitted to the water, so fish using these rapidly improving watercourses and impoundments would have gradually lost the desire to return to the sea and its hazards.

We can witness this effect still working today. In the far west of Scotland one of the many and varied factors detrimentally affecting sea trout populations is that a great many of their favoured waters are now considerably more fertile than they were, say, thirty years ago. Domestic effluent, forestry, agriculture, aquaculture and other forms of husbandry in the catchment areas are adding nitrates and phosphates into waters that once produced valuable runs of migratory fish because of their low ability to sustain adult populations. Now that the fish have not the environmental or nutritional need to run to the sea to survive and mature, most of them simply stay at home. This is by no means the sole cause of sea trout decline in the west, but it is a contributory factor.

But to return to those early days … The improving fertility of the land and its waters, both rivers and lochs, would have consolidated wild trout populations everywhere. There would have been healthy populations of migratory trout, which, as we have seen, would have led to increasing amounts of non-migratory populations.

## The Migratory Instinct

The migratory instinct of salmonids, particularly trout, is a fascinating aspect of their behaviour. We have a tendency to classify sea trout as migratory and brown trout as non-migratory, and to consider them as two separate species. This is a fallacy and does not help us understand the subject matter. Brown trout and sea trout are, biologically and taxo-nomically, the same fish. It is only in aspects of their behaviour that they differ: one stays at home (is non-migratory) and one goes to sea (is migratory). But even that is not accurate, because the brown trout that is hatched in a burn and travels down to the loch to live displays migratory instincts in doing so. The gleaming bar of silver which is a sea trout fresh from the sea may have spent many years contentedly at home in fresh water, displaying no overt migratory instincts at all until, at last, it felt the irresistible call of the sea. And, to confuse the matter even more, from almost every batch of eggs deposited in the gravel by a breeding pair of trout, fish will hatch that will show every different degree of migratory behaviour. The burn trout of more years than ounces that tries to stay in the same pool in the burn that saw its first wriggling day, and the majestic silvery torpedo (with fewer years than pounds) that will swim many hundreds of miles of salty water – both can originate from the same batch of eggs.

In Orkney there is a system of lochs, connected to the sea, which displays every aspect of migratory behaviour possible. The Harray/Stenness/Scapa Flow system is a classic case of its kind.

Harray is a typical Scottish wild trout loch with many tributary burns which provide excellent spawning facilities. Stenness is a brackish loch which connects to Harray in the north and the Scapa Flow to the south, has few spawning burns of its own, contains a mixed population of sea and estuarine trout, and relies heavily on Harray spawning burns for its annual recruitment of juvenile trout. Scapa Flow, an extension of the Atlantic Ocean, contains a healthy (well, at least it *was* healthy before the proliferation of salmon farms) population of sea trout which, again, relies on Harray spawning burns for a large proportion of its recruitment.

The spawning burns of Harray contain indigenous and migratory stock from the whole system. They take Stenness breeding fish and return juvenile trout, which can remain in Harray, do a short migration to Stenness, or continue their long downstream migration to the salt water of Scapa Flow. This is what biologists generally describe as a fully integrated and dynamic system. Cock brown trout that have never left Harray spawning burns will fertilise eggs and produce fry that will eventually swim the tides of the Atlantic or hunt sticklebacks and eels in the Stenness shallows. Conversely, Scapa sea trout will leave in that same Harray spawning burn a small portion of their progeny that will never have the urge to leave it. Members of the same brood will spread themselves throughout the whole system: in fresh, brackish or salt water. This is not by any means a unique or exceptional case. To a greater or lesser extent, similar systems and interactions exist wherever trout swim

Many years ago I remember reading a couple of interesting studies done on river systems containing sea trout populations. One was done on a sewin river in Wales (I forget which one) and the other on the River Earn in Scotland, and to the best of my recollection, they were carried out totally independently of one another. The fascinating aspect of the studies was that part of their findings on population dynamics was virtually identical – in both cases one-third of the returning fish (sea trout) were males, and one-third of the stay-at-homes in the river (brown trout) were females. This is too neat to be ignored. The riparian environment typically carrying migratory stock is very often not

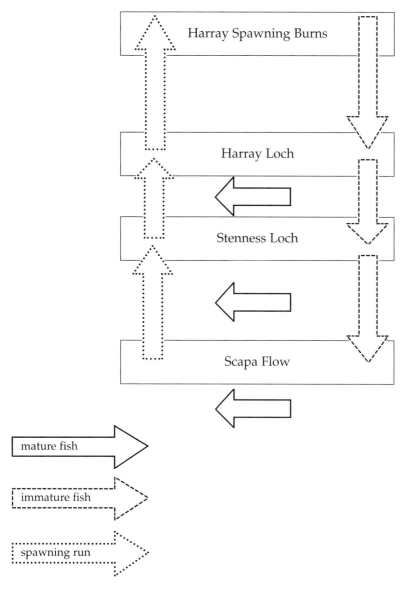

*Fig. 1    A dynamic loch system and how it works*

capable of providing the larger female fish with the nutritional requirements to produce large quantities of eggs (the ovaries of a 5 lb sea trout
may contain as much as 1 lb of eggs). But – and it is an important 'but'
– the same habitat is eminently capable of providing nutrition

adequate to form the soft roes within the males, particularly as the resident cock fish are typically much smaller than the returning/migratory hens.

But that is not the end of the story. Should there be disaster affecting either the river or the sea, elements exist in whichever is unaffected to ensure reconstruction of future populations. Nature does her level best to cover all the bets and ensure, to the best of her ability, that the population survives. Not only are all the eggs not consigned to one basket (no pun intended) – i.e. a disaster in the river or the sea won't eradicate the whole population – but also the migratory and resident populations interlock like pieces of a jigsaw: the two-thirds of resident males matching the two-thirds of returning hens, and the one-third of resident hens matching the one-third of returning cocks. The symmetry of this natural solution to a natural problem is elegant and beautiful. Mind you, introduce the destructive element of uncaring humanity into such a finely balanced system and it can all come tumbling down like a house of cards; the effects of Man are to nature's finely balanced systems what a fast-moving half-brick is to a plate glass window!

Sea trout are a fascinating development within the trout family. Their very presence, or lack of it, can be mystifying. In fact, when it comes to the study of sea trout there are more questions than answers, and I have never understood why more scientists in search of Ph.D material do not feel the need to address the problem.

The theory that migratory trout are largely a product of low nutritional productivity in their natal streams does not, however, explain the presence of sea trout in the machair lochs of the Western Isles. These lochs are highly productive, with excellent resident trout populations, but the sea trout that are caught from them every autumn are some of the finest migratory trout to be found anywhere. Perhaps the picture starts to make more sense if one considers that, although the lochs sitting on the fertile machair are themselves highly productive, the spawning streams which feed them are not, and nor are the upper lochs of the system, to which the fish are bound. We will discuss machair lochs, their trout and appropriate fishing techniques in later chapters.

Another puzzling aspect of sea trout migration is why they should be present in one river/loch system and almost totally absent in a reasonably similar neighbouring one. Sutherland's River Helmsdale has a good run of sea trout, for which the Association water in and about the town of Helmsdale is relatively famous. Just round the corner (though, admittedly, in a different county) lies the River Thurso, in which the sea trout is a very rare beast indeed. My experience of fishing the Helmsdale is not great, but when I have been on it brown trout have not been particularly evident; on the Thurso, however, indigenous river trout are common. So what have we got? The Helmsdale has good sea trout and few river browns (even if the Badanloch loch system from which it flows is heaving with the wee beasties), whilst the Thurso has hordes of hungry brown trout and no sea trout. One theory which attempts to address this conundrum has it that rivers without lochs close to the estuary tend not to hold sea trout runs – but both these rivers have lochs in their courses, and the Thurso's loch is closer to the estuary than those of the Helmsdale. If nutritional demands and population pressure should lead to a migrational movement to the sea, then the Thurso should be home to world-class sea trout stocks. It is not! If the Thurso is a good salmon river because it is a poor home for adult and developing fish (and the best salmon rivers tend to be in poor trout areas – do we have an inter-species juvenile compatibility/competition question confusing the issue?), why then does this not also apply to its trout population? If it is a good habitat for developing fish and capable of rearing them to successful maturity then why do Thurso trout rarely exceed 8 oz?

At the end of the twentieth century, Eddie McCarthy, in his role as River Superintendent, did his level best to develop a run of sea trout in the Thurso. He brought stock from the West Coast and introduced it to appropriate regions of the river – and, it must be said, had encouraging results over the period of the experiment. But when introductions of sea trout fry were discontinued the embryonic run collapsed, and the situation returned to the *status quo ante*. In retrospect, it is easy to say that the experiment was doomed to failure. All the essential criteria to create a sea trout river were already in place if Nature had wished to so categorise the Thurso. Eddie's sterling efforts were in vain simply because some intangible, unquantifiable factor was missing.

To recap, all trout have some degree of migratory instinct. The migratory imperative is, for the most part, a solution to the problem of stock density and nutritional requirements. Whether a trout moves a few metres down the spawning stream or ends up exploring the coast-line of a whole new country, the motivation is the same, and it is a migration. And the whole subject of trout migration raises more ques-tions than answers, and that's a fact!

## A Fisherman's Biology of Trout

So, apart from migratory instinct, what are the important features of trout biology that affect our pursuit of the species?

Prime amongst them must be feeding behaviour. Whenever we catch a trout it has very recently indulged in feeding activity – even though it was trying to eat something totally inedible. The two things go together: if a trout doesn't indulge in feeding behaviour when you chuck your flies at him, then you are not likely to catch him.

Trout are exceedingly voracious creatures. I once said that if trout grew to the size of sharks we'd never trail our fingers in the water on a hot day. I'll go even further than that; if trout grew to the size of sharks there'd be fewer sharks about. What trout do tends to be in miniature and largely happening to insects, so we see it as endearing and cute (the insect doesn't!). However, a trout is a cold-blooded crea-ture, an ectotherm, and its nutritional requirements and motivation towards feeding are not like ours. How often have you heard a brother angler say 'I'm going to stick it out a little while longer. They've got to eat sometime!' This is a classic anthropomorphism,* and in the case of angling, anthropomorphism totally undermines our understanding of trout behaviour. By and large, trout do not need to feed every day. They probably don't experience anything like hunger *per se*, and eat for one purpose and one only: and that is to fuel up the engine. Small, juvenile

* Just in case anyone is in doubt about the meaning of such a word I'll try to explain. We've all come across the archetypal old lady who thinks her toy dog is a child, feeds it chocolates, has wee jackets to put on it when it goes outside, talks to in the third person – 'Is doodums hungwy den?', etc., etc. The poor wee mutt will be overweight, have serious health problems including unbelievable flatulence, and be generally screwed up! Anthropomorphism is the act of turning all animals and other non-human life forms into little 'people', and imbuing them with the thoughts, desires and emotions of humans.

fish will feed whenever the opportunity arises, and because their requirements are small, this can be done on a daily basis, all things being equal. I've often wondered whether this is a dietary requirement or simply an attempt to swiftly achieve a size where everything else doesn't regard you as a succulent mouthful? Bigger trout (say from a pound in weight upwards) have a complicated mathematical equation to solve before they feed, and it goes something like this – 'There's a juicy fly sitting in the surface film. If I swim up through 1.5 metres of water to capture it (and of course swim back through the same 1.5 metres of water after I've eaten it), will I gain enough nutrition from said fly to replace the energy required to capture the sod? And what if, as I approach said fly in a cunning manner, a cheeky young whipper-snapper of a juvenile trout comes racing in and takes it off my nose – how often can I afford for this to happen before I "turn my fins up" through malnutrition?'

This is one of the reasons why we catch more juvenile/small trout than big ones. Small fish will have a go, because it is easier for them to keep their nutritional bank balance in credit, allowing them to take a chance on an unknown (your fly!); the bigger fish must be sure, a) that it is edible, b) he is going to get it, and c) that he won't be depleting his nutritional credit by doing so. This is the prime reason why, in hatch scenarios, small fish start feeding first and big fish start to feed late or at the end of the hatch. It is also the reason why big fish do like big meals, and, in wild conditions particularly, small fish are plankton (daphnia) feeders and the big fish feed on the plankton feeders: rather than chase the micro-creatures it is better to let a small fish eat them, then eat the small fish. It's a bit like eating the sandwich and the waiter who brings it, if you get my drift!

Trout alter their feeding habits to suit their environment and their own metabolism. In some environments it is true that remarkably big fish can do well on a planktonic diet but only where production of such creatures is in very large quantities – and this rarely, if ever, applies to a Scottish loch. It is a truism that big fish like a good feed. Stenness loch fish, in excess of 2 lbs, regularly contain eels up to 24 in. (60 cm) in length. This is quite a mouthful! From an angling perspective this has its drawbacks and not just the obvious one of trying to replicate a 60 cm eel with something you can chuck on a single-handed fly rod. A food item of this size can take a long time to digest, and in all probability this means that any fish with half a metre of eel hanging out of its mouth makes a poor target for a fly-fisherman.

The metabolism of any fish is slow, but for a large trout the time spent between big feeds make a mockery of the anthropomorphic angler's statement, 'Don't worry, they've got to feed sometime.' They do indeed, but that time will most likely be measured in weeks, not hours. Just the other night a TV programme about African wildlife showed a python eating an antelope whilst calmly stating that the snake would not eat again that year. Snakes, like fish, are cold-blooded creatures. Their metabolism is not like ours. So to come across an actively feeding large fish can be described as a rare occurrence, which again provides an explanation why we catch more small fish than big ones.

But, of course, things are rarely that simple. In some environments we find trout that have a genetic tendency towards fast growth and a short life, in others trout grow slow and live long. The fertile lowland or machair-type environments tend to produce the former, whilst the *ferox*-type trout from the low-productivity highland loch is a classic example of the latter. The *ferox*-type trout is a typical example of the 'big feed on rare occasions' type. Fertile-water fish, because of their tendency towards fast growth, require a feeding regime which fuels that growth rate, and can happily get by on a steady stream of small mouthfuls to do it. Fast-growing fish regularly fall for traditional style artificial flies; the *ferox* type rarely does (although it is not unknown for a double-figure fish-eating predator to succumb to a size 12 Greenwell's Glory, to the surprise and delight of the lucky angler).

Another interesting facet of trout feeding behaviour that dramatically affects our fish-catching efforts is the mechanics involved in the feeding process. Again, this is a subject greatly compromised by anthropomorphism. Now, it is obvious to even the least observant amongst us that trout, or indeed all fishes, lack hands with which to examine objects. We often examine things by touch and feel and often don't rely on vision alone to investigate the true nature of things. Gift shop owners live in fear of the average human's desire to handle objects of interest, but a trout would give them no qualms whatsoever!

Assuming that a trout wants to investigate a rapidly moving object within grabbing range, it has a range of options:

*Visual sense*   This is the primary food-identification tool. But, if in doubt, the fish will require other senses to finally differentiate between edible and non-edible. Remember that very often trout have to get by in turbid, murky water where vision will be of little, or no, help;

*Lateral line sense*   Although there may be taste receptors along the lateral line, this organ is principally used to identify vibration in water. So this sense, whilst being able to help locate vibration-producing entities that are not readily visible, isn't much use in the edible/non-edible examination of an item.

*Hearing*   Trout do have ears, but they are internal, rather than externally placed like ours. Their range of hearing is acute and used, largely, as a location device for prey or predator. Not much use in identifying the edibility of a fast-moving object.

*Taste and smell*   The taste/olfactory senses of fish are not well understood by science, but are certainly beyond human experience or understanding. This is principally because water is such an excellent bearer of olfactory sensation in comparison to air. Remember that salmon, close relatives to trout, can differentiate between the smell/taste of neighbouring watercourses to establish the natal stream after years in the sea. Imagine trying to find the street where you were born and brought up simply by using your nose! However, in a food-identification scenario, trout will presumably need a close approach to a food item to use such senses. As taste receptors exist in the mouths of fish and at the entrance to the stomach, fish regularly 'mouth' an item as the last investigation process.

Why do we catch fish whilst offering them items to eat which fail to even slightly resemble living organisms? Most small, moving things in a trout's environment are considered potential food, because … what else could they be? They move, therefore they are alive, therefore they may be edible. When we introduce an artificial fly to such an environment the trout will use any or all of the above senses to investigate the fly for edibility.

Now, what happens when a fish rejects an artificial by sight, hearing or water vibration? In all probability, unless using a floating line, you won't see that the fish has shown any interest at all. But in certain light conditions you will. Many years ago, my old mate Norman and I were blown off Harray on a very sunny but extremely windy day. We hauled the boat up under the Tenston Shore and proceeded to have a wade up and down under the sheltered banks, as the wind howled and roared over our heads. The most memorable aspect of the adventure was not the ferocity of the wind but the fact that both of us, independently, experienced a once-in-a-lifetime event. Each and every time the flies hit the water a trout would investigate, rising from the green depths to have a look at them. Sometimes these fish, whilst still metres down, would give up the approach, but the clarity of the water and the quality of the light conspired to make everything that happened visible to the naked eye. Most fish came up close, looked and turned away, but a few fish would make the whole trip and were caught. In a matter of about an hour and a half we both reckoned on seeing somewhere in the region of 50–60 fish each, at a conservative estimate. But the catch rate was nothing spectacular, and we caught only what we would expect on a normal day: we moved a heap of fish but caught only a handful. The flies we used were by most definitions a success, but they fooled only a small proportion of fish, even though they triggered some sort of response from what appeared to be every fish within range.

As I said, this was a once-in-a-lifetime experience. It is rare to see such activity (which I am sure is far from unique), but on this occasion the light allowed us to see what is usually hidden from the angler. How often do we come ashore after a blank day, cursing the lack of fish, when, in all probability, trout were paying close attention to our flies every other cast?

We are lucky that, when trout are actively feeding, they will investigate almost anything within range that even vaguely resembles a food item. Our general range of flies must be accepted as vague imitations of life – and, when you consider the quintessential traditional fly, the resemblance is most definitely vague. Palmer patterns and winged flies, such as Bumbles, Bibios, Butchers, etc., catch and have caught a whole lot of fish, but they only convince fish of their edibility because they have movement and, to the limited intelligence of a fish, movement represents life. They are intellectually incapable of understanding that an object artificially motivated cannot be alive and therefore edible.

But fish can decide that the artificial fly is not what they would wish to feed on at that time. If this were not so, fly-fishing would be a very boring pastime. Why do fish come to an artificial fly and reject it, or 'come short', as the fly-fisherman would say? This is an interesting question, and one which has bedeviled anglers throughout the history of the sport – a question which continually causes anglers to imbue trout with a whole lot more intelligence than they actually posses.

Trout, and most other fish, tend to use their mouths for feeding in a way unfamiliar to man. Very often they suck in an item which they wish to eat. This was brought home to me whilst watching fish being fed in an aquarium. As a food item falls through the water column, a fish that wishes to eat it will approach it cautiously, using all its above mentioned senses to decide whether it is edible. Once edibility is ascertained, the fish will, in effect, swallow the chunk of water in which the food item is encapsulated. To do this, the fish opens its mouth and sucks in the object and a mouthful of water. The unwanted water is ejected backwards through the gills and the food item is trapped in the mouth.

However, if the food item is restricted in its movement (e.g. it is attached to a length of monofilament nylon) and is incapable of being sucked into the fish's mouth, the fish will go through the process and will be as surprised as the angler that the fly (in this case) is not trapped in its mouth. The fish will be deemed to have 'come short', or to have rejected the fly, when in all truth quite the opposite is true: the fish has been deceived and would have been caught but for the mechanics of presenting a fly on a line. This is, I believe, one of the principal reasons for the angling experience known as 'coming short'.

Of course, if a limited amount of backward travel is allowed to the fly in this situation, then the angler may feel only a slight bump as the trout closes its mouth; the fly, which should be at the back of its throat, makes only slight contact with the leading extremities of the mouth. The best one can hope for in such a scenario is a lip-hooked fish, or, in all probability, a short, sharp tussle before the sliver of skin gives way and the fish escapes to fight another day. But trout often do engulf their prey. This is done by a sharp and sudden attack with mouth and gills open, allowing the object of attack to be swept into the mouth without

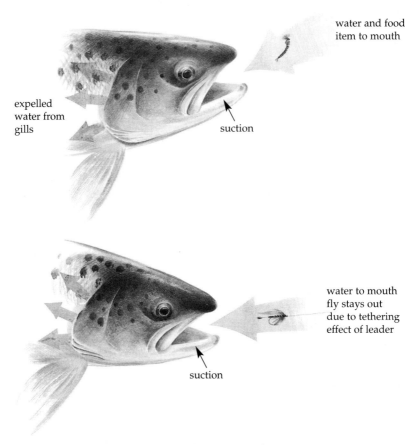

water and food
item to mouth

expelled
water from
gills

suction

water to mouth
fly stays out
due to tethering
effect of leader

suction

*Fig. 2   Coming short – one explanation*

the aid of suction. If it is done in a horizontal plane, the fish sweeping round in the attack, then a hook-hold in the 'scissors' (corner of the mouth) results. If done in a vertical plane, the hook may be found anywhere from the back of the throat to the upper or lower jaws. Either way, trout taking in this manner are almost always well hooked.

Other factors no doubt cause fish to come short. Flies that are badly presented – whether because of faults with nylon or line density, inappropriate size, motion or speed, or aspects of light – all may cause fish to reject at the last moment. It is a frustration and part of fly fishing, but understanding the problem and applying appropriate remedial action can often reduce the predicament.

## General Activity Patterns and Weather Effects

Brown trout are largely diurnal creatures, which means that they tend to be most active during daylight hours. Hence, they tend to do most of their feeding in the 'daytime'. The term daytime may need a bit of elucidation, though, as I know most of us have a great affinity for fishing during periods of *near* darkness.

Trout tend to hunt by sight, and during hours of total darkness they are largely inactive. In the far north of this country, total darkness doesn't exist during high summer, but still trout activity is greatly reduced during the darkest part of the night. And in the early months of the year, and also right at the end of the season, it becomes obvious that very early and late fishing is virtually hopeless. On northern lochs in March and early April, I generally restrict fishing activity to a period between approximately 10.30 a.m. and 4 p.m. Fish caught outside this period are rare, although trout activity can be frenetic round about midday, building up before and tailing off after.

In midsummer, the periods immediately after sunset and before sunrise can produce good rises. This is more marked in the south, where summer temperatures can be higher, restricting mid-day and afternoon activity in both trout and their preferred food items. It is, therefore, tempting to say that trout are active during early mornings and late evenings because their prey is more available then, and I don't think we are far from the truth. However, it is fair to surmise that trout do not like bright sunshine, and the occasional hatches or falls of insect that take place during such states of light are often ignored. Fish resort to deep water in such conditions but will rarely feed hard in very bright weather conditions, even when the depth at which the fish are lying reduces sunshine effects. I remember being surprised to discover that line fishermen in the sea, whose baits are fishing many fathoms down, also hate sunshine and expect to do poorly when the skies are clear. Bright sunshine generally equates with drastically reduced fish activity.

That being said, during extended spells of bright weather (measured in days, if not weeks), trout seem to become more tolerant of the light and will undertake sporadic hunts near the surface if food is available there. This is more noticeable in shallow lochs than deep ones, though.

It is, however, difficult to differentiate between sunlight and high temperatures. Trout don't like warm water, and in temperatures above 17°C can become distressed. Oxygen's ability to dissolve and stay dissolved in water is heavily influenced by water temperature, and a trout's ability to absorb oxygen from water is reduced with an increase temperature. Loch water above 20°C is a poor environment for trout. But, given the vagaries of a Scottish climate, these temperatures are only likely to be found near the surface in lochs or in very shallow water; in such circumstances trout will search out areas where better conditions exist: i.e., the deeps.

Sunshine is the destroyer of our sport, by and large. Of all the weather conditions guaranteed to reduce the catch beyond acceptance, the combination of a cold wind and bright sunshine is the number one candidate, followed by no wind and bright sun. Again, these conditions are closely linked to minimal fly hatch or aquatic creature activity. I sometimes wonder if changing weather patterns are affecting our aquatic insect life. Most of our coldest and driest weather now occurs from mid-March to late May, and quite often extending into June. This is a period when, historically, we used to have some of our most intense insect hatches and activity. Chironomid (midge), ephemerid (mayfly, olives, etc.) and stonefly species do most of their hatching and breeding in this period, and it is also very important to some of our best early *trichoptera* (sedge) species. If the present climate offers poor conditions for these insect species to carry out their normal behaviour, they are likely to decline. We ritually blame agricultural and forestry practices, or water quality, for the decline in our important aquatic fly life, but perhaps, like so many other problems that impinge on our sport, the root causes may be many and varied.

But let us get back to weather effects upon our trout. Another climactic influence that cannot be ignored when discussing trout activity and behaviour is atmospheric pressure. The gases that make up air have weight. Not much weight in small quantities, it's true, but in the vast quantities that make up the atmosphere, a noticeable amount, especially to fish. The atmosphere bears down upon the surface of the earth, and the greater the mass of air above the area of the earth in question, the greater the air pressure, and vice versa. The effect of this weight, known as barometric pressure, upon water creatures is greater than that on land-living creatures. Even minor changes in barometric pressure can have dramatic effects upon trout. In fact I never cease to be amazed at how sensitive trout (and other fish) are to minute changes in atmospheric pressure, even though I think I understand why. Most fish have an inflatable bag within their bodies that is generally referred to as the swim bladder. Trout are no different. If, like me, you suffered (I use the term advisedly) physics classes at school, you may remember being shown the effects of air pressure upon an inflated balloon. A partially inflated balloon is placed in a bell jar which has a pump attached to it that can increase or reduce pressure within the jar. When the air pressure inside the jar is increased the balloon seems to deflate, and when the pressure is reduced the balloon seems to inflate. In fact it does neither; the air trapped inside the balloon simply expands and contracts in response to the changing pressure outside the balloon. The swim bladder within the fish responds in exactly the same way to changes in atmospheric pressure with, one imagines, associated discomfort to the fish during rapid changes. Rapid changes in atmospheric pressure, such as one would experience during thundery conditions, certainly have dramatic effects upon trout activity, and it is surely logical to assume that the discomfort associated with changing atmospheric pressure must be, at least, partly to blame.

Many years ago I had a bizarre experience whilst fishing alone on Harray. I was doing moderately well, catching the odd fish on a warm and pleasant afternoon. The light breeze was from the south, there was a sporadic hatch of this and that, and trout were feeding over the shallows. Suddenly, and for no apparent reason, the loch went dead. It was as dramatic as if someone had thrown a switch. I couldn't work out what had changed, and then, from away off southwards, probably over Caithness, there came a muted rumble. A thunderstorm, still dozens of miles away, was approaching, and the trout were affected by it long before I had even heard it.

But that is not the end of the story. As the crash and flash of the storm got nearer and nearer, I fished on, more in hope than anticipation, and to no effect. Luckily, the celestial turbulence passed to the west, over the sea, and, just as it swept by, the loch virtually boiled with rising trout. It seemed as if every fish was 'up on the fin', and they all seemed prepared to slash at anything that moved. In those far off days on Harray fish in excess of 1½ lb were rarities in the catch, so it was a pleasant surprise that the first, second and third casts produced fish of that calibre. Unfortunately, my excitement at this 'all-caution-to-the-wind' feeding frenzy caused the fourth cast to go awry: I managed to throw a loop of fly line over my pipe, which was clenched between my teeth. As the flies landed, not one but two fish latched onto the flies; the line snapped tight as both trout set off in different directions, and I quickly realised that I had but two unbearable options – lose the fish or my beloved pipe. The fish thrashed and struggled as I bit harder into the pipe stem. I was sure I could feel molars slackening in my gums. But eventually the leader parted and the fish sailed away with the cast of flies and I retained my pipe. By the time I had tackled up again, the crazy rise was over.

Some years later I experienced an identical phenomenon on Boardhouse immediately after a thunderstorm. But there was one important difference – every quality fish in the loch was up, rolling on the surface, but they would look at nothing. A very frustrating experience, but one which this time didn't endanger my smoking utensil.

So, trout activity and day-to-day weather effects are closely intertwined. We should expect no less. Fish are products of their environment and closely controlled by it in all its aspects, particularly atmospheric conditions.

In my experience all weather types can be equally good or bad. Even sunshine can provide sport on the right day, and certainly won't jeopardise sport in the very early and late months of the year. Many anglers of my acquaintance hate fishing in fog and are extremely perplexed when I tell them that my heaviest wild trout was caught on a day when you couldn't see a hand in front of your face. This fish was hooked on Swannay, and although I know roughly where I caught it, I couldn't in all honesty show you the precise location. Consequently, the one piece of fishing weather lore that will help you catch a whole lot of fish is, 'You can't catch them if you stay at home'. It is easy to decide the conditions are hopeless and not go, but that is a self-fulfilling prophecy. I've caught nothing on perfect days, and filled the boat on hopeless ones. You just never know with trout.

# In the Eye of the Beholder

So we have a trout population that is not only dynamic but also migratory, to a greater or lesser extent. But, whether we look at brown or sea trout populations as a whole, we still see significant regional variations. These differences are totally external and not physiological, but they tell us a whole lot about individual trout, the quality of the environment that they inhabit, their fitness and well-being, and, with a bit of insight, something of the behaviour of the fish in hand.

The machair trout of the Western Isles bear little outward resemblance to the trout of the Highlands just across the Minch. Neither do the trout of the Durness limestone outcrop in Sutherland much resemble Shetland hill loch fish. And the same can be said when comparing Western Isles sea trout and Scapa Flow fish or, in fact, virtually any two populations of fish within the country. And yet, conversely, it is possible to trace resemblances between very diverse populations, and it is by doing so that we start to understand why trout look the way they do.

*Salmo trutta* is a spotted fish. These spots are generally black or dark, purplish brown, with a sprinkling of red (which may be totally absent, but more of this later). These spots lie on a background colour, which can vary from white, through every colour under the sun (almost), to jet-black. Relatively rare variations occur showing bright green, yellow or fawn backgrounds, but generally speaking trout are brown backed with silver, white or yellow bellies when they live in freshwater and grey backed and silvery bellied when in the sea.

In the dim and distant past, taxonomists (scientists who attempt to classify animals into distinct species and subspecies) believed that there were many sub-species of trout, which could be differentiated by their skin markings and colouration alone. We no longer believe this to be true. (There is evidence, though, to suggest that minor variations do crop up within the trout species, particularly when involving isolated populations or specific environmental impacts. These genetic variations have sprung up to help the fish adapt or conform to habitat and other varying factors which impact on their existence.) But what we can do is define the water quality of any loch by the external appearance of its indigenous trout. The marl bottomed waters of the North and the machair (shell sand) lochs of the West have a tendency to produce fast-growing, bull shouldered, small headed trout with pale skins liberally bespeckled with large black spots, and few red ones. These waters are rich and productive, supplying food of high nutritional value such as shrimp and snail. The typical highland loch trout is a long-lived, slow-growing fish with a slender body, a comparatively large head, with many small red and black spots on a brown or black skin. Although the colouration has camouflage purposes – it tends to reflect water and substrate tones and colours – spot size and quantity tends to reflect water quality, and the basic configuration of the fish will indicate the feed potential of the water and whether the fish is fast- or slow-growing.

It is a truism that wherever trout are silvery with black spots and no red ones, someone will rise up from the heather and reliably inform you that the loch was originally stocked with Leven trout. That there are lochs in Scotland, and elsewhere, that have had an infusion of Leven trout in the past should not add credence to this great myth. Uninformed and unenlightened souls assume that the lack of red spots and an overall silvery appearance belongs only to trout of Leven origin and has racial origins. Nothing could be further from the truth. There are two bodies of evidence to finally scupper this myth:

1. Take trout from Leven, put them into a black hole in a peat hag with no indigenous trout population and, lo and behold: in no time at all we have typical highland tarn trout which are stunted, red-spotted and as black as your boots!

2. Take stunted, red-spotted, black trout from an unproductive water anywhere in the Highlands, put them into a productive water (such as Leven) and, 'michty me!', in no time at all you've got fit, fine silvery trout that would grace any basket.

Trout conformity and coloration tend to reflect habitat. Colour is often, if not always, dictated by camouflage necessity. Trout that inhabit open water, generally feeding on planktonic food (for example, daphnia and midge pupae) are almost always silvery, as are oceanic open water feeders such as herrings and mackerel; fish that swim high in the water are generally dark on top and very light or silvery below. Trout that inhabit shallow, marginal water require to be camouflaged against a visible loch bottom, and are thus generally of a similar coloration to the background that they want to disappear against – i.e., black against peat, brown against peat-stained stones, very pale brown/fawn against marl, and green in mossy environ-ments. The yellow bellies that all seekers of wild brown trout love are also factors in this same camouflage game, and only belong to marginal, territorial trout.

And, whilst speaking of colour and conformity, let's speak about these planktonic feeders and others. Our native brown trout can largely be divided into two types – grazers and hunters. Grazers feed almost exclusively on planktonic (or shoaling) life forms, exist in open water situations, are non-territorial, and have, as noted above, silvery or pewter-coloured flanks with many black spots and few, if any, red ones. Hunters are identified by their more traditional coloration. They tend to be territorial in, or associated with, shallow water, reefs or sker-ries and other such features, and have a more eclectic nutritional requirement, in that they'll just about eat anything going!

Many lochs contain mixed populations of grazers and hunters. Generally speaking, trout up to 2 lb/1 kg benefit from a grazer's lifestyle, and above this weight they tend to adopt a hunting regime, although there are well-defined exceptions. It should, however, be stated – and emphasized – that the difference between hunters and grazers is purely a behavioural one and does not indicate any racial differentiation.* Trout are trout are trout, no matter how they lead their lives.

* However, long term isolation (measured in thousands of years) and selection of exclusive spawning streams can produce distinct races of trout in specific locations, and I am thinking here specifically of Lough Melvin in Ireland. An argument could conceivably be made that what started out as non-racial differ-entiations in a trout stock in Lough Melvin has, by strict evolutionary principles hammered out on the anvil of time, produced distinct races of trout showing either well-defined hunter or grazer behavioural patterns. The sonaghan show distinct 'grazer' behavioural patters, the gillaroo display only 'hunter' traits and the brown trout can show both or either characteristics as and when it suits. But it must be emphasized that this is a very rare occurrence and I know of no other similar situation within the UK. (Perhaps this is a case of the exception proving the rule!).

Leven trout are almost all grazers, as are most of those in Boardhouse, Borrallaidh, Bornish and Watten, and a significant part of the Stilligary, Stenness and Harray inhabitants. Swannay, on the other hand, is a prime example of a 'hunters" loch, and most Scottish lochs fit into this category, where best angling effort is confined to shoreline drifts, creeping round island shores and exploring rocky outcrops and offshore shallows.

These differing feeding regimes display not only a requirement to properly and fully exploit the whole environment, but also a reaction to that requirement. If trout only inhabited the shallow margins, large areas of certain lochs, and the nutritional load in them, would remain unexploited. But if trout moved into such deep water carrying their shallow water camouflage, they would fall prey to a whole host of predators it would be better to avoid.

## Geology and Topography: Effect upon Growth Rates and Life Expectancy

The rate of growth in any trout population is important, because it indicates levels of potential sport. In waters where trout grow fast and die relatively young, there must be a nutritional load capable of supporting this lifestyle. Food will be virtually always available; fish feed hard and regularly, putting on weight rapidly, and the angler can expect a good level of response on the visits, if he fishes well.

By contrast, the typical highland loch (if there is such a thing) is a poor producer of nutrition; the trout that inhabit such waters gear their nutritional expectations to suit and, perhaps surprisingly, live relatively long lives. It is anthropomorphic to imagine that trout in these waters are perpetually starving and lying, mouth open, waiting for manna from heaven – nature does not work that way. Highland loch/tarn trout tend to be slow-growing, long-lived fish with modest expectation of feeding and growth. The feeding and growing part of the year will start late for them, and finish early. Aquatic food items will be in short supply throughout the year, due to the poor nutrient levels in the water, and the late summer/autumnal terrestrial falls will be the high spot of the feeding year. Perfectly in tune with their environment, these trout are highly successful from a species point of view if a somewhat disappointing prospect for the discriminating angler.

Mind you, these are the opposite and extreme ends of the spectrum. But, though you might walk a long way before falling in a loch that differed from this rule, exceptions do occur. Lochs exist which, to the casual eye, may appear to be typically highland, but because they lie on a specific rock type (limestone or flagstone) are in fact highly productive and capable of providing spectacular sport. Others may have all the attributes of the typically productive water and only contain a host of small trout – which is fine for the beginner or novice, but ultimately disappointing for the angler in search of a challenge.

A basic knowledge of geology and land-use can be a great help here. For example, lochs in established cultivated forestry belts are likely to be productively poor because commercial tree-planting is rarely done on good soils, and the trees' leaves or needles have a tendency to lower the pH of ground water. Hill lochs surrounded by heather and peat hags also generally (but not always) fall into this type, as do the vast hydro-electric dams of the Highlands. Any deep water will fall into this category, largely because the ratio of substrate (bottom of the loch) to water volume is very low; even if the substrate is of a type that will add to the general productivity, the diluting effect of the large volume of water, low temperatures and lack of oxygen can negate any benefit. Vast upland lochs/reservoirs rarely have a chance to be anything other than on the low side of the productivity scale, because they almost always exist in areas where the land is poor, acid and unproductive. In Scotland we value our productive land too much to drown it under millions of gallons of water.

The majority of Scotland's lochs lie in areas largely made up of igneous rocks (granites, schist, and the like), and only in areas where there are intrusions of sedimentary deposits – limestone, flagstone or, in the case of the machair lochs, shell-sand – can one expect to find a jewel amongst the heather. Sudden areas of startling greenery in the otherwise blanket heather are sure indicators that there are beneficial changes in geology in the area. A loch located in such an area would almost certainly be one of these 'jewels', and the limestone lochs of Durness are, perhaps, the finest case in point, with the machair lochs of the Western Isles coming a close second. Of course, counties that have largely beneficial geology and topography, such as Caithness and Orkney, tend to have productive waters, regardless of other features.

*Headley's Rule of Thumb 1*: High ground and heather tend to imply deep water and poor productivity, whilst low ground and grass implies shallow lochs, high productivity and good fishing. Terrain scrutiny will not just tell you about loch productivity, it can also supply hard evidence of underwater features.

*Headley's Rule of Thumb 2*: If the land slopes steeply down to the water's edge, then one can expect that this degree of slope continues into the loch, thus producing deep water. If on the other hand, the surrounding land is predominantly flat, then it is reasonable to suppose that the loch will be shallow throughout.

There are, of course, exceptions to these rules. Loch Eun looks like a typical peat-hag hole in the ground, has jet black, peat-stained water, sits out in the Caithness Flow Country surrounded by miles of sphagnum moss and heather, and produces wonderful trout of trophy status. Loch Caladail sits in a deep fold of the landscape, has a cliff as

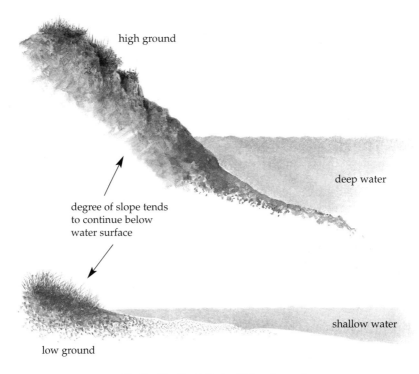

high ground

deep water

degree of slope tends
to continue below
water surface

shallow water

low ground

*Fig 3   Headley's Rule of Thumb, no. 2*

its northern coastline, and a very steep slope in the north-western corner and is relatively shallow throughout. Rules of thumb, like any other rules, are by definition full of exceptions.

As you will now begin to understand, if you did not before, trout are very much a product of their environment. This is why casually introducing trout from other alien locations into specific environments rarely, if ever works. Nature has produced trout as a by-product of countless interactions between myriad factors, and man's attempts to match this process or reinforce it in some cack-handed fashion are generally a sure-fire recipe for disaster. Scotland's wealth of brown trout is a jewel of unsurpassed value, often treated with a casual lack of respect – a prime case, if ever we needed one, of familiarity breeding contempt. Knowledge = understanding; understanding = respect; respect = care and protection; care and protection, hopefully, means our children's children will also will have lochs to fish and trout to eat.

---

### TIPS AND TOOLS

In a loch/wild trout scenario, when fish are very hard to come by, the angler who sticks to the shallows will generally have more success than those searching the deeps. A fish in shallow water is likely to be feeding; a fish which has retreated to the deeps probably isn't!

Fish-finders have their place, primarily in exploring the bottom and depth of a loch. They will show underwater features which may hold fish in an otherwise featureless piece of water. However, don't be lured into fishing exclusively in areas where many fish are discovered at depth by these machines. Because fish are cold-blooded creatures a good feed will keep them going for varying lengths of time often measured in weeks. During such times they resort to dormitories where they 'lie up', often hanging head down tail up in serried ranks. Fish-finders are good at finding these dormitories, and concerted fishing activity over these areas will result in, at best, foul-hooked fish … if you can reach them!

A good rule of thumb for fish location is 'head of the wind in the early months of the season; tail of the wind during the middle and end months'.

---

# 2  Fly-Fishing on Lochs – The Mechanics

## Loch Trout Fishing: A Distinct Form of Fly-Fishing?

What is fly-fishing? Everyone must have a definition which suits their philosophy of what they will and won't do whilst fishing with a fly. I have my own, which – certainly in recent years – I have considered to be a private thing and not something to be force-fed to other anglers, who may or may not agree with it or me. It was not always so.

If pressed, I would say that fly-fishing is the use of man-made creations designed to replicate something or anything that a fish might conceivably accept as a food item. (Does that sound like the sort of thing that would emanate from a spin doctor's office in Whitehall?). Such offerings must, of course, be launched into the wide, blue yonder via a fly rod and line.

Does that sound okay? Well, yes and no. You could drive yourself demented trying to work out why certain artificial flies are indeed accepted as food items. What the hell does a trout think a Booby or a Blob is? And you could ask the same question of many of the fancy traditional patterns of yore such as the Blue Zulu or my own Doobry. But the real crux of the matter is not that they are accepted once, but again and again, to the exclusion of much more imitative patterns and against all logic.

Another area in which my philosophy of fly-fishing tends to run aground is the realm of the more grotesque objects that masquerade as 'flies'. 'Flies' does tend to suggest light, delicate and ephemeral creations: a sparse bunch of fibres here, a wisp of fur there, and the merest suggestion of hackle to finish it off. With such a template in mind, some of the dead budgies and aborted parakeets that one sees being used to deceive and seduce trout (which, in a perfect world, should know better) are an offence to the spirit.

But the offence comes simply from scale. Take the offending object, scale it down so that it fits on a size 14 nymph hook, and you may well have a very imitative, delicate and charming little pattern. Maybe we would get close to the heart of the matter if we were to admit that the offence comes from the trout, which will accept such monstrosities, not from the angler who uses them. I want my trout to be more selective, blessed with finer manners, and it would please me greatly if every trout would abstain from eating any artificial fly larger than size 10 and would feed only in the surface film. That is a dream, and one which clashes with reality. Trout don't have fine manners and are not by any means dainty or fastidious feeders. Our dreams and flights of fancy bother them not at all! It bears repeating here that, since your average trout has the rapacity of a shark and the intellect of an oyster, it would be a greater fly-tying achievement to devise a fly that would *never* catch a trout than one which would, from time to time.

The tail end of the twentieth century saw increased use of such above mentioned monstrosities upon our wild Scottish trout lochs. It has saddened those among us who thought our wild brownies were better bred than their loutish rainbow cousins that they will, as often as not, spring upon these bizarre creations and savage them as a terrier does a rat. Most, if not all, stillwater techniques devised with rainbow trout in mind will work, to a greater or lesser degree, upon wild brown trout. And although the 'bow has a greater regard for the slow to static fly than its spotty, wild cousin, the techniques for one trout can effec-tively be applied to all.

So is loch fly-fishing a distinct style? That's a hard question, and I am tempted to say 'yes', regardless of all that is said above. Loch fly-fishing is not like river fly-fishing, because the conditions are so different – river water moves and imparts life to the 'fly', and this movement gives the river trout a lot less time, generally, to inspect the fly. These may seem cosmetic differences, but, believe me, they are fundamental. However, loch fly-fishing is vaguely like stillwater/reservoir fishing, because it was on lochs, in the dim and distant past, that techniques that were later adjusted to suit rainbows were born, although it is hard to believe now that there is or was ever any connection. Some of our southern pals like to refer to what they are doing as loch-style, but it is only loch-style in that they fish teams of flies over the front of a drifting boat. Any other resemblance is peripheral or accidental, although this may come as a shock to many southern angling pundits.

Loch fishing takes place largely from boats, although out of desperation (brought on by lack of boats, bad weather, etc.). it can take place from the bank – though we prefer to call it wading! And, it should be stressed, the boats are unanchored. In essence drift fishing is what it is. A perfect picture of loch-style fishing is a day that started with a drop of rain, a high, uniform cloud ceiling, a warm south-westerly breeze (15 mph will do nicely, thank you), a boat, two anglers (the ghillie is an optional extra), maybe a dog (black Labs are nice!), perhaps an engine (a godsend, if allowed), and a loch surface bespattered with the rings of rising trout.

But, of course, the interesting question out of all this is whether what is practised throughout Scotland today would be recognisable to our ancestors as loch-style fishing. There has been a merging of stillwater technique and traditional loch style, with the bulk of influence travelling north. Given tackle-trade influences, persistent use of hatchery-reared brown trout and the myopic focus of fishing journalism in the past thirty years or so, this is hardly surprising. Scottish recruits to the sport look to the Midland reservoirs for their inspiration, rather than the lochs of their homeland. Whilst the dyed-in-the-wool traditionalists might shake their heads and mutter hard words over their whisky glasses, it does mean that most of us are better anglers, endowed with a range of techniques which can deceive the spotty ones on all but the hardest days.

## The Changing Face of Scottish Loch Fishing

And even if all the above-mentioned influences are detrimental to traditional loch-style technique, it is not nymph, dry fly or lure fishing which will sow the seeds of destruction. No, the worst threats come from a more insidious source.

We are a pleasure-seeking race. We demand entertainment, and purpose-built recreational systems suit us very well. Given the choice between a hike to a facility- or service-free Highland loch with absolutely no guarantee of return on effort, or a day by a crowded put-and-take fishery with coffee machine and toilet at hand, an overwhelming majority of fishermen will pick the latter. In fact, to many Scottish fly-fishermen the exotic species is our native brown trout, for they see imported rainbows almost on a daily basis. I remember being accosted by a fisherman at a fishery in Ayrshire whilst I was researching a fishing guide to that area. He was holding a dead brownie and asking what it was; he knew it was a fish, but didn't recognise it as a trout!

So, if the principal quarry species is the rainbow trout and the put-and-take fishery is the delivery system, what effect is this having upon the behaviour and attitude of the trout fisherman? The very simplistic answer is that, under this regime, fish have become a commodity, and when an angler hands over his fee at the fishery he imagines he is buying fish. This quantity of fish can, for argument's sake, be termed 'a limit'. If, over a period of time, he consistently fails to catch his limit then he will blame the stock levels, the fishery management, his tackle supplier, in fact anyone but himself. After all, when the same guy goes into the off-licence and puts down his hard-earned for a bottle of whisky, and the guy behind the counter takes his money and gives him nothing, who is he going to blame but the supplier?

If you transfer this type of attitude to wild trout fishing you get all sorts of problems. Continued failure without anyone obvious to blame tends to produce statements such as, 'Wild trout are rubbish!' or, 'There're no fish in here!' This is exacerbated by the fact that the tactics and techniques made popular by the put-and-take fisheries work very well on stocked trout, but less well on wild fish. The response amongst many people in control of wild fisheries, who see dwindling interest from potential customers, is to implement unnecessary stocking of otherwise viable waters with hatchery-reared stock. So, we have a self-perpetuating cycle of degradation of wild fisheries and their natural stock because, like it or like it not, there is ample evidence, both scientific and anecdotal, that introduced grown-on stock will have a detrimental and reducing effect on indigenous stock. And then, of course, we have another self-perpetuating prophecy emerging: as you add more stockies, the wild fish diminish, so every successive year more stockies must be added to compensate for the reduced numbers of wild fish. I believe this is commonly referred to as 'running faster to stand still'.

A large percentage of anglers are no longer prepared to accept the vagaries of wild sport. Wild trout can be contrary beasts, to be sure, but for me that is part of their charm. I don't want their capture to be guaranteed. I want occasionally to turn up at the loch on a perfect fishing day and struggle just as much as I want to experience the day of simply awful weather that sees a succession of quality trout come to the net. Every capture must be a journey into the unknown and involve a creature that is as much an essential part of its environment as the weeds on the stones. I want to feel part of nature when I'm fishing, not to be catching alien fish in an altered environment that has no more rightful place in the Scottish countryside than a high-rise tenement. If it all becomes to a greater or lesser extent scripted then I won't want to be a part of it; the lure of the hunt lies in the uncertainty factor. Fishing a put-and-take fishery is, for me, like visiting a supermarket – you've got a shopping list and what you want should be there to pick up. It simply involves a cost with minimum effort.

Nonetheless, having said all that, the commercial rainbow fisheries play a very important part in Scotland's fishing environment. They provide:

- essential fishing within minutes of the urban sprawl;
- problem-free, facility-rich fishing environments for the very young and old;
- practice grounds for learning, practising and honing technique.

Without this type of amenity (and that is essentially what it is) the bulk of the population would never have the pleasure of fly-fishing at all. And, most importantly, commercial fisheries provide fishing environments that can absorb the growing interest in trout fly-fishing without inflicting pressure upon the sensitive and fragile wild fisheries that are less capable of taking the impact. Commercial fisheries are the buffers standing between our wild stock and potential over-exploitation.

But the balance is shifting. Wild fisheries now seek to emulate the commercial waters, so as to tap into the perceived popularity that the artificial fisheries engender. This brings about a situation in which the artificial becomes accepted as natural, and vice versa. I know good wild-trout fishermen living in areas with outstanding brown-trout lochs who dream of days on Rutland Reservoir and the like. This is one short step away from the introduction of the alien species into environments which already provide a first-class sporting fish.

Some years ago I wrote an article in a mainstream angling journal in which I stated that the wild-trout lochs would likely become an area of interest to the hordes of reservoir/rainbow-trout anglers of the Scottish Central Belt and England. I must admit that I missed the mark by a country mile: there has been no such growth of interest. If anything the level of interest has dropped. This, I think, is due to a variety of factors, which include the following:

1. Reservoir/rainbow trout tactics and techniques, in part, don't travel happily to the wild lochs of Scotland;
2. The contrary nature of wild fish and their ability to stymie inexperienced southern anglers can discourage potential repeat customers;
3. The lack of facilities on the average loch can disappoint anglers used to commercial fisheries;
4. 'Roughing it' in wild areas has a diminishing appeal for those used to pubs, clubs and fast-food outlets on every corner;
5. Other, more exotic, areas abroad compete for holidaying anglers and have a more general appeal to their families;
6. The well-heeled angler, who provided the great majority of Scottish tourism angling, now looks to Russia, Alaska, Argentina, the Caribbean and other such venues for his pleasure jaunts;
7. What should be a reasonably priced and available local option is very often quite the reverse;
8. Too many contributors to the national angling press, some of them even home-grown, give the false impression that Scottish loch trout are invariably small and inconsequential.

At the heart of all of the above is the perception, by those who do not know better, that our wild trout are smaller and inferior to stocked fish in artificial environments – and for this I lay the blame at the door of the angling press. To be fair, it is not their fault alone. The arena which sees the highest level of angling endeavour, of new ideas and technique development, is the English reservoir scene. So it is no surprise that the major angling journals often tend (perhaps unintentionally) to reflect this forum as the only one that really matters in the sport of trout fly-fishing. Keen reservoir fishermen are quite positive about getting their ideas in print, unlike their northern counterparts, who, by definition, tend to be reserved and more likely to keep their own counsel. The editors and professional journalists, by and large, tend to live and fish in England and tend to report the happenings on their doorstep because of familiarity, travelling costs and also because they believe their own reporting, viz., English reservoirs are where it's happening.

Over the years wild loch trout have become the poor relation, and this is exacerbated by items 1 and 2 in the above list. Excellent sport *is* available, but only if the visiting angling journalist can access it and properly tackle the fish when he gets there! The writer who only catches a couple of minuscule trout can find it difficult to suggest that the water contained lots of good fish which he was unable to catch. Who's going to believe him? And, more to the point, which editor is going to print such an article?

Scottish fly-fishing requires better reporting, because if it is deprived the oxygen of publicity it is likely to continue to decline. Certainly it has a much poorer public image than that of its neighbour and rival, Ireland, the fishing of which has always been well reported. The Irish have the Central Fisheries Board, a government body whose only responsibility is to protect, preserve and publicise that country's fresh-water fishing. Scotland has no such body, nor anything vaguely like it, and the lack of an effective body dedicated to protecting, enhancing and marketing Scottish trout fishing has threatened the welfare of our native species and its natural habitat. The Irish Central Fisheries Board has produced an enviable and unrivalled reputation for its fishing without having to go down the road of stuffing every native water with an alien breed of trout.

There was a time when any fly-fisherman with ambition wanted to

46

visit Scotland's premier trout lochs. That was then; the present reality is that, by and large, he now prefers to go elsewhere. This is no reflection on our national product, but purely a problem of image. Some notable Scottish pundits give a tweedy, antediluvian, it's-the-going-fishing-that's-important-not-the-catching-of-fish type of image which is alien to most of the modern, cash spending, angling public. But if someone has a two-week, well-planned, expensive holiday as the high spot of their fishing year, then you'd better believe that catching fish, and big ones, is very definitely important. Without the fish, the bonny blooming heather and the cry of the curlew won't put a smile on anyone's face! Time enough to look at the scenery once a brace of two-pounders have come to the boat, but until then the success of the trip hangs by a thread!

Scotland has some great fishing. World-beating fishing. I'd venture to suggest that, all in all, the best of it is a whole lot better and more dependable than the Irish equivalent, mainly because it is not so hatch-dependent. That is my considered opinion, and I've been about a bit.

## Catch and Release

There is tremendous pressure put upon fishermen to adopt catch-and-release policies whilst in pursuit of their sport. The basic principle of C&R philosophy is that a trout is too valuable to be caught by only one person. Catch and release originated in the United States, where intense pressure on trout streams meant that, without voluntary or mandatory no-kill policies, there would be no fish left to catch. The philosophy quickly found a home in areas south of the Scottish border where, because of a background of coarse fishing, there was inbuilt and entrenched resistance to killing fish. The fact that the bulk of fishing in this area is based on stock fish, and there are few waters which are self-sustaining, engenders the attitude of consideration for the fish as an individual rather than the population as a whole. These attitudes, beliefs and philosophies do not suit a country like Scotland, where the bulk of our waters are self-sustaining, where whole populations require protection, and where the shedding of crocodile tears over the death of a single individual fish is, at worst, anthropomorphic nonsense, and at best, inappropriate.

It is safe to say that I have grave reservations about a blanket acceptance of catch-and-release philosophies by those involved in fishing for
wild fish. Wild fish are a harvest which should be exploited by man,
subject to some governing principles. Such principles would include:
an objective quantifying of existing stock, and a reasonable assessment
of any surplus; an understanding of the importance of specific classes
of fish to the population (not the captor); some form of reasonable
assessment of future population dynamics, and threats to the water in
question, so that long-term viability of the stock is not endangered.

Many, if not most trout lochs in Scotland will benefit from a seasonal
cull, because most lochs in Scotland produce a surplus of fish in most
seasons. For an angler to visit a loch where there is a vast population of
fish and to return everything caught has a lot to do with anthropomorphic twaddle and nothing to do with rational assessment of good or
bad practice. But, on such a water, what is worse than a blanket 'return
every fish caught' is a policy of throwing back the tiddlers and keeping
the specimens. This is aquatic vandalism of an extreme kind. In over-
productive waters, where trout production is gross, it is the bigger fish
which should be returned, because they contain the essential and vital
genetic material that will pass on good growth potential to future
generations; the small fish should be culled, because it is likely that
they don't, and anyway they are gobbling up vital food supplies and
creating an environment that does not encourage individual growth
conditions. I appreciate that this is easy to say and difficult to put in
practice, human nature being what it is, but that should not stop us
from trying.

We should always be aware that waters stuffed with stunted individuals suit nature and the fish population as a whole, whilst waters
containing an equivalent biomass of fish, but in bigger and fewer units,
make for happy anglers. Most waters, left to their own devices, will see
individual size decrease and individual numbers increase. Selective
culling and harvesting will naturally lead to bigger and better fish,
without compromising the welfare of the stock. It is possibly helpful to
the doubters to point out that virtually all predators manage their prey
species in this way (wolves select infirm, old and diseased individuals
from the herds of caribou; lions ambush the 'tail-end Charlies' from the
massed ranks of wildebeest herds; and God help those poor individual

sardines who can't keep up with the shoal when the tuna are hovering close by) and that humans are predators on trout stocks, pure and simple. Or, at least, we should be.

On trophy-fish waters, good practice would be quite the opposite of that advocated for the too-productive waters. In environments where trout are few and grow big, probably due to poor recruitment, it can be assumed that the genetic material promoting growth is well dispersed through the stock, and so removing the big fish will not jeopardise the loch's long-term ability to provide quality fish. In such a scenario, it is wise to take home the big fish and folly to remove the small ones because there is no need to protect the 'big-fish' genetic material, which is probably carried by all. On the other hand, indiscriminate killing or removal of the small fish can reduce the whole population to a point where self-sustainability is impossible, and total population failure from outside causes (such as climate, pollution, abstraction, etc.) becomes a distinct possibility. Such waters walk a tightrope between viability and extinction, and the culling of immature fish can jeopardise the former and hasten the latter. I always advise anyone wishing to visit a trophy-fish water to resist the temptation to take more than two big fish and to return everything under, say, 2 lb. To fish a self-sustaining water into extinction, or to a point where it can only be sustained by artificial stocking is sin beyond measuring.

However, it is no sin to kill a fish if it is destined for the table. A greater sin is to kill a fish that no one wants, or to turn fish into play-things, catching and returning them *ad infinitum*, until all involved parties get sick to the stomach of the whole rigmarole.

## Scottish Trout-fishing – Defined by Tackle?

I cannot look at an old split-cane rod without a shudder running through my body. When I was a boy, learning to fly-fish, I was forced to use my father's cast-off split-cane rods or do without! I was so desperately keen to fish that I persevered with these heavy, sluggish monstrosities. The fishing days of my youth became marked by short periods of casting interspersed with long spells of recuperation, for cane rods were, by and large, hard on the arm and shoulder. The single-handed ones were not particularly good at throwing a long line. And if an averagely built teenager could get 25-plus yards out with such a rod, he couldn't do it all day. In an era of carbon fibre it is hard to believe or understand how such rods restricted fishing technique.

Many of the tactics enjoyed today would be unemployable without the versatility of modern rod-making materials. Some (who I suspect actually know better) claim to mourn the passing of cane. But, if they wished to fish a sinking line, or accurately drop a gently alighting dry fly on the nose of a distant fish, they'd be hard pressed to achieve success with the sort of rods I was acquainted with in the late 1950s and 1960s. Because of the limitations of the tackle available at the time, the widely accepted technique was to short-line with a team of wets, and this became the Celtic way of trouting. The Americans, for their native and introduced fish, used only single fly, be it a nymph, dry or wet; the English and continental fishermen were of a similar persuasion. This was a product of river trouting, which was their principal fishing style. But the Irish, Welsh and Scots fished loughs, tarns and lochs – bodies of still water – and realised the value of the team of wets.

The fly lines of the same period were also difficult tools. Waxed lines needed much attention and a good coating of dressing in order to float. Unless the angler was prepared to carry replacements, individual lines would lose their ability to float relatively quickly, and the fisherman who had set out with a floating line would return with a slow sinker. Inevitably, anglers learnt to put up with the intermediate nature of an untreated line and, because the rods of the day were inefficient in dealing with drowned lines, learnt to keep their casts within a modest range.

Leader material also had a defining influence on the development of loch-fishing tactics. Using extremely fine leader materials, as we do today, it is difficult to imagine the restrictions imposed upon previous generations by the coarse nature of the gut/nylon they were forced to use. I cannot remember using anything other than nylon monofilament in my earliest fishing trips. Possibly in my extreme youth, when everything was done for me and I was simply handed a made-up rod, there may have been a gut cast, but I seriously doubt it. Back then nylon monofilament was nasty stuff. It had more memory than a hundred metres of shire fencing; it would insist on lying on the surface of the water like so many coils of barbed wire; it was thick and frequently darkly coloured; and one simply had to look at it the wrong way and it would break. Trying to fish delicately with it was a nightmare. Long leaders were out, because they invariably tangled, due to the unavoid-able inherent memory. Using this stuff with big, heavy flies in a big wave was OK, but using it with small, light flies in a light ripple produced a three-way problem:

1. It was difficult to get the damned stuff through the eye of the small hook.
2. The leader would skate across the surface in a distressing and fish-frightening way because the light flies couldn't pull the leader below the surface.
3. Small, light flies on broad-diameter, springy nylon look hellish and fish worse.

So unless you were fishing the classic Scottish 'wee doubles', which had massive eyes to take the broad diameter nylon of the day and were heavy enough to prevent 'skate', you were fishing the big, heavily dressed traditionals that represented the other side of classic tradi-tional fly-fishing of that era.

Put all this together, and you quickly see that technique and practice evolved because of the restrictions of tackle. No one devised the tactics of the post-war, pre-carbon, era; they were imposed upon the fly fish-ermen of the day by the limitations of his gear. That beautiful technique of 'stroking the water' – in which a very short line is thrown, and the bob (and often the mid) fly fished over or in the surface film, with only the tail fly getting seriously wet – became an art form born out of the shortcomings of tackle.

Few modern anglers short-line as their fathers and grandfathers did because there is no longer a need for it. Modern tackle does not require the fish to be caught within a rod's length of the boat or lured into the surface film, and it now provides the fly-fisherman with infinite scope in tactics and technique. However, there are still times when short-lining is a very pleasurable and productive method of fly-fishing, particularly for migratory fish along the West Coast and amongst the Islands.

## Modern Tackle and Techniques

We will look very closely at technique in later chapters, but it does seem appropriate here to look at how methodology has evolved from the glory days of our grandfathers.

As we have established, fly-fishing technique in the dim and distant past was dictated by the limitations of gear. If you tried to aerialise thirty yards of silk line you stood a good chance of snapping your built- or split-cane rod at the handle. And there were no fast-sinking lines with which to search the depths, and, even if there had been, the only available materials that would have coped with thirty yards of drowned line would have produced a rod like a snooker cue. These were the days of one angler, one rod, one reel and one spare line.

Tackle manufacturers were few and small scale. One or two big names ruled the roost – Hardy's, Sharpe's of Aberdeen, Malloch's of Perth – and supplied, in a limited way, the requirements of the sport. The retail side of the tackle industry was similarly constructed, and generally consisted of a wee corner shop with an old guy sitting behind the counter, whipping eyes on a rod or lashing together a few local fly patterns. He would sell you one hook and a length of gut to tie it to, whilst his missus flogged groceries, ironmongery or fancy goods simply to keep the wolf from the door.

But, with the advent of better technology and the creation of gigantic fisheries out of the Midlands reservoirs the whole business took off like an intercontinental ballistic missile, producing what is now a very hi-tech industry. We've got the lightest and strongest rods that technology can devise; lines that make those of previous generations look like hawsers; reels that are super-functional and look like works of art; leader material as fine as gossamer, which will cut you to the bone should you be stupid enough to try and break it with your hands; and hook technology that benefits from NASA science spin-offs.

Despite all this, the wee guy in the tackle shop still struggles to make a living because now there are e-commerce and mail-order firms selling tackle to customers all over the UK, from Unst in Shetland to Chipping Sodbury in Gloucestershire. And the son of the bloke who had one rod, one reel and a spare fly line now requires a trolley to get all his gear down to the boat. My fishing box now carries twelve (yes, twelve) fly lines; ten years ago I maybe had four, and ten years before that I had one, maximum two, fly lines. (You don't have to be a rocket scientist to work out the rate of growth of the tackle industry.) But if this may seem to create a negative image of our sport, there are bene-fits. The tackle industry, in keeping pace with demand from a growing customer base, is producing some excellent products. If we look at fly line developments over the past dozen years or so, the advances made would have dumbfounded our grandfathers. We have polymer coat-ings which should last a lifetime, density compensation for sinking lines, all sorts of taper configurations and graded sink rates from negli-gible to 'look out below!'

What all this tackle development does do for the loch fisher is improve his basic ability to catch fish. In my early years on the loch, when we caught no fish on our floating lines we simply decided they were not feeding, and went home vaguely satisfied that we had done all we could. Nowadays, if the floating line fails we try an intermediate or, failing that, medium- or fast-sinking lines. Of course the rod that is eminently suited to the delicacies of the floating line and small wet flies may not be robust enough to suit the full 'sinker' and the lures that we sometimes prefer to use on it. So now we carry two rods – or a single compromise rod that does neither job perfectly but won't collapse under the inertia of thirty metres of aerialised super-fast sinker nor break a 4-lb tippet on the strike when that good brownie comes along and sips down your perfectly presented dry fly.

I have a theory that there has been a radical shift in wild-trout fishing caused by tackle trends and angler's requirements. It goes something like this. Because of the above scenario of the compromise rod (and also competitive fishing, but more of this later), the line rating of choice is defined by the lowest common denominator, which, in this case, is the perfect rating for a fast-sinking line: i.e. WF 7S, or weight-forward, size 7, sinker. Some makes of sinking line are made only in this size, or only in this size and heavier. If you are of the compromise-rod fraternity, this means that all the rest of your fly lines must conform to this rating also. A floating line in a WF7F configura-tion has a substantial diameter in the thickest part of the belly. Unless you are a master caster, putting a size 7 floater down quietly, cast after cast, is a major achievement. And it isn't only the alighting of the line that creates noise, pulling a thick section of floater through the surface will create water noise, to which trout are perfectly attuned. It is vitally important when fish are high in the water, near the surface, that you don't scare them off with an indelicate approach. Many floating-line-only practitioners that I know won't fish a line heavier than size 4, and many of them have imported American rigs that throw lines which, compared to a standard UK equivalent, have the configuration of spider's web gossamer.

When you throw a sinking line for fish that are feeding at depth, the noise of the fly line crashing into the surface probably doesn't bother them much because it isn't happening close by. And, of course, the belly diameter of the fast-sinking lines is much less than that of the same size floater. So we have witnessed a decided drift away from floating-line fishing for wild trout, because the lines we are using can have a detrimental effect on our ability to deceive fish feeding high in the water.

A few years ago, when I was still living in Orkney and competing in the local Association's matches, I grew to realise that none of the competitions were being won on floating-line tactics. Most were being won with intermediates or slow sinks, and a few with fast-sinking lines. Even when fish were visibly feeding in the surface layers, flies presented on a 'slime' line or other intermediate were getting a better response than those attached to a floater. There was one major exception, however. Billy Sinclair, the local tackle dealer and master top-of-the-water fisherman, was still getting superb catches on his very light-line floating rig. He was mightily troubled with shoulder pains and simply couldn't throw a sinking line or a heavy floater all day, and his recourse to the small-size floating line paid handsome dividends in pain relief and fish. I was forced to conclude that it wasn't that fish couldn't be taken on a floating line consistently, but that the regulation, wide-diameter floaters that we were all using were counterproductive and actually scaring fish. This thought process was reinforced by the realisation that when floating line was king and we only turned to sinkers in sheer desperation, the floaters we used were size 4s or 5s. I believe this is proof positive that tackle trends can influence fishing practice and define the nature of the sport we call fly-fishing.

## Other Observations on Lines and Line Densities

Let's start with the foibles of floaters. I remember, many years ago when a Welsh-based tackle manufacturer was first starting to market a new style of lines and we were all, to a greater or lesser extent, caught up in the arguments for or against non-stretch lines. I was walking past a trade stand at the CLA Game Fair when I noticed a static demonstration of stretch in a wide range of fly lines; the staff had erected a board to which maybe 15 yards of various fly lines were attached. Of course the display was designed to show just how much stretch there actually was in PVC fly lines in comparison to the product they were promoting. Now, up to that point I hadn't been particularly aware that there was much stretch in a fly line, but I was pulled up short by this demonstration. Some very famous brands were up there, and most of them were sagging like so many strings of chewing gum. Think on this the next time you try to hook a fish at distance and the sod 'falls off' half way back to the boat: all that stretch is capable of cushioning the strike so much that the hook point hardly penetrates the skin.

The cushioning effect of stretchy fly lines does mean that we experience a lot fewer breaks on the take than if we were using non-stretch floating fly lines. I suspect these non-stretch jobs were tested on rainbow trout, which have a tendency to 'grow' on the end of a fly line, exerting very little in the way of a sharp shock. Brown trout, because they tend to take in an exaggerated vertical movement, very often do impart a sudden strain on the leader material and the cushioning effect of stretch in the fly line reduces the potential for break-off. This is particularly true of floating lines, because, very often, trout will rise from the bed of the loch, take on the surface and dive back down to their 'lie'. Add the angler's strike to this sudden downward rush and you end up with shock, jar and intolerable strain on light leader material.

Oh, and while we're on the subject, here's a little experiment to try – feed a line and leader up through the rings of a favourite rod and get a child to hold the leader between thumb and forefinger (without hook attached, please!). Then, by steadily adding pressure (no sudden pulls allowed!) try to pull the nylon from out of the child's tenuous grasp. Your rod will be bowed into an extravagant curve and the child will be still able to hold on effortlessly. I once demonstrated this to a fly-fishing class using a double-handed salmon rod – the incredulity on their faces was a sight to behold. One would think that an irresistible force was being delivered though the bent rod, but in fact the rod is absorbing the energy, and a mere fraction of it reaches the end of the leader. The truth is that a whole lot of pressure cannot be exerted via a bent rod. This is why a fish, weighing one hundredth of the angler's weight, can reduce him to a sweating, slavering lump, especially if the fish is hooked in the 'jacket'. Food for thought?

Here's another little experiment for you to try. When using a floater, try tying on a very visible (white?) floating pattern of some sort to the point of your leader and chucking the whole lot out in the manner of a normal cast. Now count the number of handfuls of line that require to be retrieved before the point fly moves. If you haven't done this before, I think you'll be surprised: there is a whole lot of slack line and loops between the fisherman and his point fly at the commencement of the retrieve procedure. If in a normal day's fishing you are getting takes during the first couple of pulls and nothing for the remainder of the retrieve, it may well indicate that the fish require static flies or are, perhaps, taking them just at the point of primary movement.

I used to meet a guy (let's call him Jim) who would sing the praises of his intermediate line to anyone who stood still long enough to get an earful. Jim's convinced opinion was that his line, which was described on the original packaging as a neutral density, would sink so far and then sort of hover at a predetermined depth. Jim is not alone in believing that the term 'neutral density', when applied to fly lines, means that the line in question can sink so far and no further, when in truth it is a marketing term roughly equivalent to 'slow intermediate'. It is scientifically impossible for an object with no independent motivating force to act in this way – an object, not under power, will either sink or float. An intermediate line of any configuration will, given time, end up on the bottom of the loch regardless of how deep the water. A simple experiment can prove that the 'hover' line does indeed sink if left to its own devices. Wade out into knee-depth water and go through the motions of casting and retrieving the 'hover' line. The retrieved section of this magical line will sink to the bottom around the angler's feet. What I believe is actually happening is that the line's sink rate is so slow that a normal paced retrieve means that the horizontal force

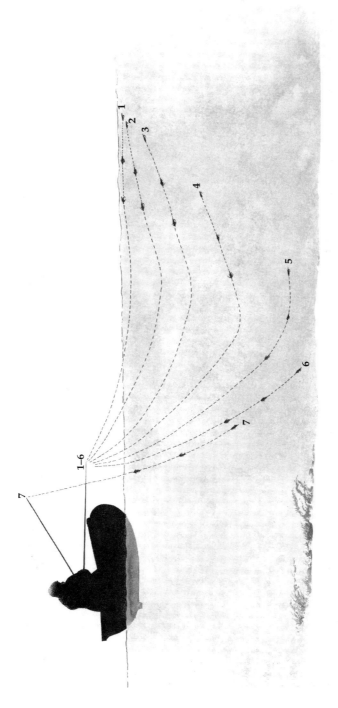

*Fig. 4  The sinking line retrieve*

applied by the fisherman cancels out the vertical force (desire to sink). Or, alternatively, the line is not in the water long enough for the human eye to detect a marked sink rate.

Faster-sinking lines carry their own confusion quotient, and this has been augmented by the density-compensated variety of sinking lines. A standard, old-fashioned sinking line will sink belly first, because that is the heaviest section of the line, and the tip will sink at a much slower rate. Viewed from the side, if this were possible, one would see the line enter the water at a steep incline, culminating at the belly (weight-forward section) and then sloping less sharply up to the leader. This in effect means that the flies are brought back in an exaggerated, parabolic curve back to the rod, fishing from the surface, down to the deepest reach of the fly line and back up. It never ceases to amaze me how many people imagine that the flies come back in a level plane, at depth, from the moment the fly line touches the water. In fact, even with the fastest-sinking line, the flies spend an inordinate amount of time near the surface. But the belief continues regardless of the number of times that the angler can see the mark on the surface as a fish take his flies, even though the fly line is descending from his rod point to God knows what depth in front of the boat (see Fig. 4).

Knowing this allows the angler to improve his catch rate. If, for example, fish are coming to the flies in the first part of the retrieve, and at no other time, there is a strong possibility that the line being employed has too fast a sink rate and one with a slower sink rate may bring more fish. However, if the bulk of the action takes place during the middle part of the retrieve then the line sink rate is probably correct and unlikely to be improved upon. But if the action comes in the very last part of the retrieve there are two possibilities:

1.  That the line sink rate is not fast enough, or
2.  It is the fast ascending fly movement that is attracting fish.

If possibility 2 is the case, then the angler would be forgiven for believing that the fish are probably feeding upon invertebrates that are ascending through the water column. These generally include midge or hatching nymphs, and spooning the gut contents of caught and killed fish may prove the concept and give the angler colour and shape information with which to match his selected patterns.

I firmly believe that wild brown trout respond better to fly lines that give this exaggerated curve in retrieve format. Density-compensated sinking lines tend to iron out the curve and bring the flies home in a more or less level plane. I suspect that such lines are designed to suit rainbow trout, which tend to feed at a specific depth and so are less impressed with the exaggerated curve adored by wild brown trout feeding at depth. To repeat my theory, mentioned elsewhere, I believe that brown trout tend to feed in a vertical plane and that rainbow trout prefer to feed in a horizontal one. In later chapters I will discuss sinking-line tactics for wild loch trout and will emphasise the importance of the 'lift and hold' technique that is so important to the catch rate when one is using sinking lines.

(a) brown trout

(b) rainbow trout

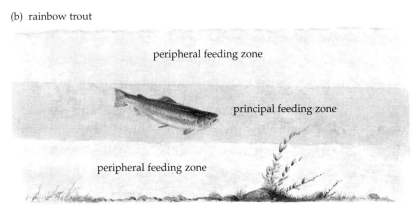

*Fig. 5   Feeding regimes*

## Monofilament Myths and Facts

We make our leaders out of monofilament nylon. Monofilament is a generic term and simply means a single fibre or filament, as opposed to multi or braided leaders. It does not describe the compounds that the leader is constructed from or any other factor.

There are a few rules which are essential when using any nylon leader material. Always wet knots before pulling them tight. Saliva is better than water because it reduces friction to almost nothing when knots are being pulled taught. It is the friction of knot-tightening which causes knots to fail, so always, *always* wet that knot.

When tying knots in fine (<0·16 mm) leader material more turns should be incorporated for security. In heavy nylons (>0·18mm) you can, in theory get away with fewer turns. In cast construction, when tying a water knot in light nylons I would always use five or more turns; in the heavy gear three turns is sufficient. But be extremely careful if attempting to knot two different gauges of nylon together. The wider the difference between the material diameters, the greater chance of knot failure: 0·16 mm water knotted to 0·18 mm will be absolutely fine, but 0·14 mm co-joined to 0·20 mm is an accident looking for somewhere to happen.

Store your nylon carefully as it is prone to weakening under the UV component of sunlight. Fluorocarbon is less likely to denature, but I wouldn't trust any spool this has been exposed to sunlight for any length of time. Last year's spools should be consigned to the bin, and, for that reason if no other, I rarely bulk-buy nylon which I may end up having to dump when the season ends. This is a good reason for the existence of the local tackle shop – mail order is fine when you can think ahead, but when you need that spool of nylon at the start of a day's fishing, the catalogue is no good to you. Support your local tackle dealer, assuming that there is still one left in your locale.

Finally, most pundits and casual passers-by will tell you that shiny mono reflects light, and the flash frightens fish. This is a prime example of a little bit of knowledge being a dangerous thing. Shiny nylon does indeed reflect light in air, because its refractive index is so dissimilar to that of air. But the refractive index of nylon and water are almost identical, and that means that when nylon is immersed in water it is very difficult to see. However, should it have a matt surface (a fad of nylon manufacturers a few years ago), it will stick out like a sore digit. Here's a wee experiment: put an ordinary piece of glass and a bit of frosted glass in the bottom of a bucket of water. Which is easiest to see? Buy shiny nylon – fish can't see it!

I must admit that details of the chemistry and manufacture of nylon leader material bores me rigid, and when I see an article in the angling press about different makes, dimensions, knot strengths, best knots and other statistics, I am faced with a difficult choice – either sit down and read the piece … or run screaming into the fields, hurdling barbed wire fences, stopping only to tear off all my clothes prior to throwing myself into any gorse bush or nettle patch I come across. Generally speaking, I find the latter course of action the least painful. So I won't inflict any pain on my readers talking about manufacturing methods and chemical compounds. Let's just say there are bog standard nylons, pre-stretched bog standard nylons, copolymers, fluorocarbons and who knows what else!

Ordinary monofilament nylon, if I can use that term, was the stuff we grew up on. Ratios of breaking strain to filament diameter were low, which meant that even 4 lb b.s. could be anything up to 0·2 mm. Nowadays we expect a whole lot more strength for such a thickness, and for surface work I would generally advise against nylon monofil-ament, although it is still popular amongst the lads who hunt migratory fish and some fast-sink line aficionados. It's fast losing its popularity amongst fly-fishermen, who seem to prefer the hyped-up, vastly more expensive, competitors such as co-polymers and fluoro-carbons. So let's have a look at these and see if we can assess the benefits of laying out a king's ransom for a spool.

## Copolymers

Copolymers didn't have a happy introduction into the sport. Although fine and relatively strong, there were serious knotting problems with the lighter gauges: knots that we had grown up with would not hold fast on copolymers. Not only that, but the original copolymers seemed very susceptible to shock strain one day and would hold a bolting horse the next. This was confusing and did not build confidence in the user.

But, it must be said that copolymers have come a long way since then, and I now use *Stroft GTM* (a German copolymer) exclusively for dry-fly fishing. Its strength/diameter ratio is definitely on the side of the fisherman, and I can't praise it highly enough. It also has a very low sink rate, and I would strongly recommend it for slow fishing of midge-imitating patterns or similar work.

### Fluorocarbons

Let me say here that I'm gradually becoming convinced by fluoro-carbon monofilament – and I'm talking of the real stuff, not the coated which I find a tad too bulky for my taste. However, for those who fish only floating lines and wet flies I do not think that this expensive form of monofilament is necessary or advisable. Nonetheless, I find that it performs very well when using sinking lines and would strongly advise the use of a reliable brand of fluorocarbon for sunk-fly work.

I've tried a few brands of fluorocarbon and found that, as with the copolymers, some brands are more reliable than others. That said, some I find totally reliable, so all I can say is try a few and stick to the ones you like. Monofilament choice is a subjective matter, and there are no easy solutions or formulas to help the customer select one that suits his taste.

Fluorocarbon has the unique quality of being heavier than water; therefore, left to its own devices, it will sink, and sink quite rapidly. (Ordinary monofilament nylon is less inclined to sink, especially in the finer gauges, and it is only the weight of the flies and degreasing agents which will force it through the water surface and its associated surface tension.) As I said above, for wet-fly fishing in a traditional format I don't think it is totally necessary, and for dry-fly fishing you'd better be using very high-riding, buoyant flies, because fluorocarbon will pull down anything else. But when it comes to nymph fishing with floater, intermediate or sinker, or when a robust but relatively fine leader is required for pulled flies on a sinking line, fluorocarbon is in a class of its own and becomes indispensable.

Knotting is fairly straightforward as long as you always wet the leader before pulling any knots tight. But then that applies to all leader material, so no problem there!

You get what you pay for in fluorocarbon leader material, so if it is cheap then it is probably the coated stuff. Buy expensive and be prepared to take the spool back to the seller and demand your money back if it fails

To sum up, leader material is second only to flies for the mythology and blind faith which it engenders amongst fishermen. One man's indispensable, totally reliable monofilament is detested and abhorred by his neighbour. My best advice is to find something that works for you and stick with it until you find something better. What you have faith in will rarely let you down.

## Leader Construction

If we remove fly pattern from the equation, nothing fails in fly-fishing more often than leaders. Hooks rarely if ever break, fly lines really shouldn't either, and rods, if treated properly, should last a lifetime. But leaders break and fail with a monotonous regularity that is a tribute and a monument to the cack-handed nature of your average fly-fisherman. First, a brief discussion of a few basic rules then we'll plough into basic leader construction for specific jobs and line densities.

Now, let's get this straight – I don't care how long you've been creating multi-dropper leaders using the double-blood knot system, stop it right now! Using blood knots in anything less than 8 lb breaking strain monofilament to produce droppers is like sacrificing a virgin to ensure rain or a good harvest! We have moved on. Face it, accept it and join up with modern trends (unless of course you really enjoy losing fish and breaking leaders)!

The double-blood is a poor and weak knot in normal trout-gauge monofilament. It was excellent for drawn gut (which our grandfathers used) but it is poor for small gauge nylon monofilament. Better (by far) is the previously mentioned water knot. What are its advantages over the double-blood knot? Both provide two possible lengths of nylon to be used for a dropper. However, the double-blood 'legs' are both equally weak, whilst the water knot has one very weak and faulty leg, and one very strong and totally reliable. The weakness of legs in both water and blood knots is due to the same fundamental flaw – when tension is imposed on the leg or dropper the length of nylon involved is pulled hard against a turn of the knot, and this, being under stress, is harder than the free nylon and cuts it. Also, the stress applied to the dropper tries to force a blood knot apart.

In the water knot the leg to use as a dropper is the one which points down to the point fly position. When tension is imposed on this length the stress and strain is immediately transferred to the main cast length and the dropper knot is not compromised. Also, when stress is applied to the dropper the force tends to close the knot. Unfortunately, because the other/weak 'leg' points back up towards the rod and holds the fly away from the leader, reducing the chance of entanglement, it is frequently chosen by the uninitiated. Disaster follows as soon as a fish takes a fly tied to the weak dropper: (1) the dropper shears off at the knot, or (2) the knot gets forced apart by the strain. Generally, when you enquire why an angler sticks with the double-blood knot style of dropper production he will tell you that he tried the water knot style and found it useless. Further enquiry to identify which dropper length (the one pointing up or down the leader) was used will lead to a full understanding of the cause of rejection. I know of no one who, having correctly used the water-knot system, has subsequently reverted to the blood-knot system.

There are other systems – some good, some flawed – with different knots and connection systems. I won't go into them, because I am quite satisfied in my own mind that the water-knot system is the best and most reliable. So why should anybody want to go further?

LEADERS FOR TRADITIONAL WET FLY

I really have only two leader types for traditional wet fly fishing: the brown trout leader and the salmon/sea trout leader. Both involve two droppers (producing a three-fly cast) and have equal distances between the fly positions.

## Leaders for Browns

The brown trout leader is three spans of my arms long. This is easily accomplished. Take the spool of nylon in one hand (most of them are round and have a central hole, into which the tips of the thumb and index finger of one hand should be inserted) and the free end of leader material in the other, then spread the arms as wide apart as they will go, running out the leader material. Then let go of the end of the leader material, grasp it again at the point at which it protrudes from the spool, and repeat the manoeuvre. This done three times will provide a perfect length of leader for a three-fly cast. (My span is exactly 72 in., thus providing me with an 18-ft cast; yours may be slightly more or less, but an inch or two more or less will not matter a jot). I thus end up with the aforementioned 18-ft cast with two droppers. The first dropper, top dropper or bob-fly position, call it what you will, is 6 ft from the beginning of the leader, the mid-fly position is 12 ft down, and the point fly is, of course, 12 ft from the top dropper.

Now that braided loops are endemic (and, I must admit, extremely useful), I don't like my top dropper a mere 6 ft away from my floating fly line – although I don't think it makes a blind bit of difference on an intermediate or sinking line. I am fully satisfied that the close proximity of the top dropper fly to the wake or surface disruption caused by a floating line is a deterrent to fish. To get round this, I either dispense with the braided loop on my floaters, substituting a 30-in. length of tapered monofilament, or simply attach a fairly heavy 30-in. length of monofilament (approx. 15 lb b.s. or 0.22 mm) direct to the braided loop and attach my leader to this. This short length of monofilament also acts as a very short intermediate/anti-wake tip and will reduce line-associated water noise in front of the flies and 'dig' them in below the surface film, which is no bad thing usually. Having the top-dropper fly 72 in. + 30 in. down from the end of the floating line makes the 'lift and hang' alternative to the bobbed fly easier to accomplish. As we have discussed elsewhere, top dropper bobbing may have had its day, and hanging a top dropper pattern static in the surface film is a better option all round.

I have experimented with adjusted middle dropper positions, moving the mid fly closer to either the point or bob fly. After many years I have decided there is little mileage in it for day-to-day fishing, although a mid fly close to the bob fly, so that both can be scraped over the surface, can be useful when fish are in this increasingly rare bobbed-fly-snaffling mood. Keep things simple is my best advice.

I first started talking in the press about 18-ft leaders in the early 1980s, having fished them since the mid-1970s. I got dogs' abuse from hordes of disgruntled anglers who couldn't understand how it was possible to fish an 18-ft leader off a 10- or 11-ft rod. How could I possibly net a fish that was 18 feet away from my rod tip? But, it is the bob-fly position and its distance from the point fly which is the limiting factor, as it is safe to pull the first 6 ft of leader material through the tip eye, so as long as your line-to-leader connection is secure. Of course, lodging the top dropper fly into the tip eye when you are attached to a spirited and far from tired-out fish is a recipe for disaster, so some definite circumspection is appropriate in the early stages, if not the whole, of the battle.

Now, the question arises, Are we talking of all wet-fly leaders, or just those employed near or in the surface film? Whilst I am occasionally tempted to switch to a four-fly cast when using sinking lines, and almost always if using the 'washing-line' technique, generally speaking most of the true expert exponents of the sinking line prefer long leaders with two droppers well-spaced apart, and my inexpert opinion backs this up. I firmly believe that, whether on a floater or a DI-8, long leaders tend to be best. Many years ago, in the article I mentioned above, I discussed long leaders and why I thought they were essential for almost all brown-trout work. To put the argument in perspective one must remember that the article was set against a backdrop of commercially available casts of 9–12 ft with two (sometimes three) droppers, and anglers coming out of the dark misunderstanding of what we were attempting to achieve and into the harsh light of modern technique. My main theory was, in a nutshell, that flies close together distracted fish, and that fish were better at targeting single items without the confusion of other targets presenting themselves within their peripheral vision. I drew a parallel with the hawk successfully attacking a single bird but failing when presented with targets bunched together. Small birds and baitfish mass together for safety sake, and the odd individual mooching along, whether in air or water, is likely to see its life insurance mature *tout de suite*! The parallel still holds good, I believe.

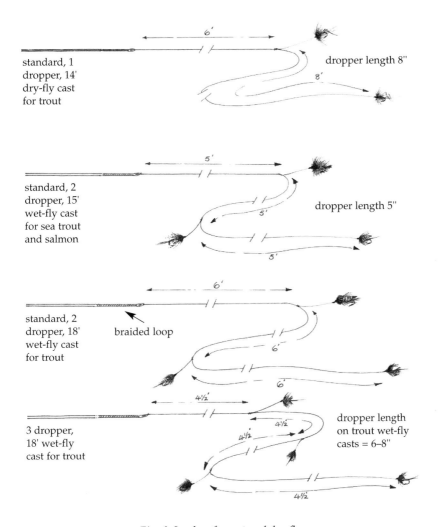

standard, 1
dropper, 14'
dry-fly cast
for trout

dropper length 8"

standard, 2
dropper, 15'
wet-fly cast
for sea trout
and salmon

dropper length 5"

standard, 2
dropper, 18'
wet-fly cast
for trout

braided loop

3 dropper,
18' wet-fly
cast for trout

dropper length
on trout wet-fly
casts = 6–8"

*Fig. 6 Leaders for wet and dry fly*

## Leaders for Salmon and Sea Trout

For salmon and sea-trout work I prefer a slightly shorter leader. This is
mainly because these species are still very susceptible to bobbed-top-
dropper tactics, and I tend to fish my flies for them slower than I would
for brown trout. My preferred length is 15 ft, which works out as two-
and-a-half spans of my arms. The three flies are still equally spaced
apart, and the shorter distance between fly line and top dropper allows

me to incorporate bob technique early in the retrieve. A shorter distance between the top and middle droppers also allows me the opportunity to bob the middle fly once the bob fly is played out, which can be a remarkably effective technique at times.

Straightforward leaders with water-knot droppers work for me, and I can rig up a new one in a bouncing boat in about two or three minutes, so I don't normally carry spares or worry about a change of leader. Once, to the disbelief and amazement of my boat partner, I changed a worn-out flyline for a new one in the time it took to travel from the Loch Leven pier to the point of St Serf's with the boat bucking like a rodeo horse in a 25-mph easterly – and that included resleeving and super glueing the backing-to-fly-line and fly-line-to-braided-loop connections. Why should the simple task of constructing a new leader hold any fears?

## Leaders for Dry Fly

Leaders for dry fly are, if anything, an easier matter. If I am setting out to fish dry, I make up a one-dropper cast laid out like this: one span (6 ft) to the first dropper and one-and-a-half (9 ft) to the point fly position. This works well for me and I have no notion to change it.

I have always done my best work on a two-fly cast, the vast bulk of the fish coming to the point fly, and if change were necessary I would fish a one-fly cast and expect to do almost as well. I know there are many very competent dry-fly fishers who always fish a two-dropper cast but I suspect there is an element of insurance in this set-up. What I think is going on is that the standard cast is made up (18 ft long with two droppers) and filled up with dries, leaving the option to quickly change to a three-fly team of wets at a moment's notice. This is a compromise, and I don't like what I consider to be fishing compromises! The best solution is always the best answer, and the only thing to do is what perfectly suits the circumstances. For example, it is as unsuitable to make fish wary of your dry flies by fishing too many of them too close together as it would be to try to thread a size 16 CDC pattern onto 0·22 mm monofilament, just because you may wish to fish a weighted lure later in the afternoon. However, regardless of what I have just said, I occasionally end up fishing a three-fly team of dries because I set out to fish wets and have changed to a dry-fly cast when the change became necessary. The better option, though, is to lose the mid dropper, shorten the cast by a few feet and fish two dries. We'll talk more about dry-fly fishing in a subsequent chapter.

### Dropper Knots and Lengths

The suitable length for a dropper can be a subject for heated debate. I know anglers who like very short droppers about 3 in. long, and others who regularly use droppers of 12 in. and more. I like to vary my dropper lengths to suit the job in hand. If I am fishing a standard wet-fly cast and am liable to change my flies on a regular basis (and it amazes even me how many times I go for a change of pattern), I will select a dropper length of about 6–8 in. Changing flies will gradually erode the length of the dropper, and the length advised above allows a change or twelve. On a dry-fly cast I like an even longer dropper length and would go for approximately 10 in., which, after a few enforced changes, would end up somewhere in the region of 8 in., which I consider just about perfect.

Salmon and sea trout leaders are not enhanced by very long droppers and, as changing flies is not always likely to change one's fortune, I tend to go for a good workable dropper length of about 4 in. This may seem very short, but given the increased diameter of monofilament suitable for the job and the sort of windy weather generally experienced, short droppers produce fewer problems.

## A Rod for Your Back?

We have discussed fly rods in a historical context and their effect upon fishing practice. But it is now necessary to consider them from a modern-day perspective and as tools for the job. However, I don't intend to say much about the technical side of rods and their manufacture, not only because the same pitfalls of boredom which beset the technicalities of monofilament science and technology affect rod manufacture, but also because I have never taken much of an interest in it myself. A rod is a rod; if it works and is suitable, then great; if not, take it back and get something that does and is!

Mind you, some observations on suitable weapons for loch fishers must be in order. I have fished rods as short as 9 ft and as long as 11 ft 6 in. My shoulder, worn out as it is with too many years of abuse from inappropriate rods, poor attempts at medium-pace bowling and thirty years of shotgun recoil, will now only accept the leverage associated with 10-ft rods. Anything longer, employed for the duration of a day, would reduce me to tears, I'm afraid! But, for those who can use an 11-ft or longer rod, I would certainly advise such an addition to the armoury. The ability to work a top dropper fly at long distances from the boat is increased in direct proportion to the number of inches you add to your rod length. Those of us who have a soft spot for sea trout and salmon fishing in lochs generally accept that the bob-fly-working and fish-bullying capabilities of the long rod have much to commend them. But, unfortunately, long rods in a trout configuration are becoming a thing of the past. Very few manufacturers include one in their range, and most modern anglers consider a rod of 10 ft or more a long weapon. Surprisingly, salvation may lie in the hands of the sinking-line-wielding competition fishers who seem to prefer the long rod because it gives them good head clearance (high-density fly lines have a distressing tendency to like to fly about at ear-level), provides good lift and hang characteristics, and raises flies up from the depths at increased distance from the boat. If enough pressure from competition sources encourages production of long rods (11 ft), then the loch fisher may enjoy an unexpected windfall.

For general purpose wet-fly work with a dash of dry-fly for variety, a ten-footer works fine, and something with an AFTM rating of 6 or 7 tends to be most popular, although if the angler is likely to restrict himself to floating and intermediate lines only, then he would be well advised to consider a lighter rod: something in the 4 or 5 range. For boat fishing a light rod is fine, but for the bank angler who may wish to throw a line pretty much into the wind, then light lines and rods won't do it, and we're back to the no. 7. I use a matching pair of AFTM 7s because, if push comes to shove, I will go to the fast-sinking option and lines of this sort of density are more readily available in 7. But if you are prepared to put up some hard cash for a rod of this designation, you need not end up with a 'poker'. A well-built, fast-actioned rod rated 7 will not only cope with the fast-sinking lines but be capable of fishing the most delicate dry fly attached to the finest leader.

So, what should we look for in a good loch rod? Well, we've already established length and line rating preferences. There's not much left except handle, reel seat and number of sections. A good cork handle is not as easy to spot as a bad one – holes, badly filled cavities and a general softness tend to give away the poor handles – but even handles that pass critical examination when new may inexplicably fail after a few months of action. (Expensive rods tend to have good handles, and if they eventually fail, there will probably be an after-sales service which will rectify the problem at minimal cost.) Reel seats are the means by which the reel is secured to the rod. Go for the good, solid metal job with a fairly widely spaced, big thread. Small-thread screw fittings are to be avoided because the merest hint of grit will jam them solid, and it will take some seriously rough action to free them up. When selecting a rod it is not a bad idea to take along whichever of your reels has the most robust foot (that's the bit that fits into the reel seat) and make sure that it will fit. Many modern rods, and a very large percentage originating from the USA, have reel seats that will take only the very neatest of feet (or is that 'foots'?) – and there is nothing worse, believe me, than unwrapping the new rod and finding your reels won't attach to it!

If I lived beside a top-class trout water and never wished to visit another, all my rods would be single-piece, and they would hang on a rack until I needed them. Every joint is a weak point and also impairs the potential action of the assembled rod. Multi-piece rods are becoming ever more popular, but, I suspect, for the wrong reasons. Firstly, the punter likes a rod that, when disassembled, can be stuffed in a suitcase, and also one that is short enough to be immune to the tender ministrations of baggage handlers. These are strong arguments for multi-piece rods, but they fail to address our desire for a 'nice rod in the hand'. From a manufacturer's point of view single-piece rods would be a great boon, but the manufacturers must also address the customer's desire to move from place to place without turning a single piece rod into a multi-piece by the careless use of car doors and assorted pieces of falling luggage. Lifetime guarantees also require that rods be pretty much immune to this sort of hazard, so the push is on for the world's shortest disassembled rod.

My favourite rod of all time was the 10-ft Sage Graphite 3 RPL for a no. 7 line. It came as a two-piece rod and would happily deal with tiny dry flies on a 2 lb b.s. cast or size 8 double salmon fly, work a Suspender Buzzer through the surface film or drag a litter of Black Cats through the depths, and it was the fly-fishing equivalent of a scalpel in the hands of a brain surgeon. Unfortunately, so many of us found that 5-ft lengths of tubular carbon fibre could not escape unscathed from closing boot-lids, encounters with hob-nailed boots or clumsy idiots falling over in boats that Sage, in their wisdom, decided that the 'best rod in the world' should be turned into an also-ran by making it a three-piece. In my humble opinion, Sage rods have never since reached the heady heights of the Graphite 3 RPLs. Too many Sage customers have been climbing into jets and heading off to the broad horizons with their multi-piece ordinary tools carefully stowed in their luggage; in my opinion, if the b***ers would only stay at home we would have better rods!

## Reel Value

This is going to be the shortest section on tackle, because there really isn't much to say. I am very much of the line reservoir school of thought, as opposed to those beloved of the tackle companies who wax lyrical on drag co-efficients, bar stock metal and the like. To me a reel is a place where the line lives when I'm not using it, and, as long as it has a reasonably wide arbor, all other considerations are irrelevant. I have one very expensive reel and a couple of moderately expensive ones, and I can't say that any of them are more useful than a 30-quid plastic job. I almost always fight my fish from the hand, using the reel during the fight only to recover inordinate amounts of line which fish have removed from the reel. As I fight my fish hard, there aren't many that are allowed to revolve my spool, so I can go for months without using a reel during a fish-fight.

In a nutshell, my philosophy is: buy cheap, reliable, maintenance-free reels. Have one for each line (changing spools is a pain in the fundament), and spend the money you save on good fly lines and expensive rods.

## Fly Lines

In the rapidly changing world of fly-fishing, fly-line innovation and development moves faster than a lure-strippers arm. We now have a fly line for every conceivable fishing style and weather type, and it is hard to keep up with new technology. However, for the sake of argument, let's just say we have floating lines, intermediates and sinkers, and we'll let that take us where it will.

### The Floating Line

Twenty years ago, if a loch fisherman had but one line then it was a floater. Nowadays, with unlimited choice of sink rates and densities available, most anglers have a range of lines. The increasing importance of rainbow fishing and reservoir technique throughout the sport has meant that the floating line is not as popular as it was. And in Scotland – especially in the Central Belt, where rainbow is king and wild brown trout are an endangered species – there is a whole generation of fishermen growing up who have little knowledge of the versatility and basic usage of a floating line. For the fishers of true wild brown trout in the regions where they abound, the floating line always has been, and always will be, an indispensable tool.

We have discussed this elsewhere but it stands repeating: brown trout feed in a vertical plane and, as they like to inhabit shallow water, are very likely to take a food item five feet down and then rise and take another from the surface a few seconds later. (Those whose fishing careers have been formed by rainbow trout fishing find this concept hard to grasp. Their favoured prey tend to feed at a specific level, and if the angler fishes out of this level he is liable to reduce his catch-rate to nil.) And catching trout on a floating line is a joyous way to fish. To see a trout appear, as if from nowhere, and engulf a high-swimming wet fly or a carefully presented dry, is the apex of trout fly fishing. Not only is the spectacle of the take a major pleasure but the use of a floating line is, in itself, also a real delight.

Almost every other density of line – from the intermediate all the way through to the very-fast-sinking lines – requires false casting to enable one to gain control of the aerialised line. Not so the floater! The angler can put out a nice long line, see a fish 'move' off to the side, and immediately lift the whole thing off in one gloriously controlled movement and gently put the flies down in the close proximity of the fish. This is, of course, in a perfect world, in which the fish will immediately take the offered fly, be landed after a stiff fight and be the trout of a lifetime! Watching an angler trying to cover a rising trout with a sinking line, which is buried 5–6 ft down at the critical moment, is to redefine the word frustration.

One doesn't have to go that far back in time to visit an era when the floating line was virtually the only line used for wild trout. But, if you go even further back, lines only floated if hard work and diligence were invested. The waxed-silk lines of the dim and distant past were basically slow sinkers that floated (temporarily) if suitably treated. The loch fisher using a waxed-silk line would normally not bother with floatation treatment, as the length of line he shot didn't allow the flies to submerge much below the surface. This technique is very similar to the modern method of short-lining with a sinker – on its day a very successful modern technique.

In the 1960s, waxed silk gave way to the plastic-coated lines we are familiar with today. And a great boon they were. I know that many pundits grow lyrical about the old Kingfisher silk lines – but who, in all conscience, would like to see the days return when lines had to be treated before fishing to make them float, and then had to be strung out to dry after every session to stop them rotting? If you don't want more than a few seasons out of your plastic floaters, then they are virtually maintenance free; otherwise a regular wash with household detergent and a polish with a soft cloth will double, treble or even quadruple their lifespan.

In the right environments the wild trout angler can expect to fish the floating line right through the season. Many southern anglers are amazed that in the Western and Northern Isles, where waters are shallow and fertile, the line of choice for opening day (15 March) would always be a floater. But wild brown trout are primarily shallow-water feeders, especially in the early months, and will always be best tackled with a team of wets cast over the shallows on a floater. A classic case in point was an afternoon that my old 'mucker', Norman, and I spent in Bankhead Bay on Harray on a pretty March day. I started in the west end of the bay; Norm went straight to the burn mouth. I finished 'the wade' with three or four pound-plus fish of pristine quality and was pretty chuffed with myself. Norman had done better! Without moving his feet he'd taken, out of a hole at the mouth of the burn, three fish for 6lb 6 ounces, and returned a plethora of smaller fish. All the fish in question were 'maidens', (i.e., fish that had not spawned the previous winter), were in prime condition and were caught on floating line and traditional flies.

As the days lengthen and warm up, insect hatches, where they still exist, will bring the surface layers of relatively deep waters into play. The lucky anglers on the fertile waters of the north and west will find fish feeding right across the lochs when the hatches are on, and dries or sparse wets fished high in the water will answer most problems. This spell from late April to mid-June can, weather willing, provide some of the finest loch-style fishing of the year, with seemingly ravenous fish throwing themselves at the flies from dawn to dusk. A good day in spring or early summer is better than the best day at any other time!

By the time the summer solstice has passed things can get a bit tricky in the surface layers and, whereas the southern anglers are now dusting off their floaters, the fish of the wild waters are now responding better to something sub-surface. But, during the first and last hours of daylight, they still sneak into the shallows to feed over the stones, and big catches of better-than-average trout can be regularly experienced by floating-line-wielders prepared to turn night into day. The best of this anti-social activity takes place in warm, overcast conditions. (If the evenings or mornings are cool and bright, forget it; you'll likely see nothing in the evening and have meagre, short-lived sport in the morning in that period known as the 'false dawn'.) As soon as the sun hits the water the fish will most likely slip back offshore. On the Durness limestone lochs in north-west Sutherland, some of the Cape Wrath hotel guests regularly turn midsummer nights into day, and spent the relatively dark hours fishing for, and catching, specimen-quality brown trout. Loch Lanlish, on the golf course, has, over the years, thrown out some magnificent fish (approaching double figures) to night anglers, and I well remember being out with Jimmy Ireland in the gloaming on Borralaidh, Lanlish's neighbour just over the hill, when big trout came up with the char. To say that there were trout the size of Labrador dogs off the south-west corner of the island is only the slightest of exaggerations.

To fish for those nocturnal trout requires that the flies be presented right in front of their collective nose and in the surface film. If the trout are up and showing, the floater is the first line to use, although in certain circumstances the intermediate or 'ghost tip' might produce better takes. However, presenting the flies below the line of sight of fish cruising just sub-surface will ensure very little or no response. A good rule of thumb is: floater when it's warm and humid, think again if there is a chill or temperature drop at dusk.

### Intermediate Lines

When fish are loath to come to the surface – and this can be for a wide variety of reasons – then it is wise to sink your flies to a depth at which they will become acceptable. This can be done with a floating line and weighted flies, or with patterns tied on very heavy hooks, and for a bank fisherman this wouldn't present much of a problem. In fact, if I was a bank-only fisherman I would fish nothing else but a floating line and subtly adjust leader length and make-up to meet varying depth requirements. However, for boat anglers to fish flies at specific depths requires boat anchoring (which is anathema) or minimal, or no, drift. The wild and windy Celtic fringe does not allow such conditions to exist often enough to permit us to do without sinking lines, I'm afraid. Generally speaking, when boat anglers wish to present their flies at depth they select a line with a suitable sink rate to get them down there.

It is an interesting conundrum that the use of floating and sinking lines tends to be totally different depending upon which region you inhabit. In the shallow waters of the north and west, we tend to start the year with the floater and, come mid-summer when light intensity increases and fly hatches tend to diminish, we reach for the sinkers. It is quite the opposite in the south. Here they start the year with the sinkers and, as waters warm up in the summer months, they spend more time with the floating line. The oft-spouted, inaccurate rule that cold water necessitates the use of sinking lines tends to come from myopic pundits who only know their own waters and techniques. In the north and west, cold water generally means springtime, and that means that feeding/catchable fish are mostly in the shallows.

But there are times when the wild loch fisher will reach for intermediate or sinking lines in the early months, and these are times when fish are off-shore taking advantage of a food bonanza that is not presenting itself on or near the surface. Such food can include snails, shrimp, midge pupae or caddis larvae. Cold winds or air can mean that the water surface temperatures are lower than those in the depths, producing circumstances where the fish and the invertebrates become more active close to the bottom, both choosing to avoid the surface layers. Flies presented below the cold water layers and at the feeding depth are likely to score where the standard tactics of floating lines will either bring no response whatsoever or produce a succession of 'come shorts' as fish, deterred by the surface temperatures, lose interest in the fly and turn away at the last moment. In the heat of a summer's day a similar behaviour pattern can be seen caused by the opposite conditions. Then surface water becomes warm, de-oxygenated and uncomfortable, and fish are again loath to enter the surface layers (although it has to be said that, in the breezy, cool conditions more prevalent in the wild trout regions, this is not a common occurrence).

During summer months sinking lines can become essential when fish become fixated upon daphnia shoals. The importance of daphnia feeding regimes was largely unknown in my youth, either because we lacked the knowledge or because daphnia blooms were less prevalent (I suspect the former). Daphnia (zooplankton) feed on algae (phytoplankton). Daphnia, sometimes called water fleas, are minute copepods that actively consume the free-floating unicellular plants we generically call algae (which make up the group more correctly called phytoplankton). Phytoplankton relies on sunshine for its nutrition because, like all plants, it converts sunshine, water and carbon dioxide into food/energy via the use of the catalyst chlorophyll. There is an optimum level of sunlight which the phytoplankton prefers for this process, so in bright conditions the phytoplankton sinks through the water column, taking with it the daphnia shoals and the trout feeding on them. Conversely, in dull conditions, the phytoplankton comes to the surface in the search for optimum light levels, and the daphnia shoals and associated feeding trout are also to be found at this level.

Hence, trout feeding on daphnia must be targeted at precise levels because – unlike larger life forms, which may be active throughout various levels in the water column – daphnia tend to stay put at a suitable level unless the light changes dramatically. And this is where sinking lines become essential tools for the wild trout fisherman.

For the sake of easy discussion we will group all lines which fish within a few feet or inches of the surface as intermediate lines; these include sink-tips, hover lines, neutral densities and slow sinkers. Such lines are generally best for the sort of scenarios described above when trout are disinclined to enter the immediate surface water, but they can be useful in other situations, such as:

- In very windy weather some anglers prefer intermediates, because they can offer a certain amount of line control, which floaters lack in a big wind. I have discussed this elsewhere. I don't endorse this policy, but it must be admitted that is very prevalent; the ranks.
- When a specific depth needs to be achieved by flies fished slowly an intermediate can be the answer. Fishing at depth is not always about fishing at high speed (in fact it very rarely is).
- There are occasions when the intermediate style line actually proves the better taker of surface-feeding fish. This is a hard one to explain, but often fish feeding high in the water respond poorly to flies presented on a floating line, and very positively to those just 'buried' an inch or two down.

Moreover, it is a sad fact of life (to those who love the floating line, anyway) that the floater can be a poor converter of chances into fish. I would have to say that, in general day-to-day fishing, a high ratio of offers to a floating line can come to nothing, and also that the solid take or arm-shuddering wrench that can so often result in nothing is more a feature of the floater than of other forms of fly line, although not exclusively so. The hooking properties of flies attached to lines buried beneath the surface are boosted by the inertia of water weight and the resistance that even a few inches of depth produces.

## Sinking Lines

Much of what I have said about intermediate lines can cover full sinkers, given that the differences are only a matter of degree. But the use of intermediates and slow sinkers goes back generations amongst loch fishers (the old waxed silk lines, if untreated, were slow sinkers), whereas the full sinking line, with sink rates up to 8 in. per second, is a comparatively new concept and requires new management skills to get the best out of it.

It has to be said here that most top-quality fishing lochs rarely, if ever, really require the fastest-sinking lines. The best of the lochs have little water in them deep enough to warrant a sink rate of 8 i.p.s. (inches per second) and, because brown trout (as I keep saying) feed in a vertical manner, they are generally willing to rise up through the water column to take a fly. In other words, it is not necessary to drop the flies to the level of the fish, because wild brown trout are accommodating beasts and more than willing to meet us half-way.

All the same, there are good reasons to fish sinking lines for wild trout on occasion. My best reason is always because I've gone through the gamut of lines, starting with a floater, then intermediates and slow sinkers, and finally find one in the fast-sinking category which produces fish – and I think that tends to go for most of us. However, sinking lines can be used in other ways than just shooting as much as you can towards the horizon then 'humping' them back until the flies appear on the surface. One of the most imitative and delicate styles of fishing involves short-lining a very short length of a very fast sinker, loaded with patterns imitating midge pupae. This and similar tactics give some credibility to fast sinking lines, and justify their employ to those of us who, until quite recently, believed their use was an admission of failure.

All intermediate and sinking lines are best loaded on the wide-arbor reels which have become very popular in recent years. The large, wide spools allow the line to be stored with the minimum of storage memory being imparted to the line. It is this memory which creates the bulk of our tangles, and the use of wide arbor reels can make tangles a relative rarity.

One little tip which I think is well worthy of passing on, and one I have found essential in producing good results, is to whip a small bundle of thread onto a point in the line where, when it hits one's index finger on the retrieve, indicates that, with the rod raised in that essential manoeuvre known as 'lift and hold', the top dropper fly will be just sub-surface (see Fig. 4). Of all the manoeuvres possible with sinking lines, this is the one which will produce the most fish. Trout, and particularly brown trout, find that a fly/food item sweeping up to the surface in a determined, hatch-imitating manner, culminating in a helpless and vulnerable hesitation just sub-surface is totally irresistible. Well, most of the time, anyway! And without that little stop knot at the appropriate location on the line – for a 10-ft rod I place the stop-knot 21 ft from the end of the fly line – it is difficult to know when the sunken fly is just at the precise point where the lift and hold technique will place it just sub-surface. With a stop knot suitably located it is virtually impossible to fail, and I use this technique on all my fly lines, bar the floaters and the ghost-tips. With those I have visual evidence of where the dropper fly is at all times – not so with any line which is, for its whole length, under the water. (See Fig. 9 on page 137.)

Nowadays almost everyone uses weight-forward format lines. When I was starting out on my fly-fishing career every fly line was in double-taper format. Because of the demise of short-lining for trout and the advent of the long-line principle, cast distance is a priority, and this is best achieved with weight-forward lines. Unfortunately, delicate casting with lines that have most of their weight/bulk concentrated in a short length near the business end is well nigh impossible, especially in the most popular size which is no. 7. This is something we have to live with. It must be said, though, that this is less critical with sinking lines than with those intended to catch fish feeding that are high in the water and therefore susceptible to surface noise and disruption. Fast-sinking lines tend to be available in a restricted variety of sizes (generally WF7–8, occasionally WF6) and only in weight-forward format. I suspect that this is market driven, and it does not seem to cause any problem to the purchasing punter.

We touched on density-compensation/uniform-sink properties earlier in the chapter when dealing with lines and line densities, but I think it is appropriate to review this matter in finer detail. Perhaps we should first identify what is meant by 'density compensation', or 'uniform sink', as other manufacturers call it. Density compensation attempts to ensure that the line sinks at a uniform rate throughout its length, rather than sinking more slowly in the thin, running line, and faster in the belly portion. Personally, I don't think that density-compensated/uniform-sink lines should be first choice for those who spend most of their time hunting wild brown trout. As we have seen, wild brown trout take in a vertical manner and have little problem rising from their selected depth to take a fly. Bog-standard sinking lines tend to sink in an exaggerated curve, which accentuates the swing-down/sweep-up path of the flies. Brown trout like this motion, but rainbow less so because it involves them moving out of their selected horizontal feeding plane to follow and take a fly. Density compensated/uniform-sink lines were designed to suit rainbow trout feeding regimes (see fig. 5) and not those of wild brown trout. After all, rainbow trout fishing and the Midlands of England are the big markets. We wild trout men have to get by as best we can, I'm afraid. So, to recap, if you're a loch fisher for wild trout and looking for a sinking line which best suits your chosen field of endeavour, avoid those with density compensation/uniform sink and go bog-standard, if you can find one!

## And Almost Everything Else …

### Tackle Boxes and Bags

Loch fishing is about boats, and to carry all the bits and pieces and cheap plastic reels get yourself a robust plastic box just like our coarse-fishing companions use. A box will keep your knick-knacks dry on a rainy day, and out of the water which accumulates in the bottom of a boat on a windy one. It will serve as a boat-seat in a poorly furnished boat (and God knows there are plenty of them for hire) and makes things easy to find if properly compartmentalised. Many anglers shy away from the box because they feel that the plastic coarse-fishing box looks incongruous in the highland loch setting, and they may have a point. But aesthetics are one thing, trying to dry out every single item of kit every day of a wet Scottish summer is quite another.

Bags are OK, but they lack almost all the above advantages of the box. However, if you like the distant trackless hills and their lochs, then a bag is a better option than a box – but a good haversack is better than both.

## Nets

Here there are two options – the boat net and the wading net – neither of which will fill in for the other. Boat nets should have a long pole, so that fish don't have to be brought right under the gunnels before netting. Fish tend to thrash when brought too close to the boat and many are lost whilst doing so. The best netting technique is to play the fish out at a distance of some feet from the boat and, keeping its head out of the water, slide the fish on its side into the waiting, partly submerged net.

There are a few recipes for disaster:

- Bringing the fish to the net whilst it is still fit and feisty. This can end up with trailing flies in the net and the fish permanently out of it.
- Retrieving too much line, so that the fish ends up suspended from the rod-tip with the angler unable to bring the fish close enough to be netted.
- Boat partners who won't wait for the fish to be brought to the net but insist on following the swimming fish with the semi-submerged net and jabbing at it in a hair-raising and ineffectual manner.
- Well-meaning souls who want to net the fish tail first. Even an exhausted fish can react quite violently to having its tail touched. Net fish head first, always.

Here is the best netting technique, which, with luck, will cover all eventualities. Play the fish out at a reasonable distance from the boat.

When the fish starts to turn on its side, make sure the net is well submerged in front of the boat. Try to bring the fish in when it looks played out – the fish lies on its side – but be prepared for a return to fitness when the fish spots the boat; if this does happen, remove the net from the water. Almost inevitably, after such a burst of energy the fish will be ready for the net. Get the head of the fish out of the water and slide it towards and over the sunken net; the net should not be lifted until the fish is well within its confines. Do not then exert destructive pressure on the net and pole by lifting a heavy fish out of the water: draw the net towards you by a hand-over-hand technique and, grasping the handle close to the net, lift the net-enclosed fish out vertically. I have seen nets destroyed by those who hadn't a clue how to net a fish properly and didn't fully comprehend the destructive powers of leverage

I have been using pan nets for some time now and find them excellent for boat work. Originally designed for the coarse-fishing market, they have made a good impression on fly-fishing boat anglers, and I think that for modest to good-sized trout they are first class. Fish seem to lie in a very docile manner in pan nets and tend not to thrash about as they do in deep, engulfing nets. For those who return the bulk of their catch, a pan net is worth consideration. However, for salmon and sea trout I still prefer my big net with its enclosing meshes.

Wading nets come in a variety of sizes and styles, and of them all I prefer the ones that look like a squash racquet gone wrong. They are neat, strong and very efficient. I had a remarkable demonstration one day when a good friend who carried such a net came to my aid as I was struggling with a seriously angry 5¼-lb wild fish. I had left my net at home and I wanted to get some photographs of this specimen. When my pal Puck arrived with his tiny net I snorted in derision because I thought he'd have trouble netting a stickleback with it. I was totally wrong! The fish, over 24 in. long, slid into this tiny net and folded up like a joiner's rule. Normally I go on the premise that a big net is best, because a small fish will go into a big net whilst a big fish won't go into a small net. I may have to revise this argument.

Fine-woven net mesh is best because it is very kind to fish and doesn't knock scales off, but unfortunately flies tend to catch in the fabric. To avoid this, spread the dry net out and generously spray it with the contents of a can of varnish. The mesh will become virtually impenetrable to hooks and also resistant to absorbing fish slime (which has a tendency to make a car interior a rather hostile environment during the long journey home at the end of a hot day).

## Drogues

For standard shoreline drifting on lochs, drogues are a menace. Too many people, brought up on southern waters, automatically employ a drogue almost regardless of wind-speed or any other factor. My best advice on drogues is use them when you must, and at all other times try to work with the weather conditions rather than fight them.

The times not to use a drogue are:

- when the wind is light;
- during a good blow, when the water you wish to drift is shallow and/or rocky or contains other sunken drogue traps;
- when you are likely to need to alter the line of drift during the course of the drift;
- whenever short-drifting onto a rocky shoreline in windy weather;
- when you may wish to repeat a drift over shallow and productive water;
- whenever you can operate without one.

Obviously there is little or no need for a drogue in light winds, so why would you use one then. If there are sunken traps which may snag the drogue, this can be an annoyance in light winds, but in a big blow this can be a life-threatening situation – the boat gets held back against the wind and wave, the rope attached to the snagged drogue becomes too tight to allow the connection to be uncoupled, and before a knife can be found to sever the rope, the boat ships water and founders. Not a situation you would wish to experience on a deserted Highland loch!

When a drogue is used it is virtually impossible to alter line of drift without hauling the damned thing inboard. As good and effective shoreline drifting invariably involves minor and major adjustments to course on a regular basis, having a drogue out the back can destroy the enjoyment of a productive drift. To attempt to row or motor with a drogue employed is at best pointless and at worst downright bloody dangerous! Also dangerous is drifting onto a rocky weather shore in a strong wind. The temptation to fish too long and only haul in the drogue when the boat is in close proximity to dangerous rocks is inescapable and part and parcel of the nature of fisherman. What generally happens is that when the drogue eventually comes inboard the boat, released from its restraint, leaps forward into the welcoming if unloving embrace of the rocky shoreline. If a boat gets trapped on a weather shore in a big wind it can become impossible to extract it, the wind and wave destroying every effort to move offshore.

I suspect that a drogue passing through the ranks of feeding fish in shallow water is unlikely to make them hungrier or more likely to accept the angler's flies on a return journey. Using a drogue in shallow water is a recipe for disaster anyway, but I cannot believe that trout (not the most phlegmatic of creatures, let's be honest) will let it trundle through their midst without batting an eyelid.

And last but not least, never employ a drogue when its use is simply not necessary. A good and accomplished angler, fishing either a floating line or a very slow-sinking intermediate, should be able to fish his flies effectively in any wind conditions it is safe to be afloat in. If not, then fishing skills need improving, and the worst way to do that is to over-employ the drogue.

Times when drogue should be employed are:

- to allow anglers to cope with excessive wind speed and rate of boat drift and fish effectively;
- when the anglers are forced to fish sinking lines and the rate of boat drift is such that the sinking lines cannot be fished effectively;
- if open water drifts are an option and the fish are in tight pockets
- to combat the poor drifting qualities of specific boats.

As I just said, loch anglers should strive to be capable of fishing in wind speeds verging on gale force, so that deals with item 1. The use of sinking lines can dictate the optimum drift rate of the boat: put simply, the faster the line's sink rate, the slower the drift rate should be. When the drift rate goes past the optimum for any line's sink rate, the first thing the angler will notice is that there is little line resistance to retrieve, or 'pull back' as we call it; then he will discover that the boat is trying to drift over the point where the line must exit the water. Four options exist – 1) retrieve faster, which generally means the depth the fish are inhabiting is not reached, resulting in fewer offers; 2) put up a line with a slower sink rate, which generally means the depth the fish are inhabiting is not reached, resulting in fewer offers; 3) head to the top of the wind, where the fish might or might not be; or 4) buy a bigger drogue!

Open water drifting offers safe and useful drogue employment. Open water drifts are rarely subject to course alteration, don't often have drogue-snagging obstacles and allow fish plenty of room to move away from the oncoming disturbance associated with the passage of a drogue. If open water drifting is coupled with location of tight groups or shoals of fish, then the angler can spend longer in the hot-spots and can control and fish his flies to suit the fish rather than the wind and wave conditions. The perfect set-up for sunk-line fishing! The only similar circumstance I can envisage for floating-line fishing is while targeting shoal fish when fishing dry-fly during a fresh wind. Overdrifting dry flies can be as annoying as overdrifting wets on a sinker.

## Marrow Spoons, etc.

One of the most useful tools to be found amongst the paraphernalia that clutters the fly-fisherman's box or bag is the marrow spoon/scoop. Mine was made for me by a knacky-handed pal who converted a 12-in. length of copper pipe into a very functional tool. To carry out a stomach contents investigation requires only that I insert the tube down the *dead* trout's throat and into the stomach, do a simple half-turn and then withdraw it. Whenever a trout has been feeding (and it's amazing how often they haven't) this process produces a three-dimensional historical record of the feeding regime of the fish – the most recent items are at the end nearest the hand and the old stuff is at the other end. A typical analysis, taken in the middle of the day, would go something like this: semi-digested fishy mush at the end of the spoon (most fry feeding in lochs goes on in darkness hours), a few orange shrimp (colour changed by digestive juices), maybe a couple of snails and a caddis case or two in the middle (as a result of some early hours of daylight mooching about in the shallows), then a great wodge of nymphs or buzzer pupae from the late morning hatch, all topped off with a smattering of adult insects – probably adults associated with the nymphs/buzzers found immediately below in the spoon (see Fig. 7).

Not only can such a result tell you how you can improve your fishing approach at that specific time, it can also provide information for subsequent trips – for the spoon graphically lays out the historical feeding regime in neatly arranged time zones. Working on the above example, a very early foray would have the angler slipping through very shallow water with some sort of fry-imitating rig in the pre-dawn spell, changing with the arrival of the light to some general-purpose wets for the shrimp and caddis larvae-bashers in the same locale, followed by a move to regions where buzzer or nymph hatches can be expected, culminating in a brief flirtation with dries to finish off the day. To discover such a feeding regime in any other way would be difficult, if not impossible, and so time consuming that by the time the feeding pattern had been established it would likely have changed.

So here's the course of action: first catch your fish, knock it on the head (you've got to eat, haven't you?), spoon the fish, investigate the spoon contents whilst still in the spoon (this gives you the timing of the feeding regime), then place the contents of the spoon in a dish of water. Your examination dish must be white, so that the items show their real colour and are more easily viewed. Poke about in the soup and correctly identify species and development stage of insect and confirm or update your cursory examination of the 'dry' matter.

*Do not spoon live fish!* I am amazed at the number of people who, because they believe it is cruel to kill fish, think it is OK to ream out their guts before returning them. There is a special place in fishing hell reserved for people who spoon live fish, where the demons carry red-hot marrow spoons of suitable dimensions, gut content analysis takes place every hour on the hour, and the spoons don't go via the mouth – and serve them right if it's true!

The downside of gut content analysis is that the information on offer can send you down the wrong road. Elsewhere we discuss the differences

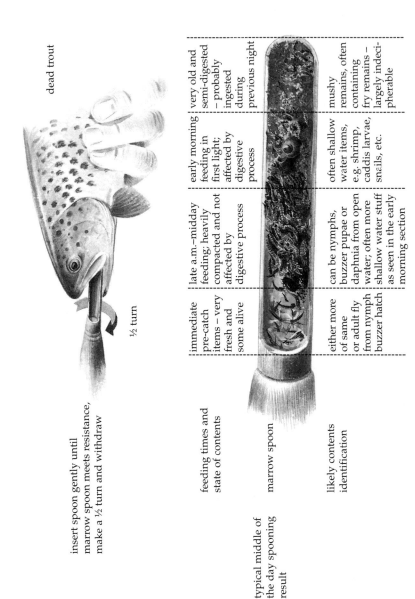

*Fig. 7 Marrow spoon use and how to read the results*

in observational process between humans and fish, transmitted light $v$ reflected light, etc. All this must be borne in mind when matching colours – and, of course, marrow spoons rarely tell you much about how a food item moves, where it was in the water column when it was clobbered, etc. For example, if you are in the middle of a good-going rise and catching lots of fish on a claret fly, and a spooning tells you that the fish are only accepting green nymphs, what are you going to do? Take off your claret killer and put on an untested green pattern? I think not! Marrow spoons provide information and are indispensable when you need some, but they are, when all is said and done, only an aid to catching fish and not a sure-fire means of doing so. Use them with circumspection and be prepared to use or reject the results of investigation as you see fit.

By the way, the marrow spoon does allow you to view the timescale of a feeding regime, and many other tools for stomach content analysis don't. I am specifically talking of the ones which pump water into the stomach and then suck out the resultant 'gunge'. It is possible to suck out twelve hours worth of food, all mixed up together, resulting in the angler trying to imitate some specific item in the contents – but one the fish stopped feeding on hours before.

And what do we do when the there are no contents in the stomach? Well, there is a fundamental fact of the life of fish hidden in this evidence. Fish spend more time fasting than feeding. It is more common to find a starved fish than one with a full stomach, and herein lies the conundrum. Do we find more fish with empty stomachs because they are easier to catch than those with full stomachs? Does fish hunger resemble what we humans define as hunger? Did the fish take our fly because it was starving, and it was a case of eat that or eat nothing? Do fish which have suddenly woken up with a bit of a hunger on become totally non-specific in their feeding and take the first thing that swims past their nose? Are fish less choosy when they are in need of food? Does the fly which took the empty fish have the same power of attraction for all fish in a similar condition? Do fish really decide to feed when there is nothing for them to eat, or is their relationship with their environment more finely tuned than that? These are all questions for which there is no acceptable answer backed up by unquestionable evidence. But in my experience it is marginally more common to catch fish with little in their stomachs than fish which have a lot; we all know how pernickety fish can be when there is plenty about to eat, and if we work from a precept that little of the human experience has any correlation with that of fish, we won't go far wrong.

## The Shirt Off Your Back

One of the big problems with fishing photography in Scottish loch-fishing circles is that, no matter in which month snaps are taken, it always looks like March. Anglers wrapped up to the eyeballs in multi-layers of thermal clothing is the norm. A normal Scottish summer tends to be nasty, brutish and short, and the boating angler will experience the worst of it. Air temperatures are almost always about 2°C lower than ambient, because of the cooling effect of evaporation from the surface of the water. So when the angler sticks his nose out of his front door in the morning and thinks 'Nice warm day! No need for the heavy jacket today!' he would be well-advised to think again. I could live in the lap of luxury if I had a 50p piece for every day I've been caught out by the difference in air temperatures over land and water.

And that's only general warmth. There tends not to be a fat lot of shelter out on the loch either and unless the boat hugs the shelter of trees or high ground (not always the best places to find fish), exposure to the elements always seems worse in a boat than on land. Rain coming horizontally across a loch can penetrate the best breathable waterproof clothing that the trade can produce. I get the strong impression that serious road-testing of sporting waterproof clothing is generally avoided by the manufacturers, and even that done in the soft, southern exposures of Midlands reservoirs doesn't mean much when the clothing is asked to deter the worst a Highland summer can throw at it. I'm afraid that the term 'guaranteed waterproof' doesn't hold much water – in fact a lot less than the gusset of your state-of-the-art waterproof trousers at the end of a wet and windy day in the far north.

Choice of clothing is a subjective matter but there are a few good rules. Multi-layers of windproof clothing are essential early and late in the season and will keep the angler warmer than a few layers of bulky stuff. Heat escapes from your collar region, so wear a scarf, snood, hooded sweatshirt or all three. Always wear a hat, because heat also escapes from your head, and a wet head will chill you very quickly. Good thick, woollen jumpers with the natural oils still in them will repel water, as will special-finish fleeces, so always wear one or the other under your waterproof, because that waterproof will fail in the foulest weather which the hills and glens can throw at you. And here's something many people discover to their horror – water doesn't just come from the sky, it can arrive over the gunnels straight from the loch on a windy day (and not just in little drops but sodding great bucket-fuls, more likely than not!).

Early and late in the season I always wear 'long johns', i.e. long thermal underwear, and thermal long-sleeved vests. I long ago gave up on waterproof trousers and prefer to wear neoprene waders where fishery rules, if such exist, allow. I wear breathable waterproof jackets but don't expect them to keep all the rain out, so I also wear something water-resistant underneath. To retain body warmth I wear a hooded sweat shirt and a snood, and have at least five layers of clothing under my jacket. Boots should be bought at least two sizes too big, so that three layers of socks can be worn comfortably if the weather so dictates. Obviously, during what we laughingly refer to as the summer months I might shed a layer or two, but not much and not for long, cold spells being a regular feature of Scottish summers.

The best advice I can give to help others stay warm whilst the elements are doing all in their power to freeze off the protruding parts is – avoid tight-fitting garments; loose, floppy items in multiple layers will see us through the coldest days. And here are two 'old saws' which will stand you in good stead: 'Any idiot can become cold – it takes brains to stay warm!', and 'If you're wearing it, you can always take it off!'

## Feets of Strength

My old granny always used to tell me 'If your feet are warm, then the rest of you is warm too!' That may not be totally accurate, but it's not far from a fundamental truth. Following up on that, wet feet almost always cause a dramatic cooling of the whole body, so it is desperately important that the angler, operating as he does very close to the water, if not always in it, keeps his feet dry.

In the good old days, real 'roughy-toughy' anglers didn't worry about boots and such; working on the premise that the skin is waterproof, they rolled up their trouser legs and got right in there! Apart from the odd blisteringly hot day I have not witnessed this behaviour much in modern times. I think it was Scrope in his writings on the Tweed that said the angler was safe as long as his legs only showed purple, but when they turned black it was considered best to leave the water. (I assume that in those far off days deep wading was followed by a period of attendance at the Vienna Boys' Choir! The mind boggles!) These days we are a much more effete bunch of nancy-boys. The merest trickle of water inside our state-of-the-art waterproof footwear will provoke a stiff letter of complaint to the supplier and a demand for replacement.

So what are our options to withstand the encroaching waters? Rubber boots, plastic boots, neoprene and breathable fabric are the popular options.

Rubber is fast losing popularity because of its tendency to perish and, more importantly to some, because in a remarkably short time the interiors have a tendency to smell like the business end of a septic tank. Plastic, whilst not having the perishable propensity of rubber, has the same malodorous inclination. It is also an uncomfortable material to wear in cold weather, because it is not intrinsically warm and quickly becomes stiff and inflexible in cool temperatures. In hot weather, on the other hand, the water vapour created by sweat (hopefully) rising from the unventilated interior causes a wet patch to develop where it comes in contact with cooler atmospheric conditions. This, unfortunately, always seems to be in the crutch area, so that when the boots are removed casual observers tend to jump to the wrong conclusions.

Neoprene sock-foot waders have few of the above disadvantages because they are more easily aired when off and won't perish, but they have an unfortunate tendency to leak at the feet end, because continual wear compresses the foam, which allows water to penetrate the material. Also the construction of neoprene waders involves seams, and when the first leak occurs it is almost always on a seam.

(Having said that, though, inflowing water quickly reaches body temperature, due to the insulating properties of neoprene, so the angler can have a sock full of water and still be warm.) Condensation can be a serious problem because the garment is designed to hug the body and ventilation can be of a very low order. The close fit can also restrict blood flow to the extremities, resulting in cold feet, though generally only during periods of inactivity. And combining hot weather, severe exertion and neoprene waders is a recipe for dramatic weight loss, if not heat exhaustion – you have been warned!

Breathable fabrics I am wary of, I must say. So much so that I have, as yet, not purchased a set of breathable waders. People tell me that as waders for wading they are totally reliable, but I don't know whether such recommendations apply to me, because I spend so much time sitting in boats and am unsure how breathable fabrics react to continual friction between bum and boat-seat. I do hear good things of them, and I hear horror stories. But I don't think I can put off the fateful moment much longer. Surely, now that such footwear has been on the market for decades, the manufacturers have ironed-out the flaws and inherent faults, and now produce trustworthy garments. Time will tell!

Under the boots, good cotton socks with an over layer of woollen sea-boot stockings is a combination hard to beat, although you can dispense with the woollen stockings if wearing neoprene waders. I was once given a pair of neoprene socks and found them the coldest footwear I'd ever experienced, because they were so tight and restricted blood flow. Perhaps a less close-fitting pair might have been a tad warmer but the thought of them flopping about on my feet did not appeal.

So that's the kit. Of course there is plenty more. One thing which defines fly-fishermen is their passion for tools, knick-knacks and assorted nonsense. My own fishing waistcoat looks like I've been pelted with the contents of a surgical supply store, and I've got enough metallic attachments to make a pearly king envious. But when all is said and done, not much of it is essential, just handy.

Now, if you are still with me, fancy a spot of fishing?

## TIPS AND TOOLS

Wait for the boat to take you to fish. To try and cover rising fish beyond your comfortable fishing range can often result in pricked or lost fish. Brown trout can take and reject a fly with remarkable speed, and covering fish at extreme range rarely allows the angler enough reaction time to respond successfully to an offer. Added to that, line stretch over long distance makes it more difficult to set hooks.

Rarely does a drifting boat move in a straight line. A good drifting boat will tend to angle towards the stern. However, oars in the water, outboards in the drive position, drogues, and weight distribution within the boat, may affect drift direction. If you wish to drift a shoreline onto which the wind is angled, turn the stern away from the shore, and vice versa. When the angle of wind onto the shoreline is too acute for 'stern out' to make the necessary adjustment, turn the boat 'stern in'. This makes for easier adjustment by motor or oars.

Possibly the best bit of information I can impart to all and sundry is – never pull your flies into the sun if you can possibly avoid it! We all know that a bright sun behind us will almost always dramatically reduce sport because, from a trout perspective, the flies are travelling towards a blinding light, and may possibly be very hard to see or identify. In the lift-and-hang style of boat fishing, whether on a floater or sinker, the angler has the choice of lifting the flies directly towards the boat or at an angle towards his sitting position. The angler who pulls his flies at an angle away from the sun will outperform those who pull their flies into the sun. Strange but very true!

# 3  A Whole Season on the Lochs

## Early-season Fishing (March and Early April)

In the early months of the season (March and April) on low-lying, productive waters, bank fishing may be the only option open to the keen fly-fisher, because the boats might not come out of storage until the risk of spring gales has diminished. My experience of big, deep highland lochs in spring is not comprehensive, but from brief experience I have come to the conclusion that the water is so cold and the invertebrate life so sparse that the indigenous trout are slow to get started. After all, why wake up and start rushing around when a decent breakfast is still months away?

Bank fishing is an unfortunate term because it presupposes that the angler can go shod in carpet slippers and never venture into the water. This is rarely the case. Wading is a more popular term in areas where this form of activity regularly takes place. But (and it is a pretty big *but*), in the first few weeks of the season trout can be found surprisingly, and sometimes distressingly, close to the water's edge. When I lived close to the shores of Harray in Orkney, a regular January activity was to walk my dog along the loch shore on a fine, calm day and count the trout arrowing away from the margins. As long as the water was deep enough to cover their backs the fish were happy mooching about in the shallows. Then when the season opened on 15 March, a walking rod close to those same, top-of-the-wind, sheltered waters could see lively, if well spread out, action. The big problem was walking quietly enough and far enough back not to spook the fish before they were in casting range, and the solution often involved making a thirty- or forty-foot cast that left a great length of fly line lying in the grass and only a few feet of line and leader in the water. Bizarre but effective!

These fish are in very shallow water for the best of reasons. Firstly, thin, shallow water in sheltered places warms up swiftly in the middle of the day, and such a temperature rise will trigger activity amongst the shrimp, snails and caddis larvae. Secondly, water can be turbid at this time of year but the shallow water of the margins allows maximum light penetration, which stimulates algal growth on the stones and gravel. This simple green plant life is the principal food of the water creatures mentioned above, and a food chain quickly becomes established in this micro-environment with the algal growth at the bottom and the trout (or the angler, depending upon your perspective) at the top. Most of the activity is in the middle of the day (or, to be more accurate, between about 10.30 am and 3 pm), developing slowly to a peak probably at or about 1 pm and declining from then on. (All these guidelines must be matched against weather conditions on the day and are offered as a broad guide only. As in all matters piscatorial the exception tends to prove the rule.)

In March the best way to avoid catching fish is to wade out into the water and chuck your flies at the horizon. The fish will be behind you (well, they would be if you hadn't scared them out into the deeps by entering the water); for the first few weeks most meaningful feeding is going on in inches, not feet, of water. But by the time we've got into April fish are starting to drift back to deeper water. Of course, 'deeper' is a relative term; from inches of water fish now prefer a couple of feet over their backs, and the spring upheaval in the midge world, and massive hatches that can be experienced at this time, will see the muddy holes and troughs invaded by trout. There will not only be environmental changes for the fish but dietary ones as well. (This is, of course, a minor slice of a trout's life and, with differing factors and scenarios, such changes will be continually repeated throughout the year as environmental changes and food sources dictate.)

Another change that takes place sometime in April is that fish will take up residence at the tail of the wind as opposed to the head-of-the-wind habitat deeply preferred in March. This is a direct result of an increase in air and water temperatures. As April ambient temperatures climb, the water along the weather shores will become suitable for invertebrate activity, and, given the presence of food, trout will move in to take advantage. Successful fishermen will still be searching knee-

**Orkney loch patterns**

Skinny Olive Dabbler

Dark Loch Ordie

Black & Claret Emerger

Magenta Slick

Orange Sedgehog

Hare's Ear
Half-Hog

Hell's Half-Hog

Swannay Viva

Machair loch patterns

Black Ke-He

Hare's Ear
Shipman's

Silver Invicta

Default
Dabbler

Green Peter Muddler

Olive French Partridge

Kate McLaren

Claret Bumble

Sea trout and salmon loch patterns

Peter Ross

Kate McLaren Muddler

Leggy Claret Bumble

Peterson's Pennell

Clan Chief

Claret French Partridge

Leggy Golden Olive Bumble

Jungle Cock Bibio

**Durness limestone loch patterns**

Hutch's Pennell

Olive Half-Hog

Muddled Hare's Ear

Olive Sedgehog

Fluo Soldier Palmer

Orange Pulling Buzzer

Olive Shuttlecock

Red arrow (variant)

**Loch Watten patterns**

Dirty Weeker

Claret Sedgehog

Green-Tailed Loch Ordie

Kate McLaren
Snatcher

Watten Warrior

Doobry Snatcher

Red-Arsed Green/Peter

Orange Half-Hog

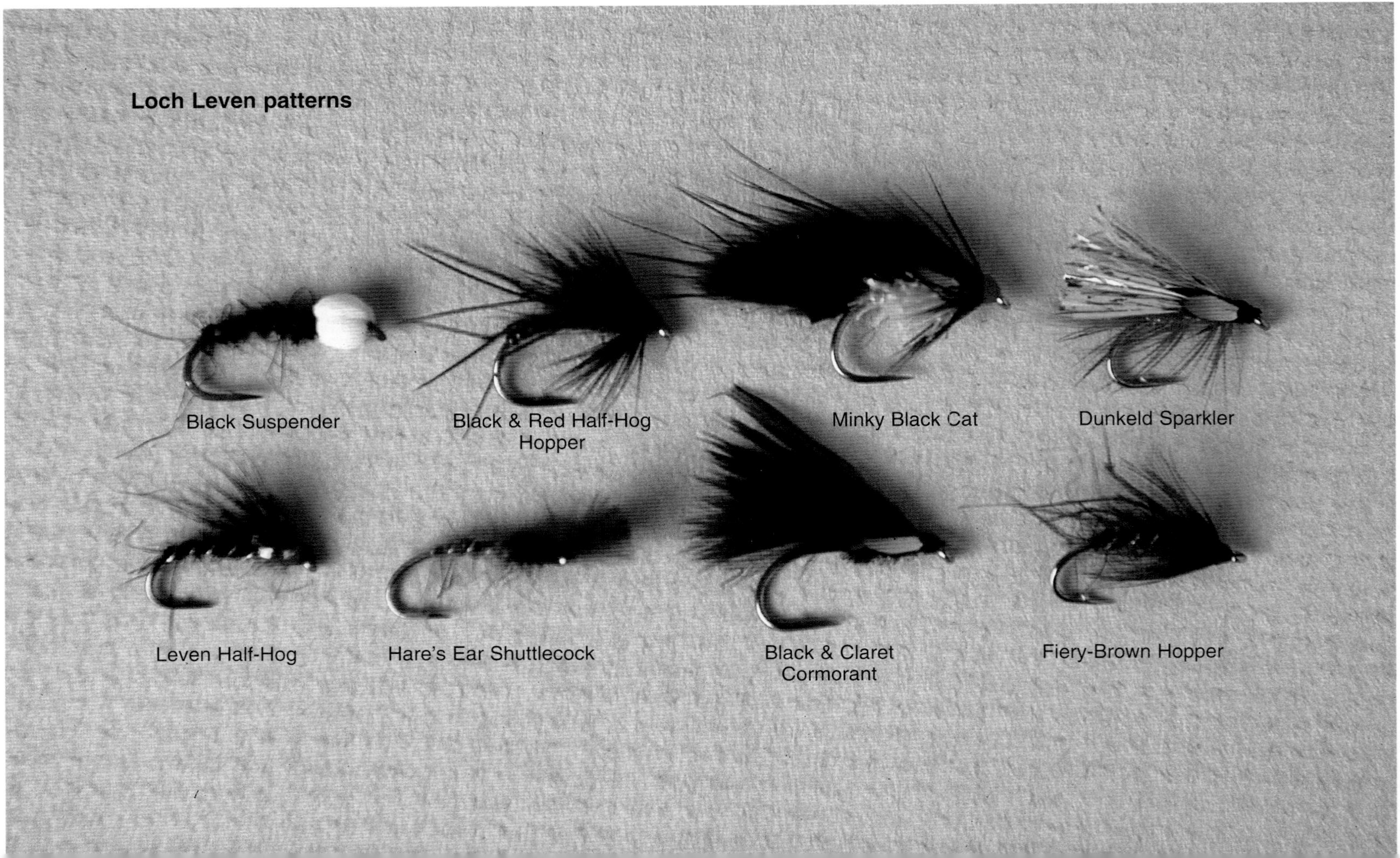

**Loch Leven patterns**

Dunkeld Sparkler

Fiery-Brown Hopper

Minky Black Cat

Black & Claret Cormorant

Black & Red Half-Hog Hopper

Hare's Ear Shuttlecock

Black Suspender

Leven Half-Hog

The last remnants of a big Caenis hatch.  Loch Watten, Caithness

Loch Borralaidh on the north side of the island and slightly east of the abyss.
Note the gin-clear water and the shocking posture of the angler!

Fish are designed for a weightless world. A fish that is to be returned should
not be lifted from the water, as this can seriously damage its internal organs

depth water for fish, because in deeper water food and fish activity will be limited, and down the weather shore the successful tactic will be 'wading out and fishing in'.

Because brown trout are largely territorial fish, and also because they prefer shallow water at this time of the year, fish are generally well dispersed, unless they've discovered a bonanza. Such bonanzas include midge in midge holes, occasional gatherings of shrimp, and windfalls at the mouths of burns and streams (I suppose we should call such occurrences 'waterfalls', but that would be unnecessarily confusing). My experience of burn-mouth windfalls extends to flushes of trout fry and bloodworm brought down by freshets, though these are not common.

Because trout are well spread in the early months, the best tactic is the 'step-and-cast' routine. Reservoir fishers and those more attuned to rainbow trout tend to stand, like herons, in one spot waiting for fish to come to them. But wild brown trout are territorial by nature, and to stand in one spot hoping for a succession of fish to pass by is generally a waste of time; within a few minutes the angler will have covered, and hopefully caught, all the trout in the area, and unless he moves on he is extremely unlikely to encounter any more. The 'step-and-cast' method is a loose term for a procedure that can involve taking a step between casts, the standing still during the retrieve, or (my preferred routine) just walking quietly and continuously whilst casting and retrieving. The latter technique would probably be better defined as 'six steps and cast'. I reckon to cover about five or six miles of shoreline in a day with this method, and fitter and healthier exponents can quite easily double that. Using such a technique means that the angler covers a multitude of fish and he won't need a high percentage response to end up catching a bucketful.

In the shallow water that trout prefer at this time of the year, wild brownies don't employ their usual vertical attack style but tend to take in a horizontal plane. This being the case it is advantageous for the angler to fish with his rod tip low and the line tight. Takes then become simpler to turn into successfully hooked fish. Fish with the rod tip high, and trout will take, inspect and eject before the angler has a chance to set the hook and the failure rate will be high. The influence of low water temperatures will compound this problem, and fish will tend to come short as discussed in Chapter 2 and for the very reasons identified. Later in the year, in warm, shallow water, the 'rush up, grab, and rush away' type of take is the most common, but at this time of year the fish tend to sidle up, suck in and turn, which reduces the chances of the fish hooking itself. Traditionally, we tended to fish with the rod tip up and a nice bow in the line, which allowed fish to take in the vertical plane and at speed without endangering the leader material, while also giving the trout time to turn on the fly. Smash takes in the spring are rare, because water temperatures are low and fish tend to take steadily, and so aren't likely to do anything in a manner that endangers fine tippet material. Keep your rod low and catch fish!

Much of what has been said above about wading – time of day, location, water depth, likely food items, etc. – is also applicable to early season boat fishing. This should go without saying, as all we are changing is the means of locomotion, and the behaviour of the fish will not be altered because the angler is afloat. But there are advantages and disadvantages to the use of boats in March and April. Assuming you can get your bum in a boat in March, the boat's design will decide whether you will be able to enter water shallow enough to hold fish (there is absolutely no point in sticking to summer drifts – the fish are unlikely to be in these areas). Unless you can get into the shallow waters where the temperatures and light penetration have got the invertebrate life active, you'll be flogging a dead horse. As I write this in mid-April, reports coming back from Loch Leven underline this advice: stockies are being caught in the waters adjacent to the harbour, but wild and over-wintered fish are being picked up in the shallows around St Serf's and along the shores below Vane Farm. If Loch Leven opened in March (God forbid!), then the draught of a Leven boat would make it unlikely that the fishermen would be able to get close enough to the margins to fish successfully. (Pure conjecture and impossible to prove, but experiences elsewhere back up this statement.)

If you are an aficionado of the sinking-line-and-lures school of thought, you may be tempted to think that there must be fish in the deeps untroubled by all the shallow-drifting boats. There undoubtedly will be, but experience tends to suggest that they will be comatose and not actively feeding. Fish that I have taken during exploratory forays into deep water in March and early April have been very thin on the ground, and almost always in very poor condition. There is little food in the deeps at this time of year, and trout tend to use such areas for hibernation – if that is an appropriate description of their comatose state.

Weather is rarely conducive to good boat fishing sport at this time of year. Since the sheltered, upwind areas tend to produce the best environmental conditions for trout to feed, this often means that the only places where a good head of fish will be patrolling the shallows are in those sheltered areas where the wind comes directly off the shore. You might be tempted to think that very calm days (when the whole loch is turned into a lee shore) should bring all the fish on the feed, but such conditions are generally associated with frosts or at least very low temperatures, and hence are a turn-off to margin-patrolling brown trout in the spring months. Light winds and warm temperatures are rare at this time of year in the Highlands and Islands; warm temperatures are closely associated with Atlantic rain-bearing systems, which are, on the whole, pretty vigorous and chock full of feisty winds. To hold a boat in the calm, warm water at the head of the wind in spring is largely ineffectual, because the boat will be sitting in the water where the trout want to be and the anglers will be chucking away from the fish. The concept of drifting in this region, and at this time of year, is only successful when there are extensive offshore shallows and – these should be fished diligently and with high expectations.

Why should warm, vigorous winds be a problem at this time of year? Well, at the head of the wind they are not a problem, but fresh winds at the tail of a drift will push you away from fish-holding regions quickly. Moreover, weed growth is at a minimum in spring, so bottom sediments will be easily stirred up in a relatively short time, making the loch turbid and fishing effort fruitless.

In March and early April wade if you can; if you can't, always try to second-guess the fish, work out where they are likely to be and stick to those areas. Random, thoughtless drifting won't bring you many fish at this time of year. And one more word of caution – keep very, very quiet in the boat. Trout in shallow water are spookier than a cat in a rocking horse factory, and when you are sitting in what, to all intents and purposes, is an underwater amplifier, one dropped item or clumsy movement will see every trout scurrying to the safety of the deeps in a microsecond.

When it comes to boat-fishing technique, in the early months the best line is without doubt the floater. Again, you might argue that a floater is a strange line to use when little surface activity is evident, but a slow-fished fly is virtually essential at this time of year, and with a long leader, a slow retrieve and shallow water the point fly of a three-fly cast will tripping along the stones and the middle fly will swim mid-water. Don't expect much to come to a bobbed top dropper pattern – this is just not the season for it – so keep your rod tip low with only a slight belly in the line and expect takes to be steady and positive. Fly patterns that I favour at this time of year generally contain black, claret or olive green, with orange and golden olive being handy for clear, uncoloured water (which, it must be said, is a bit of a rarity at this time of the year).

## Summer Fishing

### The Unbreakable Link Between Boats and Loch Fishing

It is important to remember that, from a Scottish perspective, trout fishing on lochs is all about boats. Many summer visitors from more civilised parts are either not used to fishing from boats, don't like them much, can't handle them, or get seriously concerned about safety when the slightest of breezes picks up. But we natives get a bit sniffy if compelled to fish from the bank. Therefore, those who find themselves in the heartlands of Scottish loch fishing, laden down with tackle, and compelled to fish from the bank in the summertime because there are no boats, tend to draw one of the following conclusions:

a) the fishing is not good enough to warrant the expense of a boat fleet;

b) it is too far away/high up/inaccessible to get boats there – which, more than likely, can mean that the loch has a poor fish stock, because if the fishing was good enough some Victorian enthusiast would have created a bottomless well of local resentment by having the serfs build a road into it; or

c) some worthy soul, haunted by the vision of wax-jacketed corpses sloshing about in the margins, has decided that the loch in question is too dangerous/deep/windswept to allow suicidal anglers access to boats.

Conclusions a) and b) apply most often to regions north of the Highland Boundary Line, whilst c) is most often experienced in the 'Sooth', where bureaucracy's writ, coupled with a fear of lawsuits involving compensation for loved ones departed, is a major fact of life. We, in the North, tend to have a healthy regard for the wishes and rights of others: if Joe MacSoap wants to take a leaky old tub out on a windy day on a very deep loch and thereby endanger his life (as he has done since Noah was a boy), then it's his decision and the best of luck to him –we just hope he is found quickly before he pollutes the loch!

However, boats do turn up in some seriously out-of-the-way places! Peter Gathercole, ace fishing (and other) photographer, and I once had the extremely dubious pleasure of fishing a bleak hole in the ground called the Duchess' Loch, the fishing rights of which appertained unto a weel-kent hotel in the far north-west of Sutherland. They have a quaint system of fishing allocation at that hotel (I won't bore you with it here) but it did us no favours on that fateful day. Pete and I were doing a whistle-stop trip from South Uist to Cape Wrath in order to gather subject and photographic material for a series of articles, and we wound up at the hotel late on a Monday night. All the best fishing had gone to the regular incumbents, and Pete and I were left with the dregs – and the dregs can get very 'dreggy' in that neck of the woods. Afghanistan can look positively lush and verdant compared to certain parts of north-west Sutherland (which has, with good cause, some-times been referred to as 'the last place God made, before knocking-off for the weekend'). The region does have some excellent waters, but the Duchess' Loch is, or at least was then, not numbered amongst them. This began to dawn on us when we asked the fishery manager if there were any big trout in the loch.

'Well now,' he intoned with a mixture of apathy and pessimism peculiar to the West Coast, 'I wouldn't actually call them "big". No, "big" is not the word I would use. Small might be a better description.'

'Well, at least there'll be plenty of them,' we replied, with as much carefree optimism as we could rake up in the face of his 'you asked for it, turning up late!' smug attitude.

'Ah, well, no. Not exactly "plenty" either', he replied with a faint smile playing across his homely physog (which we later found out meant, 'don't worry about the quality of the fish in the loch, because by the time you've hauled yourself up the side of Ben Stack (2,364 ft above sea level) to get there, you won't be fit to do much fishing anyway!')

The amusing side to this, at least to me and Pete, was that the proprietors expected some glowing report to appear in the magazine, painting a picture of a fishing paradise, when all they had shown us was the dark side of fishing Hell! The doubly frustrating side was that quite a few guests came back with excellent fish from waters which didn't require pack-mules and native bearers to get to. If I ever get lured into fishing a loch halfway up a mountain again, there had better be, at best a helicopter, or at least a 4WD, off-road vehicle laid on, or I'm not going! For those of you who have worked out the identity of the above hotel, rest easy; it has undergone a change of management, and the fishery manager with the well-honed sense of humour has moved on to a career better suited to his idiosyncratic view of public relations.

Anyway, enough of that! Back to boats in strange places. Believe it or believe it not, the Duchess' Loch, clinging precariously halfway up the side of Ben Stack, had a boat! I was amazed! I mean how the bloody hell did they get it up there? Did it stay from one season to the next, waiting out the winter under a tarpaulin? No! It seemed that in the bad old days (I think that was last year!) the boat was dropped off by the side of the road next to the trail at the start of the season and the guests would voluntarily drag it, bit by bit, guest by guest, in a series of increments, up the sheer slope until the loch was reached. Greater love hath no fishing man that he would drag a boat up a mountainside for the use of someone coming along a month or so later! (Nowadays they use a helicopter – perhaps the milk of human kindness runs a lot less freely nowadays when 'sod you!' is more often heard than 'after you!') Loch fishing is so much about boats that I have seen them in many surprising places. And God love them for being there, because the only time of the year when I will gladly fish from the bank is in the very early spring.

## *Midge: A Fly for a Floater*

With the general decrease in water quality throughout the region, midge (chironomid species) are becoming an increasingly important part of trout diet.* Most important (from a trout's perspective), midge species like rich waters with reasonable mud deposits where the larval stages can develop. Not all midge species need mud and silt deposits to be able to thrive. Many species have larval stages that manage well by clinging to rocks or sunken objects. But the big hatches, which create frenzy feeding amongst trout, do tend to come from midge species that spend their larval stages in mud. Just like the famous duck fly hatches of the big Irish loughs, during which the anglers seek out the mud-lined duck fly holes, so, on the fertile Scottish waters, early summer will see massive hatches emerge from similar muddy holes. And this is floating-line fishing par excellence.

There is a little lagoon on the Harray loch, called Quoyre Camp, where mild, still April afternoons would see me standing like a heron at the mouth of a burn that had created a great swathe of mud and silt at its outflow. This mud was home to millions of bloodworm (midge larvae), and in season great swarms of pupae would drift up from the bottom in a desperate attempt to successfully hatch; trout would gather in this place and leisurely fin about sucking in gutfuls of midge pupae. Although, given the right conditions, I would expect to take my first dry-fly-lured trout of the year from this hole, the default technique would be midge pupa patterns fished gently on a long leader attached to a floating line. Fishing a short line, I would position myself as close to the visibly feeding fish and carefully drop flies on their route of travel. The white flash that indicated a mouth opening would be my signal to strike. If I missed this flash, more often than not I missed the fish, and that would spook the whole shoal and they would disappear for half an hour or so. It was lovely fishing and, as I sit on an early April morning writing this, I hanker after those days and those lovely fish.

---

* The midge we are talking about here are of the genus Chironomidae, and not the little biting horrors associated with the Highlands and peat bogs. Our lovable midge are the non-biting jobs you see 'dancing' in columns in the shelter of houses, trees, etc., generally after rain.

Midge (in almost all their forms and activities) and floating lines go together like chapped lips and Vaseline. It's not often loch fishers get a chance to fish for trout that are actively feeding on the larval stage (bloodworm), but it has happened to me a couple of times. Once was in Ireland, when trout were nailing bloodworm trapped in the surface film and we caught them using bright red dry flies. The other occasion was when a small spate had washed some larvae down the burn, and the fish had gathered at the mouth to gobble them up as they drifted by. Lacking anything vaguely resembling a bloodworm in my fly box, I tried dead-drifting a Soldier Palmer in the minimal flow; I got a lot of action till the fish got the message and disappeared to places where the living was less fraught with danger.

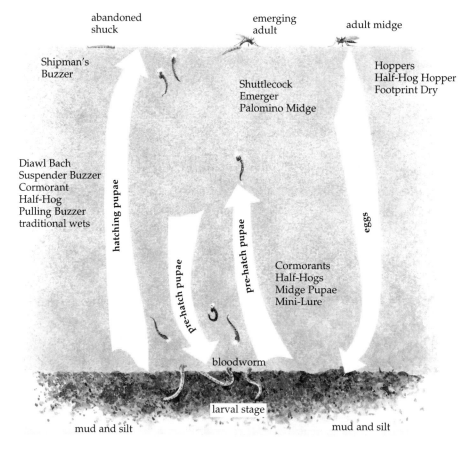

*Fig. 8   Midge life cycle and separate stage imitators*

But when it comes to fishing for trout bingeing on midge pupae, we are, often unknowingly, pretty good at it. The classic early-season flies – Black Pennel, Bibio, Viva, Peter Ross, Butcher, and anything else which involves black, claret, silver or red – are arguably midge pupae imitators, although it often takes a determined suspension of disbelief to see the likeness. The typical style of fly-fishing also reasonably represents the hatching process of midge pupae, in that a slowish rise up through the water with a brief hover in the surface film will just about convince a trout with its blood up that what it is seeing is just another hatching midge. However, when they get a bit choosy, or there just aren't enough midge pupae about to create frenzy, then the angler is required to acquire subtlety.

In the good old days when I knew little about dedicated midge-fishing techniques, my method of choice was a floating line with a Mini-Muddler on the top dropper and a few sparse and slim spider or palmer patterns below. Fishing a fairly long line, coupled with a steady retrieve was lethal in a good going hatch, and would 'pick away' during the periods before or after.

But nowadays a more sure and certain method is to 'dead-drift' a brace of buzzer patterns on the same long leader and floating line. Those 'something or nothing' patterns, comprising some thread, a strand of wire and a coat of varnish, will convince even the most suspicious of trout – but only when virtually static, slowly falling through the water column. Not all rainbow/Midlands reservoir tactics and techniques are applicable to wild brown trout, but this one most certainly is.

Whether fishing from boat or bank, the angler has to do no more than maintain contact with his flies by slow figure-8ing or, at a pinch, *very* slow retrieving, keeping the rod point down and pointing towards the flies. Takes are steady, strong and almost always unmissable. In anything approaching a good blow the boat angler should shelve this technique until the wind eases, but if the bank angler can find a quiet corner he can work wonders. Although you can fish this technique with an intermediate in deep water, it is always better to stick to a floater when fishing for early-season browns, as they are almost always in reasonably shallow water, or in holes alongside shallows.

Patterns that work well are those well publicised in the angling press and glorying in names such as Epoxy Buzzer, Super Glue Buzzer, Skinny Buzzers. My own Blushing Buzzer and Near Perfect Buzzer were designed for browns in Orkney and do very well in this context. But I am less than convinced that pattern is the most important component of success when buzzer fishing. On the contrary, I believe presentation is almost everything: Convince the trout that what they are seeing is a very slow-moving midge pupa and you'll catch them on a bare hook.

Whilst wild brown trout, all things being equal, prefer to feed on midge pupae as they ascend through the water column, there are times when for reasons best known to themselves, they will take the pupae at the point of hatching, or as a fully formed insect sitting on the surface of the water. When they are taking ascending midge pupae the only evidence on the loch surface is a series of quiet, bulging rise-forms that may only be visible as a flattening of the ripple; this is because the action is often taking place some distance below the surface. If, on the other hand, trout are taking the pupae on the point of hatching, and there are only a few about, the rise-form can be quite dramatic and explosive – strange, given that they are attacking a virtually static target. This is 'start-of-the-rise' behaviour. When the water surface becomes clogged with hatching buzzers, the trout will tend to swim, dorsal fin out of the water, engulfing their prey. If you want to have a go at a specific fish employing this behaviour, be advised that they virtually always swim in a circle, which can have a diameter of inches or feet, depending on where their nearest neighbour is and how many pupae are hatching to the square foot.

There are flies designed primarily to represent hatching midge and the most widely known is the Shuttlecock Buzzer – which, I have to say, I've found to be a pretty poor weapon for wild brownies (except on Leven, where all the rules get bent anyway!), though great on rainbows. The Palomino Midge, on the other hand, I've found to be excellent for browns (surprising, since these flies are not dissimilar). However, generally speaking, I stick with the buzzer pupae patterns on the floater and long leader until the fish get totally fixated on the emerging insect, when I usually switch straight to dries. In my experience rainbow trout tend towards selectivity more than browns, so that even when all the browns may appear to be zeroed in on emerging fly, a pupa pattern dead-drifted in their hunting zone can still be very effective. Wild

browns, due to their territorial/hunter mentality, are much more opportunistic than rainbows, or their stocked cousins, for that matter.

But on the odd occasion, when the browns ignore the pupa patterns
because they are totally focused on the emerging insect, or simply
because I want to, I will happily fish dries over them. That is not to say,
though, that dry-fly tactics for browns feeding hard on hatching midge
are always successful. Frequently you will spend a whole hatch
chucking dries at fish that are visibly knocking off hatching midge and
go home skunked. But this will be because of something I refer to as the
'trigger effect'. What I think is happening is that there is some specific
thing that the fish see during the hatching process that tells them 'Yep!
That is a 100%, copper-bottomed, gold-plated, absolutely guaranteed,
real live hatching midge!', and what you are offering lacks that certifi-
cate of guarantee. It may be colour, it may be shape, it may very well
be some sort of action that is taking place, but, whatever it is, it is part
and parcel of the real thing and missing from your fly or presentation.

Here is classic example of what I mean by trigger effect. I was sitting
out on Swannay one April morning very successfully not catching a
whole series of fish that were mopping up a sparse hatch of black
midge. It was virtually flat calm and the trout were taking the adult
flies very steadily, whilst totally ignoring my Black and Claret Emerger.
What I did know was that the trout were taking the midge, because I
could see there was nothing else available, and the rise forms were
those of fish taking something in the surface film. What I didn't know
was that the fish were taking the adults on point of emergence. As the
fly popped up on the surface film the trout would slide up and over it
and take it down. I could see the naturals on the water, and I could see
what were obviously 'adult insect' takes, so I was convinced the trout
were picking off the fully emerged adults. And I was catching nothing.
By sheer chance I discovered that if I gave the artificial a good pull, it
would become totally immersed before struggling back onto the
surface, propelled upwards by a healthy dose of Gink. As it popped up
it was taken, almost every time. It was the breaking of the surface film
that convinced the trout that here was a bona fide hatching midge.

That was an action trigger effect. Colour trigger effects are many and
varied and occur right across the insect species range. Depending upon
strength, quality and direction of light, what we see when we examine

an insect may be totally at odds with what the trout sees. We tend to view insects via reflected light: the object has light shining on it, which bounces off the objects surface and enters our eyes. We hold the insect in our hand and let the light bounce off the surface of the insect and thus we define its 'true' colour. Trout frequently view insects and items below and above surface via transmitted light, by which I mean that the object is viewed against a bright background, and the light entering the trout's eyes shines through the translucent body of the insect. So the midge pupa we see as intrinsically black may actually glow a rich claret shade, because, beneath the black skin, the insect's body is packed with bright red blood, and the transmitted light shines in varying degrees of red depending on strength of sunlight. To use a black fly in such a situation is as incongruous as using a bright yellow one. This also explains why patterns such as Grouse/Mallard & Claret and Claret Bumble, and many other with similar colouring can, in small sizes be exceptionally effective in midge hatches, and why many black patterns can be surprisingly ineffective in similar circumstances.

During the hatch process midge pump up their bodies with gas in order to split the pupal skin, and this makes the pupae, at a critical time when they are often predated by fish, appear to have a silver sheen. Irish duck fly fishers know this effect well, and most of their pupae imitations have silvery bodies (or, at the very least, a hint of silver somewhere about them). We on the other side of the Irish Sea haven't learnt the lesson quite so well, but many of us unwittingly prefer to use Butchers, Peter Ross, and other silver-bodied flies during midge hatches for, now, obvious reasons.

These are a few reasons why midge fishing can be a frustrating and perverse form of fly-fishing to the angler who is unaware of all the factors involved. And even those who know the problems, are well versed in the logic can find a loch bespattered with the rings of rising trout, the very air humming in resonance to the wings of a million midge, a source of dissatisfaction rather than fulfilment.

## Mid-year Fishing with a Floating Line

Late April until late June will see the very best of fly-fishing, and in the north and west the floating line will feature highly. It must be remembered that ambient temperatures will not be high, and May can see snow on the high hilltops. Whereas the southern regions of the UK can experience Mediterranean-style weather at this time of year, Scotland is only slowly emerging from winter. Recent weather trends have seen summer extending later and later into what was generally classified as autumn and early winter and, as a form of compensation, winter has been loath to leave until what we laughingly refer to as spring is well under way.

## WHAT THE TROUT ARE DOING AND WHERE TO FIND THEM

A good description of a Scottish year would be an indifferent summer slipping into a meek and mild winter, which gets ever more harsh and bitter as we pine pathetically for sunshine and warmth. Then comes one week of true spring weather, which generally involves hailstones, before the cycle starts again.

However, it isn't necessarily heat that triggers the onset of an aquatic summer. Light intensity is much more important. As the sun climbs higher in the sky with every passing day, sunlight penetrates deeper into the water stimulating green matter to accelerated growth rates. This has the knock-on effect of triggering activity among the invertebrates which trout favour. Shrimp, hog lice, ephemerid nymphs, caddis larvae and snails graze hungrily on the algae-covered stones, and trout feed hard. If, like me, you are a student of the marrow spoon, you will know that trout feed aggressively and virtually incessantly at this time of the year. It is almost as if they knew that living/feeding will not get better than this until next year's summer onset. Daylight hours are long, temperatures are conducive to good water oxygenation, and the sun isn't high enough in the sky to hurt their eyes. This is binge feeding time.

The best of the aquatic insect hatches take place at this time, and the totally aquatic invertebrates, such as shrimp and snails prefer these months for breeding. All this activity supports and stimulates the rapacious appetites of the trout. It's a great time for fishermen and fish.

The wading angler will find the shallows infested with feeding trout – or, at the very least, trout that are willing to show some interest in food – right through the early summer daylight hours. By this time of the year shallow water can be defined as anything up to and including 5 feet/1·5 m. Whereas the March/April angler rarely gets his knees wet, the early summer wading fisherman is in serious danger of getting mildew on his wedding tackle! My favourite technique when forced out of a boat in early summer is to deep-wade the downwind side of a loch, to the limits of a pair of chest waders, chucking the flies back into the shallow-water maelstrom where the waves break. In March/April you'd avoid this area like a plague-infested brothel, but once the air and water temperatures have climbed a bit, fish will be searching this area for unlucky items dislodged from stones or sucked from underneath them by wave action.

One of the great fallacies, carefully nurtured and passed on by anglers, is that trout like the bottom of the wind because that's where all the food ends up. There's a small element of truth in this, but:

a) If you consider the wind lanes bearing food as a gigantic, elongated conveyor belt, where would you rather be – at the very end, or working your way up it, sucking down the goodies from source?

b) The bulk of a trout's food is rarely carried on the surface but is more often found below the waves. It is the suction and destruction caused by exaggerated wave effect on the weather shore that makes this a happy hunting ground for trout and angler.

If you compare the weather-shore feeding zone to the surf of an Atlantic storm beach, where the bass and sea trout feed, you'll understand how and why the fallacy mentioned above is flawed.

Other reasons why trout favour this region are the increased oxygen levels produced by wave action on the shore, plus the cover and safety provided by the water disturbance. I actually consider the latter to be the prime reason why the tail-of-the-wind turbulence is so productive. At the calm top of the wind, not only are fish venturing into the shallows very aware of how exposed they are to predators in the quiet water, but the temperature range in this environment can make it unappealing to trout. Generally trout will only be lured into this environment during the hours of darkness, when they are less obvious to predators and when the night-time cool has improved the water temperature.

In a perfect world the bank angler should venture out early and late to find the biggest fish. It may be a tad anthropomorphic of me to suggest that by the time the season is well under way trout know best when to avoid anglers' attempts to interfere with their lives, but I am sure it is no coincidence that the hours humans consider anti-social are the ones quality trout prefer for their ventures into shallow water. However, in very windy weather or unseasonably chilly conditions the bank angler is probably best advised to stick to daylight hours, as these conditions can often discourage night-time activity amongst the fish, not to mention the anglers.

DAY OR NIGHT?

In the far north and west of Scotland in the middle of the year, the period of night-time darkness does not last long. In Orkney and Shetland it will be possible to read the printed page all through a late June night, so there is no dark to speak of, and trout activity can carry on throughout the gloaming, with a slight reduction in activity during the darkest period (generally about 1–2 am). Surprisingly, the clear, unclouded evenings and mornings produce the poorest sport, because the steep drop in temperatures experienced from sunset to sunrise cancels out the benefits of increased light. The sudden accelerated chill affecting the surface layers of water will drive the fish out of the shallows to seek more comfortable areas. Any sudden change in climatic conditions, at any time of day, will see a dramatic change in trout behaviour and almost always to the disadvantage of the angler.

If the night-time bank angler can reach relatively deep water during a chilly night he might find fish willing to co-operate if he employs a fast-intermediate or slow-sink line. But this should be a last resort to salvage a trip. Ideally he would boldly venture out, armed with a floating line, when the warmth of the breeze extends into the darkness hours, and a good cloud cover, without rain, holds in the daytime warmth. To stand in the darkness and hear the 'sloop-sloop' of unseen, feeding brown trout in the shallows is one of the sport's most exciting experiences, only outclassed by the steady, solid, heavy take of an invisible monster within a few feet of your rod point. In my more energetic youth I loved a night foray, but expected only a few per season.

In the North Isles, warm summer nights are at a premium, and June and July are the most likely, if not the only, months to supply them. Mind you, the lack of warm summer nights in those northern regions is offset by the lack of summer, heat-induced 'dog days' that can be such a problem for anglers in more southern parts. Daytime is the loch fisher's principal period of activity, and the forays in the dark are the thin icing on a fat cake.

When I think of mid-season boat angling, my memory wanders back to wonderful mornings on the Swannay loch, in the West Mainland of Orkney, with lapwings moaning over the freshly cultivated loch-side fields and snipe 'drumming' over the moor (the territorial call of breeding snipe has almost become synonymous in my mind with quality trout fishing). Somehow I have become convinced that when the trout are at their most active the waterside birds are always 'giving it laldy' in a vociferous and vocal manner. Nature seems to have its active and inactive periods and the 'slosh' of a rising trout harmonises perfectly with the sound of bird calls on a fishy morning. Unfortunately, though, the seasonal shift of latter years puts the image of fat, free-rising trout on a sparkly late spring morning, with irises, king-cups and marsh orchids winking colour from the water's edge and lapwings swooping over their kingdoms, at odds with reality. May can be a horrific month of gales, horizontal sleet showers and cast-iron grey skies, and June can be little better. Often, when the sun breaks out it is accompanied by north-easterly winds, dry and cold enough to sear the skin from your flesh. None of this makes for good fishing, but is offset by the biological imperative that compels trout to feed, and to feed hard. At no other time of the year do wild trout feed quite so voraciously.

Some of you might be surprised at the continual association with sun and good fishing, but I am convinced that from March to May sunshine is no bad thing from a trout fishing perspective. At all other times (except perhaps late September) I consider it to be anathema, but in the early to mid-summer periods, when trout need severe discouragement to stop feeding, the shallow angled rays of sunlight can be a boon.

Peat water lochs generally fish very badly in bright weather. I have always wondered at this because it would seem logical that clear-water

lochs, into which light penetration is unhindered, would be more negatively affected by sunlight. It isn't so. But, in the early months sunny
days can provide excellent and hectic sport, regardless of most other
considerations. However, come July, lose hope and learn despair when
sunshine makes peat water shimmer in the heat haze. During
uncommon heat waves on Scottish lochs of quality, sunset may see
some relief and a brief period of activity until the clear skies allow the
temperatures to plummet to levels unacceptable to fish and angler alike.

MID-SUMMER TACTICS IN WIND AND WAVE

By mid-summer trout have moved into deeper water than they
preferred in the first two months of the season. Regular forays into
shallow water will be made, depending upon what and where the best
food resources are, but general prospecting is best done from deep into
shallow and not sticking to one depth contour. While it is sensible practice for the boat angler to avoid the downwind end of the loch in the
opening months of the season, he should reverse the process in mid-
summer and avoid the upwind regions when the last few casts in the
wave-lashed shallows at the tail of the wind can be the most productive of any drift. The same can, of course, be said of the upwind side of
islands, skerries or any rocky outcrops. Getting a friend or ghillie to
hold the boat off a weather shore can be great fun for the fisherman, if
not quite so pleasurable for the poor sod on the oars (I speak from
experience!).

But I wouldn't want to leave you with the fixed idea that in any sort
of a breeze the best fish are always at the tail of the wind cavorting in
the wave-thrashed shallows, because nothing can be further from the
truth on occasion. If the wind or weather is unseasonably cold, then
fish may avoid the weather shore and lie back off it a bit, for a cold
wind will cool the surface of the water and force this chilled layer into
the shallows, where it will build up. In fact, on occasion, I've seen the
head of the wind being the only place one could expect any action at
all. An outing on Grogarry, in South Uist, in late June 2002 was a prime
example. The weather had been, if you'll excuse the expression, bloody
awful, for Orkney experienced June storms which virtually closed the
fishing season four months early. Harray (which until the storm had

been fishing wonderfully well) was turned into a gigantic bowl of oxtail soup, and sulkily refused to fish worth a damn for the rest of the season, and this scenario, in a diluted form, was repeated throughout the nation, with only a few notable exceptions.*

Anyway, Iain Muir and I were out on Grogarry, ghillied by Angus Johnstone. We were experiencing the tail end of the same storm which ravaged Harray, and only the fact that we had all spent lifetimes trying to fish fly in a flat-out, screaming gale made sense of the fact that we were there in a boat at all. There are two types of gales. One raises great waves which boom on the shoreline and sends untethered things flying high in the sky – this is a carefree, light-hearted, mischievous gale. The other is the gale from hell: it doesn't try to blow things up into the skies, it tries to blow them into the ground; it doesn't raise waves, it flattens them. Occasionally, vast plumes of spray are ripped off the surface of the loch to go dancing across the flattened waters like ballet dancers on mescaline, but, apart from the odd whimsical display of this kind, this is an evil wind which defeats oars and even outboard motors. Generally speaking, not only is it useless to fish in such winds, it is downright dangerous. I have been lifted from my wading feet and thrown bodily into the water by such a wind, and even the most versatile mind cannot comprehend the myriad varieties of boating disasters such weather conditions can cause. This was such a gale.

The one fish we caught was up on the sheltered shore. All the others which we either frustratingly moved but failed to hook or saw leaping in a carefree manner were similarly located. And we saw neither scale nor fin on the weather shore. All the same, Angus insisted on dicing with death amongst the rocks and foam at the tail end of the wind in a nerve-wracking, bowel-loosening way. As far as he was concerned, fish are to be found on the weather shore and all evidence to the contrary – fish gathered in droves on the lee shore wearing kamikaze headbands and busily jotting down suicide notes, or a signed submission from St

* Over the past few years June has produced some horrific weather. Forget all those images of early summer – high clouds scudding across a blue sky, marsh flowers nodding contentedly by the margins, lapwings mewing from the shores and the gentle lip, lap of wavelets lovingly caressing the hull of the boat. Reality paints a whole new landscape – destructive low pressure systems roaring in from the Atlantic, raging floods, storm-tossed lochs, winter-like chills.

Peter, countersigned by Isaac Walton – would not have even slightly dented his resolve. Summer gales springing up out of nowhere, especially if they blow from a west or south westerly direction, should produce sport on the weather shore, but easterly or south-easterly gales that bring along a flask, sandwiches and sleeping bag and look like they're here to stay frequently turn the laws of fishing on their head and send summer fish to the head of the wind for their chow.

Floating line fishing in such high-wind conditions can be a pain in the fundament. Of all the heart-breaking things which can happen in fly-fishing, one of the worst must be to see a whopping big fish with blood in its eye and jaws wide apart bearing down on your lovely fly, only for a gust of wind to whip the fly out of harm's way at the moment of crisis. Then to watch the same finny monster pirouetting on the spot where his lunch just disappeared from with a puzzled and hungry look on his homely face whilst your pretty fly dances the light fantastic thirty yards downwind – that only twists the knife that is already lodged in your breast.

Some pundits recommend the use of intermediates to stop this heartbreak, but I am opposed to the switch. Quite often an intermediate will outscore the floater on surface-feeding fish in a big wind, but when the floater is bringing fish up like mushrooms on a wet night, you'd be a fool to switch to a line which may lack the same pulling power. The secret is to make the pulling power of the floater work for you – and, to make sure that there is a final reward, remember to keep the rod point down and low over the water, so that the wind can't get under the line and lift it in a distressing fashion. Swinging the rod low and out over the stern or the bow will allow the fisherman to raise the flies in an enticing manner far enough out from the boat to ensure a degree of success. The use of ginked-up flies such as Sedgehogs and permafloated Loch Ordies produces a situation where a contrived bobbed fly is maintained without raising the rod tip. It is no coincidence that Ordies used as wet flies, and Hedgehogs and Sedgehogs, all originated in an area where the summer gale is a recurring fact of life. This style of pattern, the permanent bob fly, is essential fare for northern fisherman and, given an understanding of a few simple rules, provides first-class sport throughout the summer. The rules are these:

- Ensure that the flies are well treated with floatant. (I saturate mine with liquid floatant as soon as they leave the tying vice. Left to dry for a few hours and then treated with a sparse amount of gel floatant by the waterside, such a prepared fly will float all day if not interfered with, or catch a half-dozen trout before requiring attention).
- Never mount two greased-up flies on a cast that you intend to pull, as opposed to fishing static. Instead of doubling the catch rate you will almost certainly decimate it.
- On a floating line the best place for the greased-up fly is on the top dropper. On an intermediate or sinker, stick the treated pattern on the point.
- Given that conditions don't change, if you haven't had some response to your greased-up pattern within, say, half an hour, take it off and think again. Response should come about fairly rapidly if fish are going to comply. But response can take many forms. A cast with a Sedgehog on the bob may work spectacularly well without the bob fly taking a single fish, the middle and point flies being taken because the Sedgehog has pulled the fish to the cast, or, because the high-swimming bob fly has pulled the following flies ever closer to the surface film, thereby increasing their attraction.

MID-SUMMER TACTICS: DRY FLY

This brings us neatly on to the subject of dry flies for wild trout. My own introduction to dry-fly fishing was piecemeal and haphazard. A great many years ago there was a lady angler, from the south-west of Scotland, who would visit Orkney on a regular basis to wade the lochs and fish dry fly. Her success rate was phenomenal and the average size of her catch produced envy in her wet-fly-pulling contemporaries. She had spells when she could catch nothing, but when she caught, she caught big! I never found her particularly communicative; on the contrary I found her abrasive and secretive, and she had the disconcerting habit of rapidly disappearing round corners if she spotted a fellow angler approaching (given that she certainly did not have the confirmation of a racing snake, this was a sight to behold). However, for some reason she took my father under her wing and inducted him into the tiny band (total membership 2) that was the Orkney Dry Fly Fishers. Any information I could glean I got from him, but I couldn't make much of the information I inherited, and caught few fish on this revolutionary new technique for two very simple reasons. I became convinced, first, that dry fly was best in flat calms (which it most certainly isn't!), and, second that the leader must be greased as well, so that the poorly suited, greased-up wet fly would float. I probably wasn't listening properly to the advice I was given, or perhaps even my old man didn't know, but if the leader wasn't de-greased, then in anything other than a stiff breeze trout would sheer away from any dry supported by a greased-up leader. So my early induction to the mysterious world of stillwater dry-fly fishing (and this was a good decade before those charming English chaps 'invented' the art on Grafham and the like) was nipped in the bud.

R.C. Bridgett, circa 1924, devoted a whole chapter of his *Loch Fishing* to the art of dry-fly fishing on lochs. One of the best and most interesting aspects of dry fly for wild trout is that it has the distinct ability to sort out the wheat from the chaff. Big fish are very fond of dry flies, whilst small fish are, on a day-to-day basis, less so. When I really began to understand the potential and principles of dry-fly fishing I caught all my biggest fish from each of the main Orkney lochs on dry fly, the only exception being, not surprisingly perhaps, Stenness.

And an even better aspect of dry-fly fishing for loch trout is that it is a remarkably easy technique to master and apply. Here are the rules which, when adhered to, produce happy dry-fly fishers:

- Always believe that you are going to raise fish to the dries. Lack of faith is a self-fulfilling prophecy.
- Use as fine a leader material as you can without going so fine that you run the risk of regular breakages.
- Vary your flies and tactics to suit the naturals that the fish expect to see.
- Resist the inclination to fish dries when the surface of the loch is mirror-calm.
- Do not be put off by a big wave as long as you have good reason to believe that the technique will work.

- It is not important to be able to see the floating fly. Your floating line will almost inevitably point to its location, and a rise in the general area should be met with the obvious response.
- Be aware that fluorocarbon monofilament will eventually pull your dry flies beneath the waves. Well degreased copolymer nylon, which is very strong for its gauge, is vastly preferable.

Brown trout, because of their innate tendency to take in a vertical manner, are suckers for dry fly. Most anglers believe that dry-fly fishing is really a rainbow trout technique adapted to brown trout fishing. Not so! In my experience brown trout are more susceptible to dry fly because of their opportunistic manner of feeding. Rainbows, being more selective feeders, tend to be locked into one food item, and if they are not surface feeding or expecting surface food tend to respond poorly to dries. Although many would argue the point with me, I believe browns are more likely to 'come out of the blue' to an optimistic dry, regardless of what they expect to see in the way of food items. Even in waters such as Loch Leven, where the browns are more akin to rainbows in their feeding habits and are much less territorial and more depth-orientated than most other wild browns, they respond very well to dry fly. Often in what are generally accepted as pretty hopeless conditions – flat calm and bright sunshine – when fish can be expected to be very deep, the odd Leven brown will be seen to rise and may be expected to come to well-presented dries.

So much for the propaganda, now for the practical! In a perfect season dries for browns can be effective the whole season long, starting with the first midge hatches in April and petering out after the last terrestrial fall in autumn. In reality, it probably won't work out that way because of the nature of the Law of Sod, but at some time *the only and best way* to take them will be dry fly, and this is more than likely to happen in the summer months.

Aquatic fly hatches likely to instigate a general rise during a typical Scottish summer are caenis, deep-water midge, and sedges. The first and last of these are endemic and can be expected everywhere, whilst deep-water midge are generally restricted to waters which are on the tricky side of eutrophic, and are therefore rare on a national basis. Terrestrial species which can be expected are cow dung fly, daddy-long-legs and heather fly. But, and this is important, dry-fly tactics (specifically the method I refer to as 'search and destroy', can be used at any time and can reasonably be expected to produce results more often than not.

DRY FLY: SEARCH AND DESTROY TECHNIQUE

Standard wet-fly tactics for loch fishing involve setting the boat on a shoreline drift and casting a team of wets in front of the drifting boat, with the expectancy that fish covered will show some interest to one or other of the flies used. This is a relatively uncommon form of fly-fishing. Most other forms of fly-fishing rely on targeting individual fish, but the fishing practices of the Celtic fringe work on the principal that there are plenty of fish, and a (relatively) haphazard course through the trout domain will provide stacks of opportunities. Brown trout, being opportunistic feeders, respond very well to this tactic, and all our best loch fishing techniques have this at their core.

What I refer to as the 'search and destroy' dry-fly tactic follows the same principle and is often used when there is no evidence that there is anything even remotely resembling a general rise or hatch taking place. This is a strategy that takes a great deal of faith and tenacity. Whilst we are generally happy to chuck wets in front of a drifting boat patiently waiting for a fish to come along we are less inclined to do so whilst fishing dries. Perhaps there is good reason for this, in that wets operate below the water surface, where fish may be active without giving away their actions, whereas even the odd surface rise tends to be noticeable from great distances. However, stomach content analysis (the trout's, not the angler's, I hasten to add) tends to show that occasional surface items are almost always acceptable, even when almost all other food is of a sub-aquatic origin.

But, of course, we have to get pattern and presentation right. Peering myopically at semi-digested insects dredged from the deep recesses of the alimentary canals of trout over the course of many years has led me to the inevitable conclusion that small, black or very dark items trapped in the surface film are virtually irresistible to loch trout. Whenever the contents of a marrow spoon are investigated, there are almost always a few wee beetles or terrestrial flies of a dark nature. It

119

is this observation that has meant that there is almost always a small black dry pattern – black seal's fur, monofilament rib, and a sparse black hackle – on my cast. The back-up pattern is generally something seasonally right, such as a Claret or Fiery-brown Emerger in the early summer, olive or Hare's Ear in mid-summer, and something orangey/light fiery-brown with lots of legs in the back-end. Flies that are presented to look as though they are half-drowned generally outperform any other styles of dries for this tactic, and the seal's-fur emerger type with a scanty hackle, or a sparsely dressed hopper, serve very well.

The technique is, as already described, simply a case of setting the boat on a shoreline drift and search-casting in front as the boat progresses down the drift. Shoreline drifts are best, because the proximity to the land improves the likelihood of odds and sods arriving on the water with the encouragement of the breeze. Casts should be short and often, the flies generally being engulfed by eager trout within 30 seconds of alighting. In this game there is little point in long casting, because the long cast increases the likelihood of the strike being late (brown trout are eminently capable of taking and ejecting an artificial with the speed of sound, if not light). The long cast also increases the chance of the take being missed, brown trout being famous for the quiet sip-down. Forget all that old twaddle about counting to three or mouthing some nationalistic drivel, strike purposefully, gently and steadily at the rise itself – delay costs fish. But, if the fish performs one of those increasingly rare and extrovert head-and-tail rises which all anglers love, then a slight hesitation in the strike whilst you admire the athletic grace of the fish is in order. In this situation, and this one alone, fish must be allowed time to turn down on the fly; an early strike only removes the fly from the closing jaws, to the disgust of the angler. (It pains me to say it, but good head-and-tail rises are as rare as trout's toenails these days. Memory may be playing tricks, but I do seem to think that they were a whole lot more frequent in my youth, although that may have a lot more to do with the way we fish these days than with behavioural changes in trout.) Oh, and while I'm on the subject, the chances of a raised and missed fish coming to the represented fly a second time are virtually nil: small fish may accommodate the persistent angler, good fish, in my experience, never!

And finally, the dries should be presented as you would a team of wets. Cast at any mark such as known rock, or deep hole, any flattening or build up of ripple, along the edges of weed beds and always concentrate your efforts at fence or dyke-ends (a dyke in this case being a wall and not an ill-advised term to describe a muscular female tennis player!). Isn't it amazing that there is always a good lie holding a better fish at the end of a fence or wall? Which came first, the fence or the lie, or do trout just like the security of the structure?

Although search and destroy is a rarely attempted dry-fly technique, it can be remarkably effective. It cannot be stressed often enough that brown trout are opportunistic feeders and, on waters where the ability to gorge themselves on one specific item is denied, they almost always have half an eye cocked on the surface layers and warmly greet any new arrivals. Dry-fly techniques are not just for the hatches, any more than wet-fly techniques are for times when nymphs and insect larvae are free-swimming through the depths. And always remember that there is a hidden bonus with 'search and destroy' dry fly tactics: dry fly and big browns go together, and small fish are rarely a nuisance when your flies are floating.

FISHING THE RISE

However, most dry-fly fishing is practised during a hatch of insects or, as it is often referred to, a rise of fish, and quite often this is remarkably unproductive. Contrary to what many think, and what may seem obvious, periods when fish are concentrating their feeding on hatching or hatched insects are not always the best occasions to employ dry-fly tactics. Surprisingly (or perhaps not), wild brown trout feeding hard at surface level on a specific insect are often remarkably difficult to lure to dry fly, whereas opportunistic fish which are indulging in a pretty varied diet will often prove remarkably easy to deceive with almost any old pattern chucked on the water.

However, if the angler gets everything just right – and this is no mean achievement, when you consider that shape, transmitted colour, movement and precise location with respect to the surface film may have to be taken into consideration – then massive catches of fish may be on the cards. The other side of the coin, though, is that getting even one of the above criteria wrong means the angler is faced with a day of intense frustration. Fish which are tuned in to a specific insect species and its hatching regime know what is right and what is wrong, and will accept neither a crude imitation nor a badly presented perfect one. This is one of the reasons why, in the face of all the odds, the wet-fly fisher or even the lure-puller may do a lot better in a rise than the canny dry-fly fisherman. Simply put, it is better to offer the trout something completely different than something almost but not quite right!

But most loch fishers love to fish dry fly, if and when they can, and a loch covered with the rings of rising trout is an irresistible opportunity, so let's see if we can improve the odds in favour of success. As we have seen, there a number of variables involved in convincing a trout that the fly we present it with is right, natural and edible, even though it is in fact none of these things. The simplest route to success is to keep things simple and, above all, to be observant. If trout are taking a specific surface item, then matching shape and colour may not be enough. Very often it is not just the presence of the food item in the surface film that will trigger an attack but what it is doing: i.e. its movement, and how it appears to the hunting fish. (We are back to the trigger effect theory again!) Animals tend to respond to recognised movement much more than we appreciate. A good wildfowling dog will ignore a stream of other birds passing by but will immediately react when a duck or goose swings into view, recognising its precise locomotive style. Humans, however, tend to look at things in complicated ways and work through a variety of classes of information before coming to a conclusion. To return to the wildfowling analogy, if invented by a trout, that modern saying 'If it looks like a duck, walks like a duck, and quacks like a duck – then its probably a duck!' would probably read 'If it makes that duck-shaped hole in the water – then it's a duck!' We humans need the whole package, whereas trout will generally pick out and respond to one specific recognition trigger. This 'specific recognition trigger' may be fly movement, water or water surface reaction to presence, shape or, to a decreasing extent, colour. So if we can make the artificial mimic the precise factors which trigger the trout's specific recognition in the natural then we are more than halfway home.

Here's a classic example. A few years back the lochs I was fishing were covered in daddy-long-legs, but after a few days of gluttony the fish had become very particular about accepting imitations, and fishing was very tough and seriously frustrating. After a day or two of diminishing returns, I became aware of the criteria the fish were adopting to select out 'kosher' Daddies. They would only accept flies that were standing erect on the surface film and, like little sail boats, were being pushed in front of the breeze. Insects filling these requirements were snaffled confidently, whilst any which were drowned or lying in the surface film were steadfastly ignored. (This is not unusual behaviour, and I have seen identical behaviour amongst trout feeding on cow dung fly and olive duns – fish would take even poor imitations as long as they drifted downwind.) Now, the downwind drift wasn't too difficult to create. All I had to do was produce a whole lot of slack line between fly and rod so that the surface drift would move the tethered fly in the appropriate direction – not perfect, but good enough to fool one in three fish covered. But tying an artificial daddy that appeared to the fish as only half-a-dozen footprints in the surface film was a teaser. As seen from below and downwind, a Daddy standing proud of the surface film is virtually invisible, only the dimples created by the 'feet' exerting pressure and distortion on the surface film would be apparent to the fish cruising upwind and only just subsurface. Only when the fish was directly underneath the fly would it see anything vaguely resembling the whole fly, and by then it would already have made its mind up to accept or reject.

The triggering factor was the 'footprint' seen from some distance downwind, and if this footprint was compromised by anything breaking the surface film the fish would reject.

I was faced with the problem of developing a fairly substantial dry fly that would sit on the surface film without breaking it. Not only had the dressing to stay above the surface, but also no part of the hook could be allowed to penetrate the water. I solved the problem by taking a relatively light-wired hook with a short shank and a wide gape, putting it upside-down in the vice and tying in a few well splayed-out knotted pheasant tail legs, topped with a ginger hackle, parachute style – no body and virtually no weight. The parachute hackle, tied in a horizontal plane, had two functions: 1) it ensured that the fly landed, two times out of three, hook point up and well away from the surface film, and 2) it produced a splay of points to imitate the circular 'footprint' of a proudly erect crane fly. (The knotted legs were for cosmetic purposes only, more for the fisherman than the fish.) I called the resulting pattern the Footprint Daddy, and it worked remarkably well (and considerably better than any available dry Daddy patterns) considering that, to the human eye, it hardly resembles the natural insect at all. I'm sure most people, if asked to describe a daddy-long-legs, would attach great importance to the body, but in this case the trout attached no importance to it at all and were happy accepting imitations that were totally bodiless. This concept pattern has also spawned a few other terrestrial insect species imitations. (I say terrestrial species with just cause; aquatic insects seem happy to lie in, or directly on, the surface film, whereas many land-born insects sit on water as they would a solid, dry surface, i.e. with good body clearance.)

TRANSMITTED AND REFLECTED LIGHT

In the field of fly tying and insect imitation, colour is a tricky subject. We talked of this above when we were discussing trigger effects, but let's go over it again and in more detail because it is a fundamentally important aspect of fly-fishing. A large part of fly-fishing involves identifying an insect, assessing its colour/shape/size and tying a fly accordingly. We are often totally bemused when the carefully crafted imitation fails comprehensively. Our bewilderment is often increased by another's ability to slaughter every fish in the water with a pattern that bears no colour resemblance to the natural fly on the water. There is a fundamental problem here which, when understood, makes some sense out of what seems unfathomable.

Trout and humans don't necessarily see things the same way. We humans tend to see things in reflected light – we hold an item in our hand, the light hits it and bounces off straight into our eyes, and we see it. The trout, though, frequently see items via transmitted light. It looks up at the fly sitting in the surface film; the fly is translucent and against a bright background – so the light shines through it and into the trout's eye, and he perceives it.

The Irish have long known of this principle and produce fly-tying materials accordingly. They have produced dyed materials that have a specific colour in reflected light and another in transmitted light – Black Claret is one, and Balinderry Black another, the former appearing black in reflected light and claret in transmitted light, the latter black in reflected light and blue in transmitted light. If you are a trout with eyes designed to look forwards and upwards, and you live in a world in which almost all light comes from above, then transmitted light is going to be the norm, and almost everything you eat is going to be seen against a bright light source. Any food item that is not translucent will appear black (which is a very solid explanation for the importance of black in artificial fly manufacture), and translucent items will glow with internal 'fire'.

So, when it comes to matching the hatch in general and the colour in particular, what you see is not always what you get!

IN, ON OR EMERGING: MIDGE, SEDGE AND CAENIS

When we talk of location with reference to dry-fly fishing what we are specifically referring to is position in relation to the surface film. We have already discussed 'on' when we looked at dry Daddy problems, but certain insects are best represented by an artificial which can be anything from almost completely drowned to only slightly damp.

Midge provide almost the whole range of positions. Before they hatch they only just break the surface film; during hatch they are half in and half out; and after hatching they sit relatively flush with the surface. It takes a trained eye and a fair dash of luck to identify which stage of the hatch, and so which position of the insect, is creating the trigger effect response. Although far from infallible, the stage of the hatch may give the game away. Due to the influence of numbers during the early stages, when a great number of pupae may be sitting just below the surface, it would be reasonable to assume that the small number of emerged adults may well be ignored for the easy pickings beneath the waves. But the picture presented by an adult emerging from the shuck with the half-in, half-out profile tends to be irresistible, and any angler choosing this aspect of the hatching insect to imitate generally does pretty well. In my experience adult midge are rarely targeted during a hatch; they are best represented when the hatch is over and there are still a few about, when the adults return to lay eggs, or just as a prospective candidate during a 'search and destroy' operation.

Caddis flies, or sedges as anglers prefer to refer to them, are trickier or easier depending upon your perspective. They don't have an emerging stage that can be exploited successfully by the fly-fisherman, because the pupae convert to adults at such a speed that trout do not recognise this stage as exploitable. Trout take the pupae if they can and the adults if they fancy them, though this can't be said of every member of this vast tribe of flies. It would appear that the darker the adult of the species the more likely that trout will find them appetising. The best rises to adult sedge that I have witnessed have been to either dark cinnamon sedges or black ones. Although a general rise to adult sedge is not as common as to midge or olives, trout on sedge are suckers for a well-presented dry fly of correct colour, shape and position relative to the water surface.

I have purposely left the dreaded Caenis species until last, because they are a fundamental aspect of a loch summer and produce problems which cannot be solved by pure wet fly or dry fly, but are always best tackled with a floating-line rig. But before embarking on any discourse on Caenis it has to be said that there are no definitive answers to the problems they cause (what will work one night will fail the next), so your own personal experience and approach will have to be added to any advice I give, and the whole lot tempered with the understanding that the trout set the rules, not anglers.

Caenis flies belong to the up-winged flies (Ephemeroptera) which include mayflies, olives, etc. There are a number of different insects in the Caenis group but they are all very similar and for the purposes of this book may be dealt with as one. Caenis have a reasonably simple lifestyle: the nymphs live on the silts and mud on the bottoms of lochs, and they hatch sometime between June and August, although hatches have been recorded as early as May and occasionally in September. The hatches generally take place in settled weather, and most often during the evenings and early mornings, although sporadic hatches can happen during daylight hours. These can be massive involving millions, billions, perhaps trillions of individual insects. I have seen Caenis duns blowing across the Brodgar Road, which runs along the south-western shore of Harray, in such numbers that it looked like the smoke from a grass fire.

And whilst afloat on Boardhouse one July evening, I found it was impossible to see the shoreline through the masses of hatching Caenis which lay like a cloud over the calm waters. Alternatively, hatches can be sporadic and modest, and it is then that the angler can reasonably expect better results than during the massive hatches.

When the duns hatch from the nymph stages they will settle on any dry surface, split their skins and emerge as spinners, i.e. sexually mature adults capable of breeding. In a big hatch anglers out on the water will be driven almost insane by insects crawling on their skin and entering any exposed orifice, and their clothes will be covered in the vestigial dun skins discarded by the emerging spinners; those arriving at the loch side the following morning will see almost every dry surface bespattered with hundreds of thousands of Caenis remnants and the downwind margins cluttered with nymph shucks. All this frenetic activity, between hatch and death, may be measured in minutes, but during this period the spinners will copulate, the females will lay their eggs, and virtually every trout in the loch will go on a binge feed. A really big Caenis hatch and its resultant trout activity is a major natural phenomenon – once seen, never forgotten!

From a trout fishing perspective there are three distinct stages of a Caenis hatch: when the nymphs are ascending and hatching; when the females are laying their eggs; and, lastly, during the spinner fall. When the nymphs are ascending fishing can be relatively easy, or at least a whole lot easier than it is going to be shortly! Small wet flies, generally those with gold or hare's ear bodies, can be effective. If there is a major hatch in progress, and trout are indulging themselves in a feeding frenzy, they can be either impossible to catch if you offer them the wrong fly, or surprisingly easy if you offer the right one. During this stage the trout will be feeding near the surface and well-presented small wet flies on light monofilament are the best option. During the egg-laying process the trout swim very high in the water sucking down gutfuls of Caenis spinners, and wet-fly fishing becomes very difficult for a variety of reasons:

- The field of vision of trout, and most other fish, is defined by distance, or lack of it, from the water surface. When lying deep, a trout's view of the world is considerable; when swimming very high in the water its capacity to see much, if anything, is severely curtailed. So, when trout are feeding on Caenis spinners trapped in the surface film, they often swim so high in the water that they are totally oblivious to the presence of flies presented below this area in the water column.

- A dry-fly solution, which presents the flies at the level at which the fish are operating doesn't help much either, simply because one dry fly amongst a hundred thousand naturals is unlikely to be accepted. In such a numbers game the odds are stacked against the angler.

- Trout that spend large amounts of time in the surface film get very spooky, and the merest caress of a fine leader alighting on the surface of the water can send every feeding fish within casting distance crashing to the depths.

However, should the hatch be light or sporadic the angler a may expect a good return on effort during egg-laying time as fish are likely to be searching for, and targeting, single insects.

Choosing tactics for this stage of the hatch is troublesome. Given the parameters outlined above, dry-fly tactics are, on paper at least, the obvious answer, but dry fly during a Caenis hatch can be the epitome of frustration. The temptation to stick to the wets will be strong as they will hopefully have produced some fish during the early phase of the hatch, and occasionally this is the correct road to take, regardless of how wrong it may appear in the light of what we know about the behaviour of the feeding fish. But I normally put my faith in Hare's Ear Shipman-style dries, which, although far from infallible, rarely let me down. Fish two on a cast – one size 10 on the point for visibility sake (for both you and the trout) and a size 12 on the dropper – and target individual fish, monitoring their direction of travel and gently putting the flies down where the brain's computations have told you the fish will arrive, mouth open! I suppose the element of frustration exists because, of the potential hundreds of fish covered, the angler will be lucky if he comes in contact with half a dozen. Return on effort expended is low in this game!

But, if you thought that the egg-laying phase of the hatch was frustration, stick around! I know of no more fruitless exercise than trying to catch wild brown trout when they are on spent Caenis. Admittedly, by the time the egg-laying stage of the hatch is over, the general rise of trout is virtually at an end as well. The big movement is almost always during the middle phase, and the mopping up of spents is left to the determined minority. But these few can be some of the biggest, most mouth-watering individuals of the evening, and this only fuels the fires of frustration. I have no words of succour for those who would tackle the spent Caenis feeders, only dire words of warning, namely: Don't expect much and you won't be disappointed! If some tactic or other works for you, in a limited sort of a way, be happy in the knowledge that you've done very well and leave the water contented! But on no account be fooled into thinking you've got it beaten. You haven't! Tomorrow night will be different!

I can't think of many circumstances during which I would voluntarily leave a loch whilst trout were still rising, but the latter stages of a Caenis hatch certainly spring to mind. And when the season's last Caenis succumbs to its watery grave, the summer is over, and the last, fast-disappearing months of the fishing season lie before us with a whole new set of problems to challenge us. Summer is past, and there is an increasing bite to the breeze. The windy, wave-swept lochs of the autumn beckon.

## Back-end Fishing

### Back-end Behaviour

Autumn is a time of mixed emotions for the angler. On the one hand he knows that the dreaded close season is fast approaching, but the other hand holds some of the finest fish and finest fishing that the season has on offer. One of the big problems is that, to all intents and purposes, trout have almost given up feeding at this time of year, and the periods between meals become quite prolonged. Brown trout in Scotland really gorge themselves in the early months, particularly May and June, and thereafter a slow decline in regular eating takes place until by about the end of September they give it up entirely.

But, like almost all statements in fishing, this is only part of the truth. Feeding and sexual maturity are closely linked. The pampered trout fisherman eats his food primarily for enjoyment and the idea of fuel to keep the engine running is a secondary consideration. But trout feed hard in the summer months because a) they have a hard winter behind them, when food was scarce; b) they've got a tough winter to face, when pickings will be slim and they will largely be living off stored fat; and c) the biological demands of egg/milt production and the rigours of the spawning beds will require a heavy withdrawal from the banked nutrition at a time when feeding will not be an option.

The tail end of August and the whole of September see a reduction in natural invertebrate numbers. The big hatches are over and – apart from some sedge hatches and a brief spattering of late olives which may or may not be of any interest to the trout, plus the odd chance of a trickle of midges of increasingly diminishing size – terrestrials make up the bulk of the natural fly component in the trout diet. Of course, fish fry, where they are to be found, are very important too, but in the far north and west these will be stickleback fry, which don't have the same shoaling tendencies as coarse fish fry. On bonny days at this time of year there will be options for the fisherman to use all and any techniques which were successful during the summer months, because, although a large percentage of fish (the sexually mature ones) will be going off their lunch, there will still be a proportion of the stock that is actively feeding.

It is a widely based misconception that all trout breed every year. This is just not so. In any given year only a portion of the trout population will spawn, and those that don't will practise the same feeding rituals in the autumn as they did in the summer. Such fish will generally be known as 'maidens' the following spring, when they will be the pick of the catch in the early months, because they won't have had to 'mend' in the early part of the year and will be fat and well-fed come March.

However, just because a large proportion of the fish may not be actively sourcing food on a regular basis doesn't mean that they are immune to the wiles of the fly fisherman. Just as fasting salmon will, when the mood takes them, come to almost anything, so trout with empty stomachs may come to the fly with all the eagerness that they showed in late spring. Of course, when they are feeding all the tactics and techniques already described for earlier months in the season will be useful and should be employed, but it is indicative of the state of trout appetites that the most popular techniques and patterns of back-end fishing have less to do with subtlety and representation than with flash, speed, bright colour and extravagant movement.

## High, Wide and Handsome

Many years ago it occurred to me that the principle difference between early- and late-season wet fly patterns is that, broadly speaking, early flies have muted colours and are slim, sparse and understated, whilst back-enders tend to be boldly coloured and are bulky, heavily palmered and … well, not subtle! The classic autumn patterns are Bumbles, Dabblers, Mini-Muddlers, Sedgehogs and Palmers or Snatchers. Compared to the slim, fine patterns of the early summer months, these flies do not slip quietly through the water but send out lots of water noise and can be called 'water disrupters'. They aren't really designed to mimic or imitate anything in particular, but they stimulate reactions in fish which probably have little to do with appetite and hunger, and a lot more to do with aggression brought on by sexual maturity and territorial imperatives. Fished in a manner I call 'high, wide and handsome', these patterns account for a large part of the late-season catch.

A standard approach on wild-fish waters at this time of year would be to set up a three-fly cast with a Mini-Muddler or a Sedgehog on the top dropper, a Dabbler in the middle and a Snatcher or Palmer on the point. Dabblers are multi-use patterns which don't seem to have their efficiency compromised by being put in the middle position, whilst Mini-Muddlers and Sedgehogs almost must be put on the top dropper when used on a floating line, or their catch rate will plummet. The Palmer must go where there is a space left and, should anyone feel unhappy with a palmered fly as a point fly (and I used to feel this way myself, in a sort of irrational way), the Dabbler can slip down to the point and the Palmer/Snatcher can get promoted to the middle position.

Why should it matter which position any fly occupies? Well, it does and it doesn't! All-out surface disrupters should be fished on the top dropper of a floating-line cast because they will draw towards the cast fish that may, if put off the initial attracting object, be seduced by a follow-up fly. The water noise and its associated powers of attraction that these flies create should not be underestimated, and the pop-up nature of a well-greased Sedgehog can be fatally attractive to fish. If placed on the point position a Sedgehog will tend to skate rather than dip and dive, and this just won't do! The middle position is the 'death-house' for normally reliable flies. Only a limited few patterns do well here (and no, I don't know why!). It is one of angling's greatest mysteries that, over a statistically significant period of time, for wild fish and using a floating line, the top dropper fly will take somewhere around sixty per cent of fish, the point fly thirty percent, and the middle a lowly ten per cent, if that! (Of course such figures assume that we all make every effort to ensure that we put the right flies in their best positions. Religiously putting Muddlers and Sedgehogs on the point position, for example, could alter the results, but also lower the catch rate.) So, if you find a fly which works steadily in the middle position metaphorically clasp it to your bosom and treasure, it because it is a rare jewel. My own such 'jewels' are Claret Dabbler, Claret Bumble, Katie Ross, Fluo Soldier Palmer, and Kate McLaren. Flies which, in my opinion, should never be sent to the purgatory that is the middle position are Loch Ordie, Palmered March Brown, Golden Olive Bumble, any straggly hackled patterns (Goat's Toe, Peterson's Pennell, Octopus, etc.), Palmered Coch or Coch-y-Bondhu – and, of course, the previously mentioned water disrupters.

The fishing technique is simplicity itself, and can be considered as basic 'wet-fly pulling', but with a greater tendency for exaggerated bob-fly work during the retrieve. Flies – on a line with no, or any, sink rate – are chucked down the wind and smartly received with good sweeps of the 'pulling' hand. At the start of the retrieve the rod will be horizontal, and will remain so during the first three sweeps of the 'pulling' hand. As the retrieve enters its penultimate stage the rod is raised until the flies are close enough to the boat to enter the 'lift and hold' stage. This normally occurs during the fourth and fifth sweep of the 'pulling' hand. The 'lift and hang' phase is the final part of the retrieve, during which the rod is elevated close to vertical, and then either held static whilst the top dropper fly hangs motionless just in the surface film, or added motion can be added to the 'bob' fly by swinging the rod across the wind, bringing the top dropper fly sweeping across the wave tops. It is strongly recommended, that should this 'swing' be employed, that the direction of rod travel be away from the sun's position in the sky, for reasons outlined elsewhere. Generally speaking, the choice of rod travel will be from right to left, or left to right, across the body, whichever takes the flies away from the sun.

The weather at this time of year is likely to be breezy and vigorous and good 'hairy' patterns pulled just sub-surface with a good water-pushing Muddler or a popping Sedgehog in front will work well, and pull up aggressive trout from their lies. An exaggerated scrape of the bob fly over the wave tops is widely recommended and this tactic can work, but I've always preferred a 'lift and hang' conclusion to the retrieve. A bobbed fly is very effective, and almost essential for migratory fish (see Chapter 6), but of decreasing benefit to the brown trout loch fisherman. I largely stopped this method of using the top dropper about ten years ago and haven't as yet regretted the move. The lift and hang, as already discussed and described, is to me a more imitative way of portraying natural insect emergency. The only species of insects to rush to the surface, emerge immediately and then scuttle across the surface in a brief few seconds are the sedges, and to base a whole fishing technique on a family of insects which have only a small part to play in the nutrition of trout seems unwise. Admittedly, there are a few waters where brown trout rely on sedges for an important part of their nutritional requirements – Leven is the first that springs to mind – and on them a fly dragged over the surface can be dramatically effective, but they are in the minority.

Good, vigorous retrieving when the wind is busy works well and, generally speaking, retrieve speeds for the back-end are greater than for the spring or summer. Remember you are trying to stimulate destructive passions in a fish that is not likely to be much interested in the nutritional value of your flies. A good picture to hold in the mind is of the kitten responding to a piece of string dragged in front of its nose. The stimulation is the same in both cases, and with luck the outcome will be the same – indifference is impossible!

## Trout Are Where You Find Them

Now that you are rigged up and ready to go, where's the best place to find back-end trout? Well, as you can no doubt imagine, fish filling up with eggs and milt will be irresistibly attracted to the environs of spawning burns and rivers. From mid-August onwards the bays into which major spawning burns run will continue to hold greater than normal heads of fish. By the time October is reached it often looks as if it would be possible to walk dry-shod on the backs of burn mouth fish in heavily stocked waters. But by October these fish are far from attractive, either aesthetically or from an eating point of view. They will be soft, flabby, slimy and basically are best left in the water to get on with the only thing left on their tiny minds – sex! Don't be misled by their apparent attractive looks when they first come to the boat. Wield the priest, and an hour later the gleaming, colourful, firm, fit fish that you thought so lovely will have turned into a black, slimy, slug-like thing leaking eggs or milt all over the bottom of the boat.

From late August to mid-September, though, a bit of circumspection can help us select the odd fish from the catch which isn't too far gone and is still worthy of the table. There will be some seriously big fish on the go at this time of the year, and some of the biggest fish of the year get caught at the back end (though there always remains that niggling thought that the load of genetic material such fish carry would be better in the spawning burn than interned, with the rest of the guts and innards, in the rubbish bin). I have heard, and used, the argument that whether a fish dies in March or October the genetic material it contains is still lost to the trout race, and there is no logical counter-argument. But a fish that is ripe and heading for the spawning redds possibly should get special dispensation, if only because it has run the gauntlet all summer and survived. Is this anthropomorphism? Arguably it is, but it is also self-interest. There is a greater chance of a big fish producing a race of big fish than of a small fish doing so. We all like big fish so let's do a little selective genetic engineering of our own and return the 'brood mares and stallions'.

If we have the moral fibre to stay away from the burn mouths, then there is always the possibility of running across some maidens which have no biological intention of spawning in the oncoming winter. The big problem with these fish is that they are not appreciably more inter-ested in feeding at this time of the year than their sexually mature brothers and sisters. They will, of course, take full advantage of any windfalls of terrestrials, late sedge and midge hatches, and will plough into any accumulations of fry that are on offer, but the big feeding season is over and, like the over-stuffed gourmet, they may just nibble at the piscine equivalent of a wafer-thin mint. And as heavy feeding diminishes, fish tend to retreat from the shallows, where feeding was the principal interest but where security could come under threat. The deeper water beckons, and this requires adjusted tactics.

### Sunk-line Tactics

Aggression, as a factor in a trout's willingness to take a fly, is probably more accentuated in the back-end than at any other period of the fishing season. One just has to consider the fly patterns and techniques which perform best in the autumn to realise that out-and-out imitation is only a bit-part player. And, to continue the metaphor, this is the time when sinking lines and the occasional mini-lure can take centre stage.

Fishing for wild trout with sinking lines is not a great deal different from the techniques and strategies that were so useful on the floater. Many pundits have stressed the need for adjusted retrieve techniques – such as the mixed-up retrieve, which involves a variation on the theme of slow, slow, quick, quick, slow. That may be fine on the dance floor but I've never seen wild trout greatly impressed by it. Nor does the 'strip it back to the boat so fast that the dressing of the flies get fric-tion burns' technique seem to set the heather alight either. A normal, steady wet-fly retrieve of moderate pace almost always works best with the only major difference being that it is often wise to accentuate the 'lift-and-hang' section of the retrieve; wild brown trout, with their tendency to lie deep and feed high in the water, seem very susceptible to a 'hung fly'. In fact the one stable, consistent factor in wild-trout fishing through the ages is that there has always been an emphasis on a hung fly. This is a tactic imposed upon us by trout behaviour and, when fishing the sinking line, it hurts not a bit to extend and empha-sise this tactic.

So let's take a sunk line retrieve in its stages. Firstly the flies are thrown an appropriate distance downwind. I say 'an appropriate distance' because the overall distance the line is delivered will radically affect the way the line fishes. There is a balance to be struck here. A slow sinker thrown a long way will likely fish deeper than a fast-sinker thrown a short distance. A fast sinker will also have a more exaggerated curve, created by the belly of the line sinking appreciably faster than the tip and the fly-adorned leader. It is this curve which makes the lift and hold work by accelerating the flies through the arc created which should alert the trout to their presence, then making them sweep up to the surface to be held there, hovering in what we hope is an irresistible fashion. So the temptation should always be to use the fastest sinking line the water depth can stand. Remember that wild browns, being vertical feeders, will tend to locate themselves pretty close to the bed of the loch, and provided the line isn't snagging up it is extremely unlikely that the flies will ever be below the fish.

To make the lift and hold truly effective it is important that the angler knows that when he initiates the lift part of the retrieve, the top dropper fly will end up exactly where he wants it – just under the surface, no higher and no lower. This is guaranteed by the 'line stop' thread whipping. The retrieve is carried out normally until the line stop hits the index finger of the non-retrieving hand and then the angler should raise the rod from the horizontal to a position approaching the perpendicular. The flies, as already described, rush through the curve, sweep up to the surface, pausing in a 'grab me now or lose me forever' flirtatious manner – when, hopefully, a trout rushes up from the depths and takes the top dropper (or, as sometimes happens, swirls just under the bob fly and takes another fly on the way down). Trout being naturally aggressive predators get all sorts of innate predatory instincts triggered by such a manoeuvre.

Many people decry sunk-line fishing for wild trout but when it can be made to work effectively it is one of the most satisfying methods of taking trout imaginable. It is a surprisingly visual method of fishing, with trout taking flies right under the rod tip, and the angler can satisfy himself that he is fishing very well when he is catching trout in this manner.

Admittedly, in a big wind it is not easy to hang the fly for any length of time, as the boat will quickly sweep past the area in which the fly is

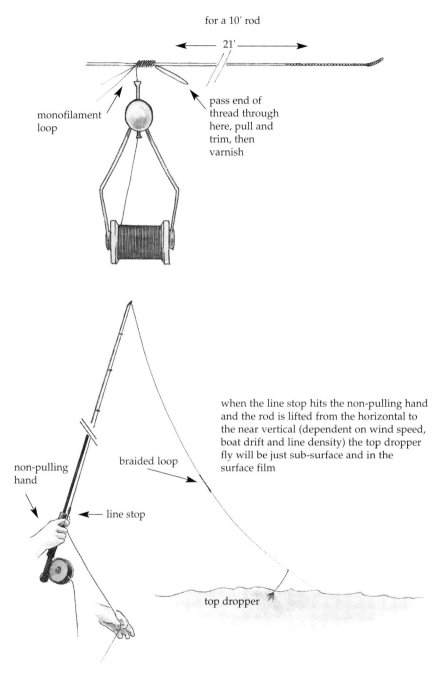

for a 10' rod

21'

monofilament
loop

pass end of
thread through
here, pull and
trim, then
varnish

when the line stop hits the non-pulling hand
and the rod is lifted from the horizontal to
the near vertical (dependent on wind speed,
boat drift and line density) the top dropper
fly will be just sub-surface and in the
surface film

braided loop

non-pulling
hand

line stop

top dropper

*Fig. 9   Intermediate and sinking line 'stops'*

hanging, but I have found that in a big wave trout are more likely to come to the pulled fly, and it is on the calmer days that the lift and hang comes into its own. And all too often there is too much emphasis put on the lift and hang. If trout are being caught during the straightfor-ward pulling part of the retrieve don't be disappointed because the lift and hang isn't working; the trout are in control, I'm afraid. OK, I don't like it either, but it is a sad fact of life that some days they will totally ignore the lift and hang section of the retrieve and only come to the pulled flies.

Do not be fooled into thinking that mini-lure-style confections are the only ones to use on a sinking line. I have a great fondness for Vivas and small Black Cats for this type of work but many of our favourite wets are equally effective. Dabblers, Bumbles, Pennells, Bibios and lots of fancy winged patterns, such as Dunkeld, Teal-Winged Butcher, Alexandra, etc., can be remarkably effective on their day, and my all-out favourite, never-off-the-cast pattern for wild trout on a fast-sink line is the Peterson's Pennell. I rarely have more than one mini-lure on the cast at any time, so that supplies some indication of how indispen-sable, or not, I actually find them.

As regards sink rates of lines, I still think that the Wet Cel 2 takes some beating for work in reasonably shallow water (up to 5 ft) but for deeper water I prefer a Hi-D, or the Wet Cel 4 as it is more accurately described. For loch brownies these two lines should be essential kit. But do not be tempted into acquiring them in uniform-sink versions. These will not provide that (to the brown trout at least), highly exciting and stimulating exaggerated belly curve. Density compensation or uniform-sink qualities tend to iron out the curve, the lines trying to come back on a level or slightly inclined plane. Another feature of uniform sink/density compensation is that to achieve their intention the manufacturers add weight to the forward section of the line – which tends to make the line plough into the water with all the delicacy of a hod full of bricks. It is virtually impossible to put such a line down with anything even approaching delicacy. For fish lying a few feet down this probably doesn't matter too much but that doesn't mean I have to like it! Uniform-sink/density-compensated lines were designed for the peculiar feeding behaviour of rainbow trout (see Fig. 5) and, in my opinion, should be used only in such a context.

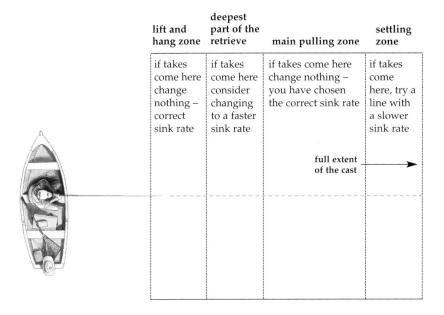

| lift and hang zone | deepest part of the retrieve | main pulling zone | settling zone |
|---|---|---|---|
| if takes come here change nothing – correct sink rate | if takes come here consider changing to a faster sink rate | if takes come here change nothing – you have chosen the correct sink rate | if takes come here, try a line with a slower sink rate |
| | | full extent of the cast ———→ | |

*Fig. 10    Sinking lines – locations of 'take' and what they reveal*

## Terrestrial Fall

The term terrestrial denotes that the flies originate from the land, as opposed to aquatic flies – such as midge, sedges and olives – which spend most of their lives in, or associated with, water.

Although there are problems associated with lochs being located in agricultural land – pollution events from agricultural wastes, water extraction, water enrichment, etc. – one of the fringe benefits is the potential arrival each autumn of masses of terrestrial flies which can spring from grazing land. The principal terrestrials are crane flies, amongst the many species of which are our beloved daddy-long-legs, and the cow dung and heather flies. Other species do exist in the southern regions of Scotland such as hawthorn fly (a close relative of the heather fly), but they are of limited interest to those fishing the best of Scottish lochs.

Daddy-long-legs, unlike most of the crane fly family, are renowned for massive hatches. The larva is an unprepossessing little horror called the leatherjacket, which makes its living gnawing away at the roots of plants. (I have seen whole fields of barley eradicated by the activities of leatherjackets, and when rooks descend en masse onto arable or grazing land it is generally these grubs that they've got in their sights.) The grubs pupate in the summer months and the hatch, if it comes, takes place in early to mid-autumn. The hatch can be of mammoth proportions with the grass literally moving with the countless numbers of insects emerging from it. If the wind is light, the Daddies will take to the wing in mass migrations to find suitable homes for the next generation. During these mass migrations countless individuals can appear on the water to the growing delight of the trout, whose response can be varied but generally takes a recognisable form. In the first few days the daddies are ignored as if they were poisonous, then gradually the odd fish will cotton on to their scrumptious qualities, and, almost overnight, the whole loch will go crazy, with trout rising, slashing and engulfing every available insect. (I have seen fish leap out of the water to take passing Daddies, such is the intensity of their passion.) This stage keeps going for a while (it can be weeks in a bumper hatch), but slowly fish start to specialise and will only take flies in a particular state: e.g. drowned or totally erect, standing high above the water surface. Then, towards the end of the hatch, when numbers are starting to seriously wane, trout can be pretty snooty, letting almost every available fly slip past. The angler will get poor response to his imitations but, surprisingly, spooning shows that almost every fish has one, or sometimes two, Daddies in his gut, even though there is no visible rise.

That is the form of the bumper hatch. Lesser hatches can omit some of the stages outlined, and often there are so few Daddies about in the autumn that the trout don't get past the initial phase ignoring them completely. And so my own tack with Daddy hatches is not to get too fired up by seeing a few of the beasts on the water. I wait until I've got hard evidence that the trout are taking them before I reach for the Daddy box.

It is a fact of life that Daddy hatches fail. More often than not the hatch is poor – so that when the bonanza comes it is majestically impressive (although the housewife shovelling the corpses and cripples out of the house every morning may have a different perspective). Two of the reasons for hatch failure are agricultural intervention (spraying the crops against leatherjackets), and dry weather at the back-end of the year (wet soil encourages the hatch). Farmers loathe the larvae, which are capable of decimating their crops, so spraying takes place regularly on arable land, though it is rarely economically viable to spray grazing land. Dry soil is a deterrent to the big hatch but whether this is because the pupated leatherjackets don't like it or because the adults avoid laying their eggs in arid soils, I don't know. Wet autumns are more likely to see a hatch than vice versa, but a wet autumn does not guarantee a hatch.

The lowly cow dung fly is a surprisingly pretty insect, given its origins. The males are a startling brassy-golden colour with a hint of olive, the females being more demure, clothing themselves in a greyish, olive-green mantle. The males are larger than the females but tend to hatch throughout the year and are only gregarious when there are nice, fresh cow-pats to paddle in. You hardly see a single female until the autumn, when they can explode out of the cow pastures like some biblical plague with bad breath. Let's face it, no matter how handsome the males are in their brass armour, only a female cow dung fly can welcome the embrace of a lover who thinks the next best thing to sex is hot, wet bullshit. And do cow dung flies have bad breath?

Cow dung fly hatches are as sporadic as daddy-long-legs hatches. There probably is a cyclical nature to terrestrial hatches, but agricultural interests can also affect the lowly dung-eater. Farmers give cattle anti-parasite drenches to keep them free from all sorts of nasties. I am guessing (with little hard evidence, I admit) that the pharmaceutical content of cow dung – which is, after all, nursery of this species – is probably hazardous to the health of a larval fly. What I do know is that hatches have diminished over the past twenty years, paralleling an increased use of drenches. This state of affairs is a great pity for the fishermen because trout love cow dung flies, and to see a loch covered in them, and the fish going loopy, is a sight to behold. I remember once venturing out on Boardhouse and being surprised to see a gigantic new weed bed where no weed bed had been before. What I thought were the little florets of the weeds sticking up through the surface were in fact hundreds of thousands of cow dung flies sitting on the calm surface. This was the day of their first arrival, and the fish were still looking at them with a sort of puzzled eye. But that didn't last long, and ritual slaughter started up very soon after.

Whereas I am well acquainted with both Daddies and cow dung flies, I have had a lot less experience of the heather fly. This is surprising, since the Latin name for the beast is *Bibio pomonae*, the literal translation of which would be the bibio/gnat/whatever from Pomona, Pomona being the old map-makers' name for the Orkney main island). So, obviously, heather fly were, at one time, synonymous with Orkney where I served my fishing apprenticeship. I can tell you that heather fly are not now common in Orkney, and are very rare visitors to the lochs. I have seen them on Swannay in numbers enough to stimulate the fish but only a handful of times over the course of two decades. I suspect that in bygone days they were much more common, widespread in fact, because I also suspect that the famous Orkney fly pattern, the Ke-He, is an attempt to reproduce the natural in wet fly form. However, heather fly do crop up all over the place on the mainland of Scotland and probably in the Western Isles too, and trout are renowned for their love of the whole Bibio clan, so it is well worthwhile keeping an eye peeled for the wee blighters.

The big problem with matching any terrestrial is the fact that it does hatch from land. Most aquatics are best imitated in a pre-hatch or hatching phase, the adult phase being less productive, but this is not an option with terrestrials. So we are, like it or not, left with one option – imitate the adult. And the reason this is a problem is that we have only a tenuous understanding of how the eyes of a trout work and how the very rudimentary brain of the trout actually interprets the visual signals sent by them.

Dry fly fishing with terrestrial patterns can be very productive one day and frustratingly fruitless the next. This I put down to the interaction of fly with water surface, and the signals which this interaction sends out to the trout. For example we've already talked of the trout's view of its own world, and the mirrored surface effect outside the trout's window. When the fly is directly above the fish (in the trout's window) it can see it as we do, all legs, wings and body, but outside the window the trout will recognise the insect only by the effect it has on the mirrored surface film. So, rather than imitating the visual aspects of the fly, at times we must imitate the physical effect the fly will introduce to the surface film. This confusing state of affairs explains why, from time to time, the very best visual interpretation of a terrestrial insect that human hand can fashion can be totally ignored by fish picking off naturals all around the imitation.

Cow dung fly are noted for sitting high on the water surface, balanced on the tips of their toes, and making as little contact with the water as possible, and in a breeze they fairly zip across the surface film like skate boarders on something illegal. A trout, positioning itself head to the wind, will intercept these skaters as the breeze brings them to him, moving to left or right to intercept those which are off-line. The trout, being high in the water, will have a limited window in which to view the whole insect; there will not be a chance for a good look at the fast-moving insect until it is a few inches off the point of the trout's nose, so it will rely on visual disruptions to the surface film to warn of dinner's approach. The best analogy that springs to mind is of a dog

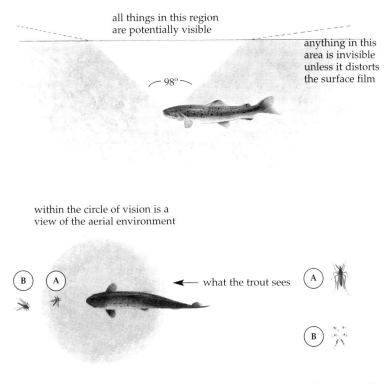

all things in this region
are potentially visible

anything in this
area is invisible
unless it distorts
the surface film

98°

within the circle of vision is a
view of the aerial environment

B   A   ← what the trout sees   A

B

outside the circle of vision the trout sees only the aquatic environment and the water surface is represented as a mirrored image of what lies below

N.B. visibility outside the water will be compromised severely by wind and wave effecs and in rough weather nothing will be visible above the water

Fig. 11   The visible world of a trout

143

hunting through long grass. The human eye cannot see the dog at all, just the movement of the grass stems as he passes, but the mind's eye paints the dog into the visual image our physical eye sees: the dog is invisible, and only its interaction with its environment tells us that it is there. That's exactly what the trout experiences when a terrestrial is approaching its position.

Nor is it only the imitation of the effect of the fly's presence that poses us problems, so also does its means of locomotion. Terrestrials almost always drift downwind, in front of the breeze, and trout know this. A dry fly tethered against the breezes stimulates suspicion, so it is not easy to replicate downwind movement when the angler is casting with the breeze and the imitation is tethered to the fly line. The amount of downwind motion available to the fly is extremely restricted. To cast upwind does not solve this problem, because the inertia of the leader in the water also restricts downwind motion. The only solution I've found when trout insist on some downwind motion in the imitation is to chuck a short line across the wind, raise the rod tip and virtually dap the greased-up fly across the ripple or wave.* Of course, the obvious answer is to dap, but how often do we actually carry dapping gear (if we even had any) on an average day's fishing.

Dry-fly fishing during a terrestrial hatch offers the best and most exciting back-end fishing available. That it is often frustrating and relatively unproductive, given the massive numbers of feeding fish on show, only adds to the experience. At no other time is the trout's ability to tell right from wrong more accentuated, and, hence, at no other time is the ability to fool them more of a triumph. The odds are stacked against the angler as he wanders in a world he does not understand and attempts to obey laws of which he has only scant knowledge. Terrestrial hatches and the rise of trout associated with them underline an empirical truth: that fishing is at its testing best when there is plenty food on the go and the trout know exactly what they are looking for. Fishing is easy when the trout throw all caution

---

* Some slack thrown into a cast downwind will allow some pattern drift in front of the breeze until the line straightens, but it will be minimal and often ineffective.

to the winds and will accept any old fly, but when they get picky (and they are never pickier than in a good going hatch), then it takes real skill to catch them consistently.

## A Trout's View of Life

Trout are visual hunters (in that they use sight almost exclusively to find food). However, their visual sense is markedly different from that of humans. I therefore feel it is important that we fisherman fully understand these differences, because, in the final analysis, we rely on trout being aware of (seeing) our flies in order to catch them.

The fundamental differences in visual sense between ourselves and fish stem from the fact that light, by which we both see, is noticeably affected by its passage through water. We are aware of the fact that light is bent as it passes through from air to water. We know this because, although we can see an object on the bottom of a pool of water, and our eyes locate the precise spot, when we attempt to pick up the object it is in fact elsewhere. This anomaly is caused by the bending of light as it passes through water.

The visual sense of trout is also affected in that not everything above the water is visible, and, due to light's peculiar behaviour in water, some objects below the surface may appear reflected and thus show twice. In Fig. 11 (page 143) there is a depiction of the strange visual world of the trout. Light entering the trout's eye must arrive within a cone of approximately 98 degrees. Any light striking the surface at a shallower angle will be reflected by the surface film. Any light trying to escape from below water out with the restrictions of these angles will be reflected back towards the bottom of the loch. This means that the deeper the fish swims more of the world above the surface becomes visible. Not only that, but the area out with the said cone appears as a reflection of the bottom of the aquatic environment. A rock on the bottom of the loch will have a mirror image reflected on the surface lying outside the trout's 'window', which is the area within the cone. A nymph or angler's fly presented just subsurface in the area outside the cone will appear replicated as a mirror image in the surface film. In the late evening and early morning, light coming from the light source – the sun – will probably be arriving at such a shallow angle that, for the fish, true dawn will occur later in the day, and dusk earlier, than for humans. And, perhaps most importantly, in windy conditions, when the surface is ruffled by waves and ripples, the view out of the water will be seriously restricted if, indeed, it exists at all.

All this may be, and assuredly is, confusing to the human observer, but is part and parcel of the trout's life. It also goes a long way towards providing insight into trout behavioural anomalies such as 'coming short', differing responses in calms and ripples, reactions to dry fly in varying situations. For example:

perhaps 'coming short' is caused in some small part by the confusion of mirror images;

and maybe flat calms reduce our sport because fish see too much, and good 'ripple' conditions improve our sport because their vision is impaired;

it is reasonable to suppose that the angler's fondness for late evenings and early mornings stems from reasons given above.

And understanding the physical limitations of sub-aquatic vision certainly helped me to appreciate why trout feeding very high in the water seem oblivious to flies presented close to them – their visual field is so reduced by their proximity to the surface that they simply can't see the angler's fly.

*Another Season Gone*

As the last Daddy lifts off the waves and heads for the nuptial bed in the grass, the twisting, writhing lines of grey geese hasten across the lowering skies, and mallard explode from the rushes at the boat's approach, the angler knows the best is gone, and it's time to leave the loch for another year. The trout, or at least most of them, have work to do in the spawning burns, the insect larvae will be battening down the hatches in an attempt to survive the winter, and the fisherman has long neglected tasks to confront at home. Another season has been added to the list of seasons past, and it's time to look forward to the one fast approaching.

## TIPS AND TOOLS

When fishing dries I generally ignore trout rising behind the drifting boat. Experience leads me to believe that the success rate with fish behind the boat is a mere fraction of that on fish down the wind. Whether this is due to poor presentation when pumping a fly up the wind or to line 'noise' close to the fish, I'm not sure, but dry fly down the wind catches more fish and results in fewer tangles.

Wild brown trout are by nature opportunistic feeders and something lying trapped in the surface layers will be, at least, investigated by surface or near-surface feeding trout. A dry fly, even when not a fish is to be seen 'rising', can often salvage some success from perceived disaster. And, importantly, very often the bigger fish are more susceptible, small fish being surprisingly less attracted to dry flies.

In turbid, dirty water always fish shallow and avoid deep water. Turbidity is reduced in shallow water, and only fish which can see the fly are likely to be caught.

# 4  Scottish Loch Flies

## The Evolution of Scottish Fly Patterns

Evolution is a term generally reserved for living things. To use it in conjunction with inanimate objects such as trout flies may seem bizarre, but I believe that the usage is valid. Why? Because, as a student of trout fly trends throughout the ages, I see definite trends in development, and the best way to describe those changes is to refer to them as 'evolution'.

It is simply amazing how the appearance of trout flies change. When I was young (and that wasn't yesterday!) the Scottish loch fly was either a very gaudy winged pattern or a buzzy, bulky palmered fly, whereas nowadays, with few exceptions, the emphasis is on drab and sparse. But even as long ago as the middle of last century the elements of modern pattern development were in place, even though the greater preponderance of flies were most definitely of their age.

In those days few fishermen tied their own flies and those that did were still likely to purchase a substantial proportion of their overall requirement. This allowed the commercial supplier to dictate pattern popularity. I remember seeing a Malloch's of Perth catalogue, from the early 1950s, which had a wide range of flies, mostly of the gaudy variety such as Saltoun, Freeman's Fancy, Gold Butcher, Assassin, etc. But at the end of their general selection they offered the same patterns, all tied on wee double hooks and adorned with jungle cock eyes. This no doubt reflected the company's proximity to Loch Leven, where patterns of this type were in great demand. But, because there were fewer suppliers in those days, recipients of the catalogue throughout Scotland would understandably assume that the contents reflected general trends in fly popularity, rather than over-the-counter demand in a Perth tackle shop. After all, why would the punter not assume that trout are trout, and therefore that a fly designed for Leven brown trout should also prove attractive to a Shetland hill loch trout? But more often than not it won't or, to put it more accurately, two days out of ten it probably will, but there are better patterns to offer Shetland trout if one wants an improved return on effort.

It is often difficult to reconcile oneself to the argument that trout fly trends tend to reflect human choice rather than that of fish, but the evidence is strong. In this day and age few trout flies are tied with wings. Some could justifiably argue that to tie wings on a fly that is designed to be fished under water is, in itself, folly. But the truth is that tying wings on flies is a tricky business, and one that few modern 'home rollers' can be bothered to learn. So with each passing year the number of competent wing-tiers decreases, resulting in fewer and fewer winged flies being produced or fished; check through the magazines, and you will see few patterns emerging (no pun intended) that possess wings. Meanwhile, those of us who can still wing a fly will tell you that winged patterns are an essential component in a comprehensive collection of flies.

This is a form of fly pattern evolution that has nothing whatsoever to do with trout preference. In fact, given that a trout has a brain only marginally bigger than a match-head (and therefore must have a learning speed only a tad faster than a jar of piccalilli), it is hard to believe that there is any evolution in trout preference. OK, maybe the trout's dinner menu has changed over the years, and a whole host of stonefly, sedge and ephemerid species have disappeared from many waters. Perhaps modern trout eat vastly more bloodworm, midge pupae and other life forms more closely associated with rich or mildly polluted waters than they did in times when all waters were clean and wholesome. But is an animal with a mind that moves more slowly than a glacier capable of looking at a hatching olive representation and working out that all ephemerids disappeared from the loch decades ago and therefore one shouldn't be swimming across its face? I somehow doubt it. After all, Sedgehogs catch trout where no sedge flies flutter; Muddler Minnows lure fish where no sculpin minnow ever swam; and Montana Nymphs catch fish, wild and stocked, many thousands of miles from any spring creek in the foothills of the Rockies.

And if the preponderance of midge, in all its forms, as part of a trout's diet means that they come to favour slim patterns which remind them of the aforementioned midge, why then do Boobies and Blobs have so many adherents and users on water where midge make up the great preponderance of food items?

But, taking all that into consideration, there is a form of fly pattern evolution that is dictated by trout preference – although perhaps preference isn't the right word, because this choice is one that trout would rather not make. Let me explain. I am convinced that one of the most obvious effects of continual heavy fishing pressure on lochs with totally wild stock is not, as one might imagine, a drop in stock levels. Good self-sustaining waters, carrying high levels of stock, and being subjected to heavy fishing pressure frequently, if not invariably, will experience changes in what the bulk of the fish are happy to accept as a 'fly'. Almost without exception, all really hard-fished waters that I am acquainted with have seen the form of the successful fly change as fishing pressure has increased. Slimmer and slimmer flies regularly outperform the traditional concept of the heavily hackled, tightly palmered wild brown trout loch fly. Flies with wispy wings and no hackles, bodiless flies, one strand of peacock herl and a suggestion of cdc, are the order of the day. Meanwhile, back on the underfished lochan in the middle of a thousand acres of moorland, where the annual number of visiting anglers can be counted on the fingers of one hand, trout still go doolally over flies we stopped fishing seriously on hard fished waters decades ago.

## Evolution and the Learning Process

But there is a problem with this theory. It presupposes that trout can learn, and learn reasonably quickly – and we have already decided that they probably lack the grey matter to do so! Obviously caught and killed fish are incapable of learning (unless there is more to this reincarnation lark than I believe), but are caught and released fish capable of learning? My experience leads me to believe they may be. I suspect that trout require some sort of 'learning from experience' talent, as they have no other means of acquiring knowledge, apart from basic instinct. And what is instinct but an innate reaction stemming from some sort of acquired knowledge gained from an uncertain or undisclosed source? Is there any point (again, no pun intended!) in a stickleback having spines if its predators are not capable of learning that eating sticklebacks is going to involve some pain, and may be, on balance, not worth the discomfort?

Is the existence of such deterrence proof that trout and other fish are capable of learning? Is a trout capable of matching factors in a present, unfolding scenario with those from an unpleasant past experience, putting two and two together, and resolving the situation by taking avoiding action? I have certainly witnessed trout behaviour that may be interpreted in this way: for example, when fishing with floating lines it is not unusual to see a fish come for a fly in a determined fashion, only to take drastic avoiding action at the fateful moment. I have actually observed fish throw themselves backwards away from a fly just at the point where I thought the take was assured (we are not talking about a missed take, or a 'come short', but about radical avoid-ance behaviour). The only explanation I can give for this response is that trout recognize potential danger in the situation and act accord-ingly. Trout may not be the Einsteins of the animal world, but they must have some ability to know what is of their environment and what is not, and to embrace the former and positively avoid the latter.

On the typical small-scale, hard-pressed commercial waters where fish are commonly caught and released, it is possible – virtually inevitable – to build up a percentage of the stock that has learned a valuable lesson and is, to all intents and purposes, uncatchable until something not previously experienced comes along. Given those different causes and effects is it possible that catch and release, or the lack of it, will have a minor hand in fly pattern evolution? I suspect the answer may be yes!

And if you are still with me, and your brains haven't shut down due to overload, here's something interesting! There would appear to be a sequence of events that mark a traditional fly pattern's fall from grace on the hard-fished waters. At first the fly will work well on any density of line in virtually any conditions – it is very popular and widely used. Then, gradually, this changes until success only comes during extreme circumstances, such as a good wave/big wind; the fly has now become a finely-tuned tool for specific circumstances. The penultimate step is that the pattern works reliably only on sinking lines or (for some strange reason) on migratory fish; it is now largely unused except by a small band of believers. Finally, the pattern just doesn't seem to do anything for anybody and ends up on the 'remember that pattern that used to do well here?' list. I recall an acquaintance who had been a very successful competition fisher but had given up the competition scene because of other commitments. He returned after a gap of almost twenty years and struggled to gain any form at all. I remember meeting him on the street one day, and during our discussions he said something which backs up almost everything said above: 'My flies don't catch fish any more!' He was mystified and bemused by this failure of his beloved and trusted patterns which had caught him vast numbers of fish in the past but were now subjected to total contempt by the trout. I know how he feels. My list of essential patterns for today's fishing contains not one single pattern that I relied on twenty years ago, and the same can be said for every other successful angler that I know! Now do you believe in pattern evolution?

## Wet Fly – The Backbone of Scottish Fly-fishing

The definition of a wet fly is a fly that is pulled, as opposed to moved slowly (nymph/buzzer) or not moved (dry fly/buzzer), and is not a lure. This is a simplification but one which is accepted by most still-water anglers. A pulled fly is very attractive to brown trout, much more so than to rainbows. A mere generation ago virtually all wild-trout fishing was done with wet flies to the exclusion of all other forms of flies. The wet fly was the backbone of Scottish traditional loch fishing for trout.

The Celtic peoples (Welsh, Irish and Scots) have a strong affinity for the wet fly, but as the best of wild trout and almost all the true still-water wild trout exist in Wales, Ireland and Scotland, this probably reflects the preference of the fish rather than the preference of the angler. To put it another way, the popular forms of fishing are the ones which work best most of the time. Wet fly fished from a drifting boat, or by a step-and-cast wading angler, suits the territorial, opportunistic, hunting temperament of the wild trout.

## The Form of the Wet Fly: Art Imitating Life

The wet fly requires movement to be attractive to a trout, because, in all honesty, it poorly imitates any life form upon which trout normally prey. This is a quintessential 'chicken-and-egg' situation. Which came first, the appearance of the fly which suits movement, or the movement which suits the appearance of the fly? I suspect the former. Our angling ancestors knew that movement stimulated the predatory instincts of the trout, and fly patterns evolved to suit this successful style of fishing. Most experienced wet-fly anglers shy away from trout flies which too closely resemble invertebrate food items. We all know that the carefully sculpted 'more alive than the real thing' style of fly is largely useless as a pulled wet, because, surprisingly enough, looks are not enough; the imitation which would fool nine out of ten human observers will not fool one out of ten trout. Here we are returning to that same old problem of the difference between the recognition points the human eye searches for and those that satisfy the fish.

Some of the best wet flies resemble nothing which swims, crawls or flies, but when they are pulled on a line, trout will gladly accept them as food. Why, when they have already turned up their noses at the virtually perfect imitation, should these fish gladly accept an item which, to the human eye, bears not even a passing resemblance to the real thing? The answer is, again, in the way trout see and what they recognize as 'life'. Motion is one of the keys. To the simple under-standing of the fish, what moves must be alive. It is beyond the comprehension of a trout that movement may be imparted to an object from an outside source. Therefore, if it moves, then it must be alive, and therefore edible to a greater or lesser extent. And the pulled component of the presentation also presents the trout with a dilemma – if I don't grab it now it will be gone, taking with it my chances of an easy meal!

Mobility within the dressing of the fly is another key factor. Many of the best wet flies are very mobile, with 'kicking' fibres and animated components. A fly composed of mobile fibres will change shape with every movement imparted by the hand. This again represents life. The most successful wet-fly types over the last few decades – Dabblers, Bumbles, Palmers, Spiders, and a whole host of other types of wet flies

– work because of a high level of mobility built into the construction of the fly. And, again, that which moves must be alive/edible. Wet flies work because they answer the most relevant question asked by a trout: is it alive/edible?

Colour is another key factor in the imitation of life. In a world where almost every prey item appears back-lit against a diffuse light source, colour is a very important factor in whether things look wrong or right. Claret represents black items packed with haemoglobin, gold and silver reflect their surroundings and shift colour in a natural way, seal's furs and some other dubbings sparkle with fire and colour in a life-imitating fashion, etc. To the simple understanding of a trout, whatever looks alive is alive! And for those who believe in that somewhat discredited theory that all fish are colour-blind, would you really be happy with a selection of flies solely comprised of varying shades of grey?

## Area Signature

As I mentioned above, there is a regional component in wet fly choice which I call 'the area signature'. In my book *Trout and Salmon Flies of Scotland*, I said:

> I have always thought that I could fairly accurately place the waters that a Scottish angler fished by looking through his boxes of loch wet flies. Big, bushy, colourful and wingless [flies] for the far North; drab, slim sparse and winged from the South-west and Border regions. Central Belt patterns tend towards tinsel bodies, sparsely Palmered; the Western Highlands like silver ribs and bodies; whilst the Isles patterns are notable for their dubbed bodies, heavily palmered, stoutly ribbed and with a hint of the Irish about them.

I can't really improve upon that statement.

The area signature is heavily influenced by, if not totally a product of, the national increase in home tying. Bulk commercial fly production tends to act against the concept of the area signature, offering all comers the same selection of patterns constructed abroad, and professional commercial tyers tend to export their own area signatures to other regions. The result of this state of affairs is that the attractions of tying one's own becomes irresistible to those who want to do better, catch more and address local problems with local solutions. It is an inescapable fact that the most successful anglers in any area will tie their own flies or, at the very least, have them tied to their specifications by a colleague who appreciates the area signature. The signature concept is best defined in wet flies, though, and is largely unreliable for other categories of patterns. This is perhaps not too surprising, given that other classifications of flies – dries, nymphs, buzzers and lures – are new arrivals on the loch scene, and the regional differentiations haven't had time to have an effect as yet.

I am a great lover of the wet fly. In no other category of loch flies is there so much room for interpretation, diversification and innovation. Wet flies are also very versatile and can be used on all densities of line and in all states of weather. Some of the other categories require specific line densities and weather conditions: for example, trying to fish mini-lures on a floating line in a flat calm for wild brown trout would be no more likely to produce sport than would dries on a fast-sinking line in a gale. But I can't envisage any set of circumstances in which a properly fished appropriate wet fly pattern selection would not nor could not be used. For years I thought that mini-lure use was mandatory when fishing sinking lines for wild trout, because of the tendencies and preferences of anglers from other areas fishing for stocked trout. I now firmly believe that, with a few very limited exceptions, modern wet flies will outperform mini-lures for wild trout. (Lures have their place, but reliance on them will not serve the loch angler well.) However, for the wet fly to stay top of the heap requires a continual process of updating, of absorbing new materials and concepts, and accepting that evolution in wet-fly patterns exists.

## Wet-fly Styles

Wet flies come in a variety of styles. The traditional classifications are winged, spiders, palmered and hackled. To these we now add Ordies, Sedgehogs, Muddlers and Dabblers, and more new recruits clamour to join the ranks with every passing season, amongst them Wet Hoppers and Half-Hogs. Not one of the above is a simple tweaking of an existing style, but each stands alone in method of dressing, use and purpose.

The old styles wane in popularity. Heavily dressed palmers were mainstays of loch-style fishing for decades but they reached their climax with the explosion onto the scene of the Kingsmill Moore's Bumbles. Apart from some use on sinking lines and for loch salmon and sea trout, heavily dressed palmers are now largely consigned to the sub's bench of history. Some will contest this view, but those that do will probably be found to practise their arts on lightly fished waters where time moves more slowly.

Winged flies are also fading from the active list for reasons already mentioned, proving, if proof were needed, that it is the mainstream of populist fly tying which supports pattern popularity. I find that there is a definite place for winged patterns in modern-day loch fishing, but not the fancy, brash attractor-type patterns of the 1950s and 1960s so loved by previous generations. The ultra-slim, sparsely dressed, under-stated variations on established patterns fit in very well with present successful trends of 'next to nothing on a hook fished slow'.

Of all the ancient wet fly styles, only the Spider pattern family buck the trend towards oblivion. Spider patterns come and go in popularity, and there is reason to believe that they fit in more with modern concepts of acceptable pattern style than they did on their inception. Modern styles such as Pulling Buzzers, Sparse Dabblers and even Wet Hoppers owe much to the sparse straggle of the archetypal Spider pattern and most competent anglers would be able to pull out of their fly box a game-hackled pattern of this type in which they have total confidence.

MINI-MUDDLERS

As regards the modern standards – Muddlers, Dabblers, Ordies and Sedgehogs – their longevity and ability to stay with the game, there are indications that evolution is catching up with them. When I started fishing Mini-Muddlers, in 1980 give or take a year, they were the hottest thing in my fly box. I was fishing the Orkney lochs pretty hard in these days, and size 10, 12 and even 14 Mini-Muddlers fished on the top dropper of a floating line rig were *de rigeur* on almost every loch in the county, from the start of the season to the finish. I amassed massive catches of fish on Mini-Muddlers on Harray, Boardhouse and Hundland, although Swannay and Stenness fish seemed less enamoured of them, and any standard pattern with a muddler head added would out-perform the original by a substantial factor. The impressive run of results racked up by the Orkney Trout Fishing Association's travelling competition team from the late 1980s to the mid-1990s was largely built on Mini-Muddler use. There is no such thing as a totally fail-safe pattern, but the Mini-Muddlers template carried all over the UK by the top Orcadian rods came pretty close. All things must pass, and now, a half-a-dozen years on the reliability of Mini-Muddlers has been seriously undermined. They just don't perform as well as they did, and whether that's due to changes in trout or human preference is open to debate. Perhaps a bit of both!

LOCH ORDIES

The story of the Loch Ordie as a wet fly is a very interesting one. The original, the prototype, was a dapping fly. Like all dapping flies of its time, it looked very much like a chicken which had inadvertently fallen in a box containing treble hooks. Then someone had the novel idea of scaling the thing down (but not by much), dressing it on a single hook and using it as a bob fly to terrorise unsuspecting trout, and in this role it had the same revolutionary effect upon wet-fly fishing as did the later Mini-Muddler. For a time it was the fly to fish, and when the wind blew the white froth off the tops of the waves, everyone did! I knew guys in those days (late 1970s) who did nothing other than short-line, and it was their practice to tie their casts direct to the fly line leaving a long leg to which was attached a size 8 Loch Ordie. Just imagine it! Hanging three or four inches below the fly line itself was a lavatory brush with a hook in it. Purely there to pull fish to the normally presented mid and point flies, it did account for a surprising number of fish. When the heavily dressed Ordie wets (a size 10 could hold 8–10 hackles) fell from grace, greased-up Ordies had a brief moment in the sun, but they were a nightmare to keep floating especially when trying to support a couple of normal wets hanging below. And then Ian Hutcheon launched his Anorexic Ordie concept, and the train took off again and ran almost to the present day. It would seem that, without an injection of innovation, anglers and trout alike get bored with the original concept and go looking for something new.

DABBLERS

This sort of process hasn't seriously hit the Dabbler clan as yet, but the writing is on the wall. Donald McLearn's original Dabbler was a typically Irish fly in that it looked like it needed a damned good wave to make it work, although this was far from true in practice. I can remember being deeply surprised by the effectiveness of Dabblers on my home waters. Initially I wasn't too impressed by their look and didn't feel they incorporated the ultra-high levels of mobility I thought an essential requirement in a top performer. But I had to be impressed by the fly in action. Dabblers of all sorts of colours became almost indispensable overnight, and they became a sort of default pattern, so that almost every cutting-edge angler, responded by trying a Dabbler when all else failed.

Evolutionary principles are already having an effect on Donald's fly. I still love it in its original form for sunk-line work, but for general-purpose use my Dabblers are now much finer, sparser patterns, with little bits of flash and sparkle and nothing even resembling a hackle about them. For all that, though, they are still instantly recognisable as chips off the old block and I'm sure that the elements which made the original work are still present in the new models.

There is versatility in the Sparse Dabblers which the original Irish pattern lacked. The prototype pulled fish because of what it did – i.e. acting as a typical top dropper pattern, pushing water and disrupting the surface film – and if the trout weren't in this sort of mood the Dabbler would fail. But the Sparse Dabbler works because it looks right.

One of the hardest scenarios in wet-fly fishing is taking trout that are totally focused on ascending and hatching olive nymphs of the species *Cloeon simile* or *dipterum*. The nymph rockets up from the bottom with one thought, and one thought only in mind – getting shot of its shuck and away from the underside of the surface film as fast as 'insectly' possible. (And in this it is remarkably adept: there is a split-second of sub-surface hover as the emerging adult climbs out of its pyjamas before the dun bursts forth in all its splendour.) Trout tend to specialise during the olive hatch; some cruise about attempting to snaffle the nymphs on their trip from loch bottom to the surface (no easy task, as the nymphs seem jet-propelled), whilst others only move to hit the nymph as it disrobes. I always used to suffer from mixed emotions during an olive hatch. It was wonderful to see the great, bulging rises of the sub-surface interceptors, and the water bespeckled with pristine duns, sailing along without a worry in their empty heads – but trying to make inroads into the trout population during such a rise could be hell on earth! Nothing regularly fooled the trout and all the much-lauded olive-imitating patterns were worse than useless. On the odd occasion when the trout, for some reason best known to themselves, would switch on to the adults, dries would do a bit of work, but this was a very rare occurrence. There *had* to be a reliable wet fly or nymph for those days when the trout were ultra-selective, but in twenty-odd years of fly-fishing I had not discovered one. Then the Olive or Hare's Ear Sparse Dabbler came along, and now I long for olive hatches, where once they filled me with woe. I use the Olive Sparse Dabbler in the early days of the hatch when the nymphs are darkest, and switch to the Hare's Ear version as the hatch dwindles and the lighter nymphs put in an appearance. The Sparse Dabbler is the best imitator of ephemerid nymphs that I've come across yet. If I find something better, you'll be the first to know!

## SEDGEHOGS, HALF-HOGS AND HALF-HOG HOPPERS

Very few modern patterns can claim to be innovative. Most are products of evolution, in that they take an aspect from here, a feature from there, pick up the merest dash of original thought en route, and emerge, blinking in the sunlight of a new day. The Doobry was a prime example: take the body and orange hackle of a Dunkeld, the tag, palmering and head hackle from a Zulu, add a dash of Kingsmill Moore's influence, stew it in the brain for a couple of days, *et voilà*, a new-ish pattern. The lists of modern patterns abound with creations of this sort. But occasionally something revolutionary pops up that does seem to come from no recognisable source. The Hedgehog/Sedgehog concept is a whole new limb on the evolutionary tree, which has already thrown out other branches such as the amazingly versatile Half-Hog family, and the Half-Hog Hoppers, of which more later.

Although known as the Hedgehog in some parts, the more widely accepted name is Sedgehog and this is the one I'll use here. In truth the Hedgehog lacks a hackle whilst the Sedgehog wears one with pride – a minor variation, you might think, but because of the hackle a Sedgehog makes the better dry fly, and anything which adds a little kick to a fly that spends much of its time being pulled is a positive factor. Sedgehogs have come a long way in the dozen or so years since their inception. Used primarily as a greased-up, top-dropper, pulling fly for a floating or intermediate line, the Sedgehog supplanted the Loch Ordie. The dense band of deer hair fibres in the Mohican-style strip down the dorsal length of the hook shank proved, when well treated with floatant, to be virtually unsinkable (and even when pulled sharply below the surface would quickly re-emerge with a defiant 'pop'). As a wet fly, this was the Sedgehog's single most important characteristic because, in all honesty, it doesn't have an awful lot more going for it. This re-emerging trick makes it the eternal hatching fly and as such it is almost totally irresistible to trout.

Another strong quality of this pattern is that it tends to work very well or not at all! If you have fished a properly treated Sedgehog on a floater or intermediate for half an hour or so without positive response, it can be removed from the cast without qualm and replaced with some other pattern. If nothing has looked at it in that space of time then, rest assured, nothing will look at it until there has been a radical change in the attitude of the trout!

Mind you it is not only the 'pop-up' that can prove irresistible. I well remember a foul night on Boardhouse when a north wind was bringing low, thick, ominous cloud hurrying from the Arctic. It was 'Baltic', as they say in these regions, where memories of the herring trade with the Hanseatic League remain surprisingly fresh. I was fishing with Norman Irvine, my longest-serving boat partner, and we were struggling to make any impact on the trout stocks using standard tactics of wet flies above or below Sedgehogs on floaters and intermediates. Norm decided to try a sinking line and selected a Hi-D from his box, rigging it up with the same cast. 'You're not going to fish a Sedgehog on a Hi-D!?' I enquired in shock and disbelief. 'I'll give it a coupla chucks!' Norman replied with a chortle. It is the central tenet of Norm's fishing philosophy that the rules were made for everyone else, and, as everyone who has ever fished with him will know, one should never be surprised by the arrival of the unexpected when out on a loch with Stormin' Norman. As we have already noted in the section on sinking lines, the tail fly takes a long time to respond either to the sinking effect of the line or to pulling from the hand, so Norman's Sedgehog, which was on the tail, all greased-up, would sit for a lengthy period before the forces of technology and science caused it to slip quietly beneath the waves. And just as it did so, it was taken. And this happened again, and again, until we quickly realised this was not chance but preference. The trout would not accept the fly sitting on the surface, and totally ignored it when it popped up as per normal, but just as it slid under the surface film a succession of trout would come out of nowhere and nail it! Of course, only Norman with his chaotic attitude towards fly-fishing could stumble on this esoteric and unlikely technique. Or, to put it another way, don't try this at home, kids!

A spin-off of Sedgehog technology is the Half-Hog, and I would venture to suggest that this is more versatile and useful than its source pattern. Half-Hogs can be fished as a surface-disrupting bob fly in a similar fashion to the Sedgehog, though they lack the quantity of deer hair of the latter, and hence are not so capable of the 'pop-up' trick. But H-Hs can be fished as dry flies, semi-emergers, nymphs or wet flies, and I have had success with them in all these forms. Well greased up they sit very high, and if they boast a hackle (not all manifestations of this pattern do) can imitate fully hatched insects. Greasing up the wing only, allows them to fish semi-emerged like a hatching insect, and in this form they will outfish many of their more recognisable competitors such as Shuttlecocks, Palomino Midge, etc. Figure-8 a team of H-Hs on a floater or intermediate and you have a killing method for trout intercepting nymphs or buzzers on their way to the surface – assuming, of course, that the colours are appropriate. In shallow water this trick will seriously sort out trout grazing amongst the stones for nymphs, shrimps and all sorts of creepy-crawlies. And pulled on any line, from top to bottom, these are as successful a breed of wet fly as you will find in the ranks of modern traditionals.

It is as an amalgamation/compromise between the semi-emerger and the figure-8 nymph that I find Half-Hogs most successful, because you have the trout coming and going. Lightly grease up the wing, chuck them out and leave them for 60–90 seconds, then slowly figure-8 them back. Most other semi-emergers will try to skate over the surface if pulled slowly back to hand, but H-Hs slip under with no fuss and immediately become nymphs/buzzers and ready to fulfil their alternate role. I know of no other style of fly with this range of versatility, but I do know of individual anglers who never fish without at least one H-H on the cast, regardless of venue or trout behaviour on the day. You can't say fairer than that!

Half-Hog Hoppers are relatively new but look full of potential. This year alone they have caught me sea trout, browns and rainbows in a variety of settings. They perhaps lack the versatility of the straight H-H, but are superior pulling wet flies, and have done some impressive work when standard patterns have failed dismally. On sinking lines, using the classic lift-and-hang technique, they have outperformed almost every other option, and I strongly recommend them .

WHAT TOMORROW WILL BRING

I'll be honest with you; I don't have the foggiest idea what we will be relying on as first line of attack for wild trout on natural lochs in the seasons to come. Nobody does! But what we can be sure of is that somewhere out there someone is developing new patterns and techniques which will consign many of today's essential tools to the scrap-heap of time. But that is what is so fascinating and exciting about the world of modern-day fly-fishing – stand still and you'll be left behind.

Of course many of us love the slow passage of time that can be found in loch fishing and want nothing more than to be left behind. To know that there are places where the patterns and styles beloved by our forefathers will still catch a parcel of fish is a consolation. I meet many anglers in faraway places who hang on to the past, and I sympathise with them in their distaste for the excessive inroads that modern style has made into the pretty fishing ways of an earlier time. But I also enjoy the new, and wish that the best parts of it could be happily reconciled with what we look on as traditional loch fishing. Unfortunately it is not just tackle, technique and pattern that are making inroads into modern day loch fishing, but also attitudes – limititis, poor etiquette, resentment against those more skilful or plain lucky, fish as a commodity, etc., etc. It is down to each and every one of us to set a good example.

But what of the modern fly patterns developed for reservoirs and their rainbows? Will they have an impact on our wild trout sport? To a large extent they already have. Mini-lures are an inescapable fact of life on waters where deterioration in water quality and fly life mean that patterns imitating sedges, olives and stoneflies, to name a few, are a thing of the past. Harray – at one time the finest top-of-the-water loch in Scotland, where buzzy, bumbly, top-dropper patterns fished off a floating line would catch fish nine days out of ten – is becoming more and more a mini-lure/sinking-line water, solely due to poor water quality and demise of indigenous fly life. I can remember, many years ago, stating that I didn't think that reservoir tactics would have a serious impact upon traditional fly-fishing; I was firmly convinced that rainbow trout and wild brown trout had differing views on what consti-tuted an acceptable fly. But nowadays the borders are blurring. Sad to say, my revered wild browns will gladly accept confections on hooks which I look upon with disdain. How can they do this to me? It is like watching a much-loved, well-brought-up, bright young daughter selecting an unwashed, Mohican-haired, body-pierced, knuckle-drag-ging retard as the love of her life. Nasty flies, like unsuitable prospective sons-in-law, should be ignored in the hope that they go away!

However, there is hope! Wild brown trout seem resistant to some of the least wholesome of the rainbow standards: Boobies don't particu-larly set the heather on fire, and Blobs (bloody awful things – the death of the art of fly tying!) are even less acceptable, thank the gods!

But not all imports have been bad or had a coarsening impact. Midge tactics and patterns are a wonderful blessing; as are the refurbished arts of dry-fly and nymph fishing. To sit out on a quiet loch, flicking dries or midge pupae to rising fish is one of the prettiest and most satisfying ways to take trout, and a whole lot more successful than continually dragging a succession of Butchers, Pennells and Soldier Palmers across the path of rising fish in the vain hope of triumph.

*Fly Pattern Selection*

Over the past few decades Scottish fly-fishing journalism has been blighted by a few practitioners who have promoted the concept that there was something slightly demeaning in being a successful fly-fisherman. These few tweed-girt individuals wax lyrical on the bonnie bloomin' heather, the birdies, the wee flowers hidden in the bankside grass, the Spartan repast taken in the lee of the big rock, and the twenty-mile hike over the hills to get to a loch that no one else wants to fish anyway because it is full of twenty-year-old trout that all weigh four ounces. The intuitive reader quickly realises all this twaddle exists for one purpose and one purpose only – to hide the fact that no trout were caught, and that the writer actually has difficulty in remember the last time a trout worthy of the name *was* caught. It may come as no surprise to anyone that the same pundits are the ones who promote the concept that one team of flies will do for anywhere. There is a very well-known book on Scottish lochs, where to find them and what to do when you get there, which also provides some potted advice on fly patterns recommended for said venues. If I took every trout fly named in it I could pack them all in a match-box … without first removing the matches!

I can assure the reader of one thing – set out on any half-decent loch with half-a-dozen patterns, all created when Isaac Walton was a laddie, and the chances of success are slim. Of course, success is a relative term. But I find that the 'cry of the curlew' becomes sweet in my ear only after the first decent fish has come in over the side of the boat. Anyone who says they don't care whether they catch or not, and that it is just a pleasure to be out, is someone who is more than just reckless with the truth, he's a damned liar! Turn to him when you've caught your fourth two-pounder and he is waiting for his first offer, and ask him whether the flowers look as pretty or the birds sing as sweetly as they did when you set out? Nine chances out of ten the look on his face will fully answer your question.

Tying on the right fly at the right time (and, sometimes more importantly, replacing it when appropriate) is one of traditional fishing's highest art forms. Some learn it by dint of experience, but it is, oh, so much better to collect it at birth in the package of in-built instincts. I know of a few such blessed individuals who will scan a fly box and, by sheer magic, pick out the only pattern to suit the fish. It is always fruit-less to ask such lucky sods how they achieve these minor miracles, because they don't have a clue or a system. Something happens between the eye and the brain: the fly looks right, and so it gets selected – it just doesn't seem to be any more complicated than not. But if you lack the skill, resign yourself to the fact that it cannot be learnt!

I work with a system which, regrettably, relies upon the trout responding logically to identifiable factors in water, weather, insect activity, time of year, and a hundred other minor things of which even I am sometimes only subconsciously aware. There is only one thing wrong with my system – it relies on the trout doing what I think they should, co-operating as I hope they will, and being good little boys and girls. Unfortunately, playing silly buggers comes as second nature to wild trout, and they are often not greatly impressed by the fruits of human logic.

So, allowing for the fact that few of us have a natural gift for fly selection, how does one go about it? The first thing to do is establish the parameters, which include: water characteristics and loch features; time of year and trout feeding regime; and weather.

## Water Characteristics and Loch Features

The changing aspects of water and loch head this list because they probably have the most profound influence on fly selection. Loch water comes in many forms: it can be gin-clear, turbid, full of algae of varying hues, and/or peat stained; it can be shallow or deep; it can be acid, neutral or alkaline – the list seems endless, and each and every variation can affect fly pattern selection.

### CLEAR-WATER LOCHS

Clear-water lochs are a rarity in an era when enrichment of standing water is a fact of life, but they do exist, and they are, generally speaking, providers of our finest fishing. By clear water I am talking about the stuff that would pass for gin. (Many fishery managers or estate factors talk about their waters being clear when they mean there is nothing floating about in them. But the fact that the water in question is see-through but as black as the Earl of Hell's waistcoat doesn't make it clear. Clear is clear!) So what effect does clear water have on fly pattern selection? In the simplest terms clear water generally indicates subtle tones rather than harsh primary colours, and small flies rather than big ones. Tinsel-bodied flies and olive shades dressed sparse to anorexic are my own preferred weapons, but never underestimate blacks and clarets when the light conditions favour their use. Natural tones and shades, mimicking as they do the colour of natural invertebrate life forms, are generally best. Clear water allows trout to inspect flies from a distance and the overstated, brash patterns normally won't succeed.

PEAT-WATER LOCHS

Conversely, peat-stained water can stand the use of brighter, more stand-out colour schemes, because of the light-filtering effects of peat stain. Subtle tones can work, but generally in mid-summer months, when the levels of peat stain are at their lowest. Peat stain also radically affects the way in which colour is seen: e.g. blue becomes green, orange becomes a yellowish olive, yellow has a creamy hue, green lightens dramatically, and even the brightest colours are muted. It may come as no surprise then to learn that flies containing blue, such as Bruiser or Blue Zulu, tend to work better on peaty lochs than on those with clear water, and eye-wateringly bright shades of red, orange and green don't seem to put off the fish one whit!

Peat stain is not a constant factor. Some peaty lochs have water the colour of a rich, dark sherry, and others more resemble a vat of pale malt whisky, and the effect of these varying degrees of colour on fly selection is a study in itself. The general rule is that the darker the stain, the darker the shade of fly required. The very darkest waters really perform well to black, dark brown and 'black' claret patterns, whilst the medium or lightly stained waters respond well to the range of bright colours mentioned above. But available light has a dramatic effect upon colour acceptability – we will deal with this below, in the section dedicated to the effects of weather on pattern selection.

Black flies are without doubt the most effective weapons in the armoury of the peat-water loch fisher. Why this should be so is easily demonstrated. On a bright day watch birds flying against the sun.

Regardless of colour, they all look very dark, if not black. Light is diffused very rapidly upon entering peat water so that the whole of the trout's 'window' becomes the light source, not simply the sun. Black fly-tying materials tend to be extremely opaque, and their intrinsic 'blackness' must make them startlingly visible to fish which live in a sepia-tinted world. Flies tied with lighter coloured materials will be less visible to the fish in similar circumstances. 'Get noticed, get eaten' is a simple rule of fly selection.

## TURBIDITY

Turbidity, the result of undissolved particles being held in suspension in the water column, can be caused by wind and wave action or by gross imbalances in the chemical nature of the water. It is most common when aquatic plant growth is least pronounced, as in spring and early summer. A strong wind blowing from a set direction can produce strong flows in 'still' waters, and if these flows become strong enough they are quite capable of scouring loose detritus from the bottom and spreading it through the water column. Plant forms reduce this effect in two ways: a) by blocking the flow through the water column simply by being in the way; and b) by binding the loose and friable material with their roots.

Turbid water is a curse, because its light-filtering effect generally means that underwater vision is restricted (in a worst case scenario, to inches), and fish that can't see the flies are unlikely to be caught. Also, turbidity is much more a feature of productive water than those with low productivity (I've lost count of the occasions when a long awaited trip to a trophy-fish water has been ruined by a week of gales). Primary colours and fluorescents, especially peach or yellow, on big hooks form an essential combination for turbid water – but, even then, don't expect too much, or, indeed, anything at all.

## HIGH- AND LOW-PRODUCTIVITY WATERS

Alkaline water is often remarkably clear, as is very acid water, but lochs with a high pH will be much more productive than the acid ones. It is reasonable to expect fish from lochs with a high pH to be well-fed, choosy and have a tendency to specialise on one specific food item at any given time. Trout from low-pH lochs may be more opportunistic but within very well defined limitations: i.e. they know what to expect on the menu and won't accept just anything.

Acid lochs generally have low populations of modestly sized fish, with the odd monster (ferox) thrown in, and the run of the mill fish are conditioned by the environment to expect little and not too often. If anglers visiting this type of loch/reservoir expect the indigenous trout to be starving little monsters willing to throw themselves on the first fly offered, then disappointment is almost guaranteed. They can be remarkably selective, at times even more so than their well-fed and pampered cousins.

On a hydro-electric dam way up in the hills of Easter Ross I had a seminal experience which serves to underline this point. It was a lovely fishing day, and I could see the odd fish rise in the margins as I tackled up. It was quite obvious from the lack of any growth above or below the surface level that productivity on land and in the hellishly deep water was of a seriously low order, so I was prepared for smallish fish widely spread. What I was not prepared for was the fact that I couldn't catch any of the wee sods. I covered about 400 yards of marginal water (water in which I seen fish rise) and didn't get a 'knock'! This was disturbing. I'd gone through all my favoured, first-line-of-attack patterns, and these famine-afflicted ingrates had turned their scaly noses up at them. In sheer desperation, I put on what seemed to me a ridiculous choice, a Diawl Bach, and, goodness gracious me, trout seemed to come from all over this massive water for the privilege of impaling themselves on this one pattern. I killed a couple for the barbecue and discovered that their stomach contents consisted of a few Claret nymphs (*Leptophlebia vespertina*) and nothing else. The Diawl Bach was a pretty good imitation of the nymph, which is one of the very few invertebrates well-suited to these inhospitable waters.

Generally speaking, productive waters, those that have a neutral or alkaline pH are relatively easy to read, and when the fish are feeding they prove reasonably straightforward to catch. Problems arise when fish are sated and just not interested in feeding, then they can be the very devil to catch. If possible, the angler should attempt to get a broad understanding of the available food items, when they can be expected to be accessible to the trout, and what the fish will accept as a reasonable

| Time of Year | Day or Evening | Food Item | Appropriate Fly |
|---|---|---|---|
| April/May | Day and Evening | Shrimp (*Gammarus*) | Invicta; Soldier Palmer; Green Peter |
| | | Aquatic beetles | Bibio; Palmered Coch |
| June | Day | Corixa | Muddled Hare's Ear; Silver Invicta |
| | | Shrimp | Invicta; Soldier Palmer; Green Peter Muddler |
| | | Lake Olive nymph | Sparse Olive Dabbler |
| | Evening | Midge (chironomid sp.) | Kate McLaren Muddler (size 12) |
| July/August | Day | Corixa | Muddled Hare's Ear; Silver Invicta |
| | | Sedges | Sedgehog; Half-Hog Hopper |
| | Evening | Midge (chironomid sp.) | Kate McLaren Muddler |
| | | Caenis | Caenis Muddler (size 12); Hare's Ear Shipman's; Claret Shipman's |
| September | Day and Evening | Stickleback fry | Silver Invicta |
| | | Daddy-long-legs | Footprint Daddy |
| | | Cow dung fly | Olive Footprint; Olive Hopper |
| | | Aquatic beetles | Bibio; Palmered Coch |

facsimile thereof. Above is a table which gives an example of a season's feeding regime, with flies to match, for a small, highly productive, trophy-fish water with which I am acquainted. Of course, this doesn't take into consideration all the myriad variables which can affect fly selection, and probably won't be relevant to your own favourite loch, but it does is provide an insight into the ways these highly productive waters work.


ALGAL BLOOMS

Algal blooms are a sad fact of life these days, appearing on waters that never knew them in my youth. They can vary from a light speckling of 'dust' in the water to the sort of occurrence which almost destroyed Loch Leven in the 1990s. I was out on Leven the day before 'the day the loch died'. In the southern reaches of the loch there were mats of dead algal material lying on the surface so dense that even a fast-sinking line would not penetrate them. It was a horrific sight and one that I'll never forget. I had an English journalist with me, and I was embarrassed to have to tell him that he was out on Scotland's premier wild brown trout water. 'What,' he must have thought 'can the others be like?' Surprisingly, I caught a fine, fit brownie of 2½ lb up near the Green Isle where the algal bloom was marginally less dense; twenty-four hours later fish started to die in great numbers.

Algae can come in a variety of forms, but the one that most affects fly selection is the soup of living unicellular plants which free-float, suspended, in the water column. Because they are light-sensitive, the individual organisms are capable of rising and falling through the depths and selecting depths where the light levels best suit photosynthesis. Of course, they can only do this when alive; the surface mats of scum associated with gross blooms consist of countless millions of dead cells accreted together. The effect on water quality and indigenous animal life when tons of this stuff starts to rot is catastrophic.

But we are straying from the point. Most algal plant life is, to a greater or lesser extent, green. It may be yellowish-green, blue-green or brownish-green, but the presence of essential chlorophyll will give a green component to the bloom, and any light passing through an algal bloom will have a green tone, due to the fact that other colours in the light spectrum will be absorbed by the colour of the plant life. We are all aware of the belief that daphnia-feeding fish like fluorescent greens and hot-orange. Daphnia, being microscopic animals which feed on unicellular plants, are strongly associated with algal blooms. In fact, these blooms are to daphnia what the grasslands of the veldt are to wildebeest – the better the grass production the bigger the herds. Daphnia-feeders like fluorescent green because this is the colour that shows best in the filtered green light that passes through algae-laden water, and in very bright conditions hot-orange also shows well, regardless of the green filtered light. Black and white are to a lesser extent enhanced or unaffected by green filtered light, but all other colours are strongly muted by the light-altering effect of high concentrations of algae. Of course, when the algal presence in the water is low this effect wanes and the necessity for every fly to have orange or green aspects lessens, if not disappears completely.

## Time of the Year and Trout Feeding Regimes

### THE EARLY MONTHS

Many of us do almost all our loch fishing in high summer because that's holiday time, but for those who live with a few minutes drive of wild trout waters the season can start early and finish late. An understanding of the passage of the months and their effect upon fly selection is helpful.

Following the changes in fly colour and shape as the months pass is a bit like watching the grass grow – a bit of perspective is needed to notice any difference at all! At the start of the season trout are generally mooching about in the shallows, in a desultory fashion, either honing in on one specific item (in the Northern and Western Isles that's almost always freshwater shrimp or cased caddis) or totally opportunistic, accepting whatever Mother Nature puts in the way. Something broadly the colour and size range of acceptable naturals should work, though turbidity and all its associated effects upon fly selection can be a serious and unrelenting problem at a time of year when wind speeds are generally high and the presence of binding plant growth is low. The fact that trout can be, and often are, found in very shallow water tends to reduce this problem, because, for a variety of reasons, turbidity is lessened greatly by shallow water. *Headley Rule of Thumb 3*: In seriously turbid water, fish shallow (knee depth) and catch a few, fish deep and catch nothing!

LATE SPRING AND EARLY SUMMER

A few weeks of good weather will see the fish out of the very shallow water. And once this phase of very early season trout activity is past, midge feeding will become more important, and this means slim, sparsely dressed flies. Colours associated with hatching midge – blacks, reds, clarets and silver – will also become an important factor in fly selection.

Trout will *still* be closely associated with shallow water at this time but not necessarily consistently *in* it. This is where the snail, shrimp and cased-caddis harvest provide an acceptable alternative to the midge explosions, which will only occur in suitable hatch conditions. The big offshore move to take advantage of the summer zooplankton blooms, where such migrations take place, is still some time away, and fishing should still be of a traditional and imitative nature. Sparsely dressed palmers, Mini-Muddlers and good, old-fashioned stuff like Sooty Olives, Grouse and Claret or Greenwell's Glory can be expected to do a job for those who still stock a selection of old-timers in their fly boxes.

HIGH SUMMER

As already suggested, the dog days of summer tend to be a time of feast or famine. Daphnia swarms reach their peak now and if big, deep-water midge are present late evenings will see them emerge in clouds, hopefully luring the fish away from the hellishly unproductive (to anglers at least) Caenis hatches. In between times things can be tough, with spasmodic flurries of sedges and late olives offering brief respite. In the middle of the season I always seem to be caught between floating lines with dries and sinking lines bearing mini-lures and wets, never knowing when I set out for the day which is likely to be the better option.

The slim and sparse imitative wets of the early season are starting to be replaced with attractor-style wets – Half-Hog Hoppers, Mini-Muddlers, Anorexic Ordies, Sedgehogs and the like – and competition-sized lures cannot be ignored for those desperate for some action on a loch which at times will seem to be totally devoid of life. The evenings should see some response to midge patterns and Caenis-simulating dries but the emergence of the naturals will be weather dependent and not to be relied upon.

Colour choices should be cross referenced with water clarity and type and available food item colour. For the daphnia feeders, the already mentioned fluorescents of green and hot orange, plus black and white, cannot be ignored, and dries in hare's ear, claret and fiery brown should meet most requirements.

THE BACK-END

Fly selection in the latter months of the season can be problematic, due to the trout's decreasing interest in feeding. Admittedly there will be a variable fraction of the whole population that will not become sexually mature as the season wanes, and these fish will still feed normally. But, even so, nature ensures that fish feed avidly when there is a harvest, while in leaner times their appetite shrinks to meet expectations, and food is not plentiful in the back-end of the year. The hatches of aquatic insects that do occur are poor things compared to the phenomenal natural events of the late spring.

Some fry feeding may take place, but in the lochs of the far north and west coarse fish are non-existent, and such fry as are available are likely to be stickleback or, very occasionally, perch. Stickleback fry do not tend to gather in huge shoals so 'fry bashing' can be a solitary occu-pation for the fish and not characterised by the wanton violence and mayhem associated with trout attacks on the dense coarse fish shoals of southern waters.

We should be strongly reliant upon attractor patterns by this time, and successful flies will be characterised by bulky bodies and strong palmering, and will bear little resemblance to the thin, wispy, anorexic patterns of the spring. Sedgehogs, Wet Hoppers, Dabblers, Muddlers and mini-lures of all sorts will feature strongly, and colours will continue to strengthen and darken. Blacks, dark clarets, reds, hot oranges and even blues can all prove irresistible at this time of year, when aggression can replace appetite.

The one redeeming feature of this period is that, unlike aquatic insects, terrestrials choose it for mass mating, and insects such as heather fly, crane fly and cow dung fly can all make significant visits to the loch surface. Cow dung fly are strongly associated with agricultural land as, to a lesser extent perhaps, are daddy-long-legs. Heather flies come only from stands of heather (i.e. non-agricultural land) and appear in late July at the earliest, and more regularly in August and September. A quick glance at an Ordnance Survey map should give some inkling of which terrestrial is likely to put in an appearance on the loch of your choice.

There appears to be a cyclical nature to the life styles of terrestrial species. Some years have hatches that are almost of plague proportions, and then in following seasons one could be forgiven for thinking that the insect had become extinct. The use of insecticides and drenches in agriculture tends to reduce population densities of crane and cow dung flies, but heather flies are just as erratic in their appearances and are generally unaffected by agricultural practice.

Some of the finest, most exciting and frenetic fishing of the year can be when a fall of terrestrials coincides with a visit to a loch. The canny angler should contrive to arrive at the water when the 'fall' has been under way for, at the very least, a few days. The willingness of a trout to take an adult fly depends on the size of the individual insect coupled with the number of days that species has been present on the water. The first Daddy to arrive on any loch is virtually guaranteed immunity from fish attack, but the same cannot be said for one arriving a week later. This 'safety zone' is less for the smaller heather fly, and may not exist at all for the poor cow dung. Fly selection for these events shouldn't pose too many problems for any angler with a reasonably well-stocked box of dries. Hawthorn Fly patterns and Black Hoppers will do perfectly well for feeders on heather fly (and in all honesty, fish on heather fly are not renowned for being overly picky), but more dedicated patterns are required for fish clued-up on Daddies and cow dungs. Daddy patterns are legion and widely available, but you may have to get the vice out for cow dung fly feeders. In Orkney, where these insects can sometimes be seen in vast numbers in the back-end of the year, small Sedgehogs are popular, but Footprint Dries in appropriate shades of olive are better.

## Weather

The effects of weather on fly selection merit a book in itself, but I'll try and cover the salient features as best I can in the space available. I shall start by discussing light intensity, because, as noted earlier, light has a central role in fly selection. I will also take the opportunity to discuss not only weather effects on fly selection but also weather effects on fish.

### LIGHT

Of all the aspects of the conditions of the day, light will have the most profound effect upon fly selection. Light is made up of a mixture of colours. A rainbow is just normal sunlight that has been split into its constituent colours by being shone through natural prisms, i.e. rain-drops. As light shines on a coloured material, all the constituent colours of sunlight will be absorbed and the colour of the said material will be reflected. Although this is not a strictly scientific description of what happens it is the best and easiest way to describe why we see colour.

At varying times of day and under specific atmospheric conditions sunlight is altered and will contain different ratios of its normal colours. For example, in the late evening on a good summer's day it is common to experience one of those wonderful orangey-red sunsets. Under such circumstances the ambient light delivers a very high ratio of colours from the red end of the spectrum such as, naturally, red and orange, and flies which have those colours in their make-up will shine very brightly and will be more than just noticeable to the fish. As the sunset fades, darker colours, such as dark magentas and clarets, will respond in a similar way to the ambient light, until eventually, as dark settles in, black becomes the colour which shows up best.

One of the truly magical fringe benefits of living in the far north and west of Scotland is that the quality of the air and the wide open vistas allow the observer to see the changing light of the day more clearly. In my early adulthood, as I learned more and more about trout fishing, I became totally absorbed by changing light and its effect upon pattern acceptability. I quickly became aware that trout could, and often would, switch from one colour combination to another as the light subtly altered, even though their choice of food items would remain constant. I soon realised that it was the way that trout saw the fly that governed its acceptability, and not the shape, the size, nor necessarily any attempts by the creator to mimic specific life forms.

It was common to experience situations which spectacularly demonstrated this reality. I could be drifting down the loch, 'moving' and catching trout on a satisfyingly regular basis to a team of flies and, say, a cloud would pass over the sun; although fish would continue to rise naturally, they would now treat my flies as if they'd been dipped in a lethal poison. As the sun re-emerged the catch rate would pick-up where it had left off. Another common experience, which occurs when the sun moves round in the sky, is that fly patterns cease (or begin) to be accepted by trout. This is, I firmly believe, caused by the differing way the light hits the flies and/or enters the water, making the said flies look different to the trout.

We have already discussed how trout use their vision as a prime means of identifying edible items, and how material translucency is of critical importance in matching insects. As light shines through fibres, dubbings, etc., it will be seen in a specific way with precise qualities. Should the light alter in intensity or direction, then these qualities will also change, and the perceived image of the fly will alter.

Now, I know that every angler really wants answers to problems rather than a do-it-yourself kit, so let's see if we can provide some solid ground to this theorising.

The following table attempts to provide a very rough guide to pattern colour selection in varying states of light. Nothing in fly-fishing is absolute, and neither is this chart; many other factors may impinge on what the trout find acceptable, but as a general guide this will help when the angler finds himself 'stumped' as to what to try next.

| Colour | In Bright Light | In Good Light | In Poor Light |
|---|---|---|---|
| Black | Can be very good | Not a first choice | First choice |
| White | First choice | Occasionally | Can be excellent |
| Claret | Not good, generally to be avoided | Occasionally good | Indispensable, first choice |
| Red | Not a first choice but occasionally good | Good | In specific circumstances (e.g. a red sunset), first choice. |
| Orange | First choice | Occasionally good | Not good. Avoid it. |
| Yellow | Occasionally very good | Good | Poor |
| Green | Occasionally | Very good | Not often good |
| Blue | Very good | Poor | Occasionally good |
| Pink | Not good | Normally poor | On occasion very good |
| Peach | Occasionally good | Occasionally good | Can be very good |
| Olive tones and fiery brown | Not often good | Very good | Occasionally good |
| Hare's Ear | Not a first choice | At its best | Occasionally good |
| Silver | First choice | Occasionally good | Can be excellent |
| Gold | Occasionally good | Very good | Generally poor |

It perhaps goes without saying that the table assumes good water quality and clarity. Peat stain, algal discolouration and/or turbidity can all affect the issue and should be taken into consideration when using it. In my experience only gross discolouration will affect it radically, but others will have to make their own assessment.

Light has differing effects upon trout feeding regimes in differing locations. While it is generally accepted that trout will not feed close to the surface in bright weather, this does not hold true in the Isles. I have a photograph taken during a spectacular day I shared with Peter Gathercole on Loch Bornish in South Uist (I can't remember how many fish we caught but there were a lot, and most of them were well over the pound mark). The photograph distinctly shows there is hardly a cloud in the sky, and that is how I remember it. My favourite conditions on Harray, before the Canadian Pondweed disaster and associated water-quality problems, were always bright days with a stong wind and a good wave pushing the boat up to and over the skerries. Hundland, a small prolific loch in Orkney, is the only distinctly peat-stained loch I know that can fish its socks off in bright weather conditions.

Clear-water lochs seem more likely to produce bright-weather sport; peat-water lochs less so. We should not assume that bright conditions guarantee poor sport, but what we can be relatively sure about is that the direction of the sunlight in relation to the wind direction can be critical. Trout, in a loch, will tend to lie head to the wind; anglers drifting down in front of a wind will tend to pull their flies in an upwind direction, encouraging taking fish to follow suit also! With the sun behind the angler, the fish is then asked to take with the sun shining directly into its eyes – or, perhaps more accurately, with the fly disappearing against the brightness of the sun. I suspect that it is not the sun shining in the trout's eye that is the problem; it is more likely to be that the trout has problems visualising the fly as it moves towards the brightest area in its window of vision. The same fish certainly doesn't seem to have a problem seeing the fly when the sun is behind it, but in this situation the fly will have the spotlight of the sun on it, reflecting its colour and sparkle for all to see.

The table above shows which colours I believe work best in bright conditions, but if you are cursed with a bright, low sun shining over your shoulder, a combination of orange and gold or, even better, orange and yellow may be your only hope of success.

At all times try to avoid pulling the fly towards the sun. If the sun is to the side, shining onto your left or right shoulder, angle the retrieve away from it, thus encouraging the fish to take in a direction in which it has the sun behind it, not in front – this is crucial when working a bob-fly. Normally I tend not to use definitive statements about fishing, because words like 'never' and 'always' have little place in angling, but in this case I am prepared to make an exception. *Never* pull your flies into the sun if you can possibly avoid it. *Always* angle them away whenever possible. This may seem to be advice solely for those fishing in, or near, the surface film, but it is not. Even flies fished off the fastest sinking line will prove more acceptable pulled away from the sun and most certainly in the latter part of the retrieve.

Cloud is the great friend of the fishermen. Even those who ply their trade on the deep sea and bounce their baited hooks off Davy Jones' locker hate the sun and prefer the cloudy day. Fish do not, of course, have eyelids and probably lack the ability to protect their eyes from bright lights in the way we do (and I'm not talking of Polaroid sunglasses!), but I suspect that the prime reason for poor fishing in

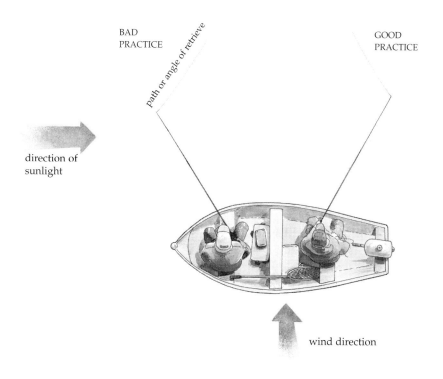

*Fig. 12   Good and bad retrieve directions relative to position of sun*

bright light has more to do with the physics of light in water. On a calm day a trout lying some feet below the surface will see the world as we would if we were in a round, mirror-lined room with a window directly above us in the ceiling. The 'window' allows the trout some view out of its world into ours, but the bulk of its visible environment will be what lies around it and the reflection of this in the surface. Light entering the water is bounced back from the mirrored surface. On very bright, cloudless days with copious amounts of light filling this environment, everything existing below the surface has a mirror-image displayed on the 'ceiling'. I wonder if it is anthropomorphic to suggest that trout probably get a headache in such conditions. Imagine being incarcerated in a room lined with mirrors with someone shining a spotlight in from the only window located in the ceiling. You'd be justified in taking your complaint to Amnesty International. But that is the lot of the trout, and the only suffering it endures is that such conditions of excessive light actually make things harder to see rather than easier.

Because of this mirrored effect underwater trout see things in ways which are not immediately obvious to us. For example, sunk objects, such as our flies or natural objects which are above the trout, will have a mirror image reflected on the underside of the surface so that instead of seeing one object the trout will see two. An object lying in the surface film, for example a hatching midge, will have its mirror image attached to the real thing and will, therefore appear twice as large as normal. An insect sitting on the surface film will, if outside the "window", not appear at all, but its points of contacts, legs or feet, will make dimples in the mirrored surface and distort it, showing that something is most definitely there. This last effect is the one which sometimes triggers specific attack on insects such as daddy-long-legs and cow dung fly which sit high on the surface. If the perfect imitation is sitting *in* the surface film, more often than not it will be ignored, to the confusion of the angler.

READING THE WEATHER

In my youth and early manhood I used to pore over Met Office weather charts as seen on BBC weather forecasts and became reasonably adept at forecasting weather for my own area. Nowadays, in keeping with the Nanny State, the Met Office has decided we are all too thick to understand barometric pressure charts, with their confusing isobars, and have replaced them with patronising little images of cheery suns and sad clouds. A barometric chart can be read and interpreted; a map with sun and cloud symbols is about as much use to me as a ice-maker to an Eskimo.

But let's have a look at what I learnt from weather charts before the Met Office decided to patronise me. There are two basic types of weather systems, low pressure and high pressure, and they have associated features such as ridges, troughs and fronts. The lines on a barometric chart – the isobars – link points of equal atmospheric/barometric pressure just as on an ordnance survey map the contour lines link points of equal height. To expand the comparison, the low-pressure systems are valleys and the highs are mountains. Fronts show areas where sudden changes in atmospheric pressure, changes in temperature and water loading of air masses exist. As a low-pressure system approaches the atmospheric pressure will fall, and as it departs, hopefully, the pressure will rise. In a low-pressure system the winds travel in an anti-clockwise direction, the opposite being true of a high. (However, this is only true in the northern hemisphere; wind directions around weather systems are reversed in the southern hemisphere. Bizarre, but true nevertheless!)

What the angler will generally experience as low pressure passes over is that the wind will pick up from a south-easterly direction, move quickly to the south-west (without ever seeming to have come from the south), linger as a westerly and have a brief period as a north-westerly. That is typical northern Scottish low-pressure sequence of wind directions. Rain will almost inevitably arrive with the south-easterly. But should it continue to fall from the south-westerly, the wind will most definitely blow from the north-west, and blow hard! The north-westerly wind almost always heralds the approach of either a high-pressure system or ridge of high pressure.

Low-pressure systems in your area can easily be located. Simply stand with your back to the wind and the centre of the low is on your left-hand side. If this places the low anywhere from north-west to south-west, the weather will improve. If (and no pun intended), on the other hand, the centre of the low is between north-east and south-east, the weather will deteriorate. So, the next time you see someone at the side of a loch with his arms extended, spinning like a top, ask him for a weather forecast!

If you draw a north–south line through a low pressure system, the area to the east of the line will be characterised by falling pressure and that to the west by rising pressure. Do the same with a high-pressure system and you will find that the areas of rising and falling pressure will be reversed. And the isobars which join up all the points of equal pressure can also tell us a lot. The direction of these lines indicate wind direction (taking into consideration the direction in which winds circulate around weather systems), and their closeness indicates wind speed – the closer they are, the windier it will be.

Rising pressure means that rain is less likely, and vice versa. Cold air holds little moisture, so that north and east winds tend to bring clear skies, sunshine and, in season, frosts. Warm air can become saturated with water, so that west and south winds can be expected to bring cloud and rain.

And that's about all a fisherman really needs to know to interpret weather charts.

ATMOSPHERIC PRESSURE

Barometric pressure is the more scientific name for atmospheric pressure, but we will use the older, more commonly used description for ease of understanding. As noted in the chapter dealing with the physiology of fish, changes in atmospheric pressure have a profound effect upon trout behaviour. The rise and fall of atmospheric pressure can trigger an increase or decrease in activity, and such activity will include feeding behaviour. Generally speaking, the sharper the rise or fall in atmospheric pressure the more extreme will be the trout's response to it. And a further general statement is that falling pressure produces poor prospects for the fly-fisherman, while rising pressure provides improved sport. And now it gets really complicated and confusing, because extended periods of stable high and low pressure are generally poor for sport, but *gradual* change from one to another is to be welcomed. Sudden changes, however, in atmospheric pressure are disastrous.

Anglers are frequently aware of the effects of fluctuations in atmospheric pressure, although unaware of the causes. Recently I took a three-day trip to fish the mayfly hatch on Lough Erne in Northern Ireland. On all three days the atmospheric pressures were chaotic – brilliant sunshine followed swiftly by low cloud and drizzle; flat calm one minute a raging storm the next; all interspersed with hellish rain and hail showers that battered the lough surface flat even in a brisk breeze – and the fish sulked as only Erne fish can! The mayfly hatched in droves but the trout, unable to stand the plunging and rising atmospheric pressure, were largely unimpressed and did not feed. Occasionally there would be a brief spell of stability, and the loch would be spattered with the rings of rising fish, but, just as we thought 'Here we go!', off they went, and we cursed, swore and shook our fists at the heavens.

I have already mentioned my experiences during a thunderstorm on the Harray Loch. Meteorologically speaking, what happened there was that, as the storm approached the atmospheric pressure dropped dramatically, and the fish 'went off the feed'; then, as it departed, the atmospheric pressure soared equally dramatically, bringing on the frantic feeding frenzy in the trout population. Thunderstorms are extreme weather conditions and, therefore, produce extreme and bizarre reactions from fish.

A less intense, but still noticeable, reaction can be the result of more moderate weather phenomena. I've frequently been out on a loch, catching at a steady rate when suddenly, for no apparent reason, the fish have switched off, then, after a lengthy passage of time, they have gradually come back 'on'. Checking the weather charts later in the day has shown that a frontal system passed over the loch at or about the time of the break in the trout's feeding regime. Even weak fronts can have this effect, though generally to a lesser extent. The passage of a frontal system over your area is almost always betrayed by a sudden shift in wind direction; this shift may be only a few compass points, but it should be noticeable to those who are aware and monitoring the situation (and, let's be honest, it would be an unwise and careless angler who didn't notice even a slight shift in wind direction!).

We have all been out on one of these hellishly frustrating days when the wind has veered and swung all round the compass, with no two casts travelling in the same direction. Can anyone of us, hand on heart, say that this has led to good fishing? Changing wind direction is a sure sign of fluctuations in atmospheric pressure and fluctuations in atmospheric pressure mean poor fishing. In addition, sudden falls/rises in wind speed can also herald pressure changes, some to good effect, as far as the angler is concerned, and some to bad. Massive, towering cloud masses looming against a bright blue sky are a sure-fire sign that weather and pressure fluctuations are on the cards. Under each of these looming cumulonimbus towers is a deep area of low pressure, which, as it passes, will cause the trout in the area to respond negatively to the sudden change in atmospheric pressure. Under these circumstances we tend to experience 'off, on, off, on' behaviour from the fish, as the clouds advance and retreat.

One of my pet hates is a day when the wind has backed instead of veered. A wind 'backs' when it follows an anti-clockwise direction round the compass, and 'veers' when following a clockwise course. A backing wind means falling pressure, and a veering wind means a rising glass: steady rise = good; steady fall = bad. To be out on a loch when the wind travels, say, from westerly, through south-westerly and ends up strengthening from the south-east means that, ninety-nine times out of a hundred, I'd be better employed elsewhere, far from trout and water. Of course, all things being equal (and, by definition, they never are!), the opposite conditions should make the perfect fishing day! The old saw that north and east winds are bad, and west and south winds good relates to this weather feature; when it is understood that it rarely blows from north or east except in a backing wind, and that south and west winds are generally a feature of a veering wind, it all becomes clear. (Of course, on the rare occasion that a westerly or southerly does occur on a backing wind, it causes disgruntled anglers to moan 'I thought west and south winds were good for fishing! What the bloody hell is going on?' All weather features must be judged in context to get some idea of how they will affect sport.)

So, in a situation of changing atmospheric pressure, don't change flies so much as change tactics. During periods of falling pressure fish may be expected not to frequent the surface layers as much as they may normally do, and in periods of rising pressure one can expect fish to be more co-operative generally. Hatches are generally stimulated by rising pressure and curtailed by a sudden drop.

PRECIPITATION

An old fishing pal of mine always used to hold the belief that it was impossible to catch fish whilst it was raining. Even if I caught fish when it was raining and held it in front of his nose, he would pay no attention and would carry right on with his belief. Mind you, he was a Shetlander, and they do things differently up there!

To a certain extent his theory has some truth to it. Rain most often occurs as a low-pressure system approaches and, as we have learnt, falling atmospheric pressure is associated with advancing lows, and fish react negatively to it. The heavier the rain, the steeper the fall in atmospheric pressure, and the more marked the effect on trout behaviour. However, some rain can accompany a *rise* in atmospheric pressure, generally the lighter stuff. This sort of rain, and the associated hatches of insects that like moist conditions, instead of deterring fish can herald spectacular rises – although in truth the rise most often starts as the rain fades away.

Hail showers are closely associated with cumulonimbus clouds, and we already know what that means – short, sharp drops in atmospheric pressure and sudden cessations in trout activity. Snow, on the other hand, is more often associated with a mass of moist, warm air pushing into an existing mass of cold air. The associated rise in air temperature is beneficial to fishing effort. I have experienced the onset of snow on cold spring days when salmon fishing and have been aware of the sudden slight rise in temperature. Nothing could be better for the spring salmon fisher, and, if there are fish about, they almost always react positively. A few years back, on opening day of the trout season (15 March), I went down to the Stenness Loch to see if I could get a trout for dinner. The weather was a tad sharp, frosty and bright, and Stenness was my best bet for a fish. Normally I would have gone searching on Harray for the first fish of the season but the weather ruled that out. I fished for an hour or two and had seen nothing when great banks of cloud started to build from the west. A few flakes of snow appeared and there was a distinct softening of the chill. Just when the air was filled with great gobs of snow and anything more than twenty yards away had disappeared behind a wall of white, I got my first fish, a chunky yellow-bellied Stenness fish of about pound-and-a-half. Fifteen minutes or so later I got another, and they both looked fine lying in the thin layer of snow that had fallen. Another memory involves a December day when I was goose shooting along the side of Harray. There was a thin layer of ice in the marginal water at my feet and, when the snow started, midge pupae started emerging from the mud on the bottom of the loch and rose up and banged their heads on the underside of the ice layer. It was a bizarre thing to watch, and the memory stays fresh in my mind.

Precipitation of any kind is no sure indicator of trout activity, whether negative or positive. I have seen fish come to the boat when massive raindrops, like marbles, were battering the surface into a welter of spray. An unusual occurrence, admittedly, but not unheard of. In fact I'd rather have some rain than none at all. Moisture in the air is a good thing in moderation; totally dry air is almost always an indicator of total lack of sport.

As regards fly or colour selection associated with precipitation I would always advise the hatching midge colours of black, claret, silver and red. Rain generally heralds some sort of midge hatch – perhaps only sparse and sporadic, but the increase in humidity levels always increases the chance. And trout may also associate the pitter-patter of rain on the surface with the possibility of a double-midge supper, so there's little to lose.


WIND

The loch fisher in Scotland can face all sorts of wind speeds, so the ability to be able to fish in conditions approaching gale force will stand him in good stead. Wild loch trout seem actively disposed to feed in conditions which many southern anglers would consider to be totally unproductive. In fact, we in the far north and west, routinely venture forth in conditions which, in southern areas, would see boats confined to base. Therefore, an understanding of what is likely to happen in varying wind speeds will help those more generally acquainted with fishing in clement conditions.

Calm to light winds were generally shunned by the mainstream angler when I was a boy. This had more to do with tackle and technique than any preference shown by the fish. The heavy end gear, coarse leader material and bushy patterns that were *de rigeur* back then meant that trout were likely to be deeply suspicious of fly-fishing activity, and the resulting poor catches meant that in gentle weather anglers stayed at home. But trout do feed actively in such conditions, all things being equal, and modern-day tackle and fishing trends mean that we can now fully exploit such weather states.

Perhaps surprisingly, I find that almost as many people have problems coping with very calm conditions as struggle in a big wave. Many of us need a bit of wind to help get the line out and to straighten the leader before it alights on the surface. To successfully target rising fish in calm weather takes good technique and line control. Fish that are within inches of the surface are understandably spooky and about one nano-second away from panicked flight if anything disturbs them. There is only one route to mastery of such conditions, and the milestones on that path are a quiet approach, fine tackle, a light leader, not too many flies on said leader and, above all, practice.

I quickly adopted light tackle as it became available in the late 1970s, and a whole new world opened up to me. For example, Swannay, back then, was generally considered a loch which required a good blow and the use of big, bushy flies for those in pursuit of a 'good 'un'. I actually found the opposite to be true. During the 1977 season, when the loch was arguably at its big-fish-producing peak, I took thirteen trout over 3 lb from Swannay all in very calm weather and on light nylon and small flies. I became convinced that if the angler could seduce fish in calm conditions with appropriate gear, then the chance of catching specimens was actually improved by light winds. As I remember it, Norman Irvine (the only one amongst my fishing pals who shared my beliefs) and I always seemed to have the loch to ourselves when the winds dropped away. Regardless of venue, no experience since then has seriously dented this belief, as long as brown trout were the target. Mind you, sea trout and salmon are a different kettle of fish, if you'll excuse the pun.

It seems to me that most aquatic insects prefer light wind conditions in which to hatch. Admittedly hatches do occur in strong winds, but rarely with the frequency and intensity experienced in calm conditions. Some insects, midge and Caenis primarily, will actually terminate the hatch if wind speeds pick up, whilst olive species, on the other hand, seem to like a brisk breeze for a hatch, but only up to a moderate point. Terrestrial species will stop flying when winds freshen, and the old belief that a strong wind was required to bring them to the loch is more than just questionable.

Light-wind tactics should be well differentiated from those adopted in strong winds. If you are using a floating line, multi-fly casts should be avoided when the wind is very light to avoid flies skating or overly disturbing the surface film. I frequently use a two-fly cast, with a distance of ten to twelve feet (two arm spans) between the dropper and the point fly. Very occasionally two flies may seem too much for the floater in such conditions, and then I tend to switch to a very slow intermediate or an intermediate-tip. In light winds avoid bushy, heavily palmered flies; select slim and sparse dressings instead, and fish them off the finest leader material that you can get away with. As I have hinted, my line of choice in such conditions would be a floater, and this is because it allows me to fish slowly whilst still keeping the flies in the area of action, which in such conditions will generally be the surface.

Midge-imitating patterns are always worthy of selection in a light-wind scenario, and a wet/dry combination is not to be sniffed at unless the wind disappears entirely (then I would remove the dry, as being too disruptive of the surface film). We tend to think that more fish rise in very light winds, but the truth probably is that we can actually see more, and over longer distances, in a virtual or actual calm. It is a characteristic of wild brown trout (in fact all trout) that they are drawn to the surface in quiet conditions and, assuming that the boat angler slips about as silently as a mouse, should be targeted there.

Moderate blows are generally more productive than calms, because fish tend to lose some of the extreme caution that marks their behaviour in very calm conditions. In a reasonable blow the angler can get away with clumsy casts that, in a calm, would have every fish rushing to the depths. Another advantage of the blow is that the trout's vision is restricted by the chaos and confusion of the waves, and the appearance-disappearance-appearance of a wet fly being pulled through a vigorous wave formation arouses their opportunistic nature. This goes a long way towards explaining why takes in calms, when the fish can see more clearly, tend to be steady and purposeful, whereas the take in a wave is often more violent and sudden.

The over-used argument that wave action produces vast quantities of food on the downwind shore should not be relied upon. There is no doubt that some items and creatures will be shaken loose by the suck and blow of wave action, but most invertebrates and others which inhabit the margins have developed and adapted to withstand such effects. To put it another way, ducks float on water because they are designed for life in an aquatic environment, goats don't fall off mountainsides because clinging to narrow ledges is a way of life for them, and nymphs, snails and shrimps don't immediately lose their grip on security and fly around in the water like confetti in the wind just because a wave has lashed the shoreline. Of course, ducks may occasionally sink and goats from time to time do fall off the mountainside, but nobody got fat on the proceeds. The increase in action on the wave-lashed shore may have more to do with optimistic opportunism on the part of the trout and also an increase in their activity rate brought about by improved levels of dissolved oxygen in the area.

To improve chances in a good wave, use standard wet-fly techniques with highly mobile wet flies bearing good straggly hackles and reasonable quantities of palmering. Flies which use extra long gamebird hackles such as Peterson's Pennell, Leggy Claret or Golden Olive Bumbles, Octopus, Wet Hoppers and Palmered March Brown are likely candidates for this chaotic environment where mobility is everything.

For those who will eventually fish in the next best thing to a howling gale – if you frequent and fish the wilder regions of this country, then I'm afraid this is inevitable – its important to know that this will bear little resemblance to fly-fishing in moderate or calm conditions. Firstly, there is little likelihood of a hatch, so imitative patterns are not likely to be required. Also, the turbulence of the water will require the use of flies that are, how shall we put it, brave! The sorts of flies that our fathers used – big, bushy, bumbly patterns in primary colours – still have a place in a world where subtlety is surplus to requirements. Historically, the best fly for such conditions was a fully-dressed Loch Ordie, but present trends tend to suggest big Sedgehogs and the like; others which can perform sterling service in a storm are bushy, well-hackled Grouse and Clarets and Bibios. The patterns already recommended for the more moderate wave will also always be worth a trial.

In a big wind the boat will be drifting fast even with a drogue out the back, so to avoid overdrifting the line, a faster than normal rate of retrieve will be required. The boat drift speed relative to water drift speed will tend to cancel out the faster-than-normal retrieve rate and, although the arm is moving so fast it is almost a blur, the flies may be virtually static or merely idling along in the flurry, jumble and confusion that is, or was, the surface film. Takes can be surprisingly steady in such conditions, and the angler rarely has more to do than hold on as the fish hooks itself. The temptation to fish outsize patterns should generally be resisted, as standard flies will do the job perfectly well. If mad, slashing rises are experienced that result in no contact or the merest of touches then it is very likely that the flies are too big. A reduction in size whilst maintaining the same pattern should bring a positive result. (And, while we are on the subject, fish arcing over a fly without taking it is, regardless of weather conditions, an indication that the fly is too small. This is certainly not a common occurrence, but it does happen, and when it does appropriate action needs to be taken.)

Trying to trip a bob fly across what passes for a wave top in a big wind and wave is generally a waste of time for three reasons:

1) in a very big wave trout prefer to make fast rushes into and out of the turbulent surface area and prefer a fly presented static and just below the surface to one dancing crazily across the top;

2) because of the way the eyes of fish work and the physical nature of light in water, in situations where the surface is seriously disturbed by wave action fish will not be able to see much which is not actually immersed;

3) the likelihood of line control in winds of this sort of speed is remote to negligible, and there is nothing worse, more frustrating, than having a fish commit itself just as the fly is whipped away downwind.

Keep the flies in the water and at the end of the retrieve simply hold the flies static for as long as circumstances will allow. If nothing comes along to interfere with the flies, then a simple roll cast, throwing the flies up into the wind, will be enough to deliver a 20-yard-plus cast downwind.

A minor technique in such conditions which has worked well for me and my colleagues is to short-line with a fast-sinking line. Delivering a short length of line (approx 6–10 yards) coupled with a fast enough speed of retrieve will ensure that the flies will never be far from the surface. The sinking nature of the line will hold the tail and middle flies down in the water, allowing better control of line and flies, and trout find the steep angle of ascent to be highly stimulating. It works – try it!

TEMPERATURE

It is rare in Scotland to experience the sort of water temperatures which make fishing a waste of time. The sort of high summer temperatures which bedevil more southern regions are not common north of the Border, and the mild, temperate winters we enjoy (!?) rarely mean frozen lochs once the season has got under way. The best of Scottish trout fishing exists as a direct consequence of the tempering effect of the North Atlantic Drift – in other lands which share our northerly latitudes winters can mean total freeze-up well into the spring months. So the next time you are out on a Scottish loch in the early part of the season, and feeling a mite chilly, be thankful you are where you are – everyone else on our latitude is likely to be fishing through a hole in the ice wondering if the sensation will ever return to their fingers and toes, not to mention more sensitive areas in between!

In our neck of the woods temperature will have a lot to do with wind direction, rather than hours of sunshine. In shallow water sunshine will heat the water indirectly, by first warming up the bed of the loch; in deeper waters temperature will be directly influenced by the ambient heat, or lack of it, of the wind. We have already discussed weather systems and how they work, and we know that west and southerly winds tend to be moist and warm whilst north and east winds are cooler and drier. Cold water means plenty of dissolved oxygen, and as the temperature of water rises, its ability to hold oxygen declines. Trout require high levels of dissolved oxygen to exist, and that is why they are creatures of the sub-arctic regions, high mountains in warm countries, rushing rivers and wave-lashed lochs. In areas where trout do not flourish species such as coarse fish, which require a lot less dissolved oxygen, thrive. Scotland is a trout region because of its climate, and the most important factor in that climate is seasonal temperature.

So far most of the features of weather discussed have been slow-working, and not ones which would tend to have an immediate effect upon angling endeavour. But air/wind temperatures can help and hinder fishing effort in very direct and immediate ways. For example, we've all been out on very pleasant evenings with the wind dying away nicely and a nice hatch just starting to bring the trout 'up', when suddenly a chill wind picks up from nowhere, the hatch stops, the fish disappear and the loch goes dead as a stick. The sudden chilling of the surface layers will stop the hatch and the rise just as if someone had pulled a switch. Mind you, a wind picking up in the evening is frequently a sign of atmospheric pressure drop, so here we have two negative factors working in conjunction.

Knowing that all things to do with temperature are relative, it is easy to understand that, although trout prefer cold water, there is little about a Scottish summer that will cause them discomfort. Frequently in the summer months, fish will be deterred from entering the surface layers because a chill wind has dropped the temperature in the top few inches of water. The overt indications of this are:

- fish coming short to flies fished in or on the surface film;
- the floating line failing and slow or fast sinkers taking all the fish;
- negligible fly life hatching;

My own fishing waistcoat looks as if I have been pelted with the contents of a surgical supply store

Sometimes it is appropriate to get out of the boat. A beautiful evening on
Loch Sarclet, Caithness with the odd good fish on the move!

In high summer, when the weather is hot and bright, the late evening offers
the best chance of a good fish. Loch Sarclet, Caithness

The best fish are not always to be found at the tail of the wind.  Loch Sarclet, Caithness

Catch and release is a conservation tool which requires knowledge and understanding if it is to be correctly used

A silvery, black-spotted appearance is a sign of good feeding and a pelagic lifestyle. A fine fish from Loch Watten, Caithness

Drifting the machair edge on Loch Bornish, South Uist. To do this successfully and effectively requires a good ghillie

Great sport can be had from modest sized fish. Loch Watten, Caithness

Fish of this quality challenge the theory that the typical Scottish trout is small, nasty and black!

What the spoon can show. This fish has been feeding heavily on shrimp, but with the odd midge pupa and terrestrial fly thrown in for good measure

The author looking for a trophy fish on a machair loch. Loch Sandary, North Uist

A wild day on Loch Stilligary, South Uist. Note that the anglers have both sets of flies well separated by keeping both rods well angled away from the centre of the boat, and the rod-points are low to avoid the wind interfering with the retrieve

Drifting the machair edge in perfect weather conditions. Loch Bornish, South Uist

Pick your clothing to suit the worst possible weather conditions. Any fool can get cold and wet; it takes brains to stay warm and dry!

- fishing effort being more productive where wind effect is lessened, i.e. the head of the wind;
- the water actually feeling warm on the skin.

The last of these indicators seems to confuse many anglers. The easy (but wrong) conclusion to draw is that the problems stem from warm water temperatures when the true dilemma is that the air is colder than the water. Our hands are acclimatised to the low air temperature, so that when we put them in water the warmth we feel is only relative to the coolness of the air. This is a fairly common experience in the early months of the season when water temperatures, though only a few degrees above freezing, are frequently higher than air temperatures. (You really know you've got problems when the odd fish caught is capable of warming your frozen fingers.) For good fishing we require that, at all times, the air is warmer than the water, so water feeling warmer than air is a sign of poor fishing prospects.

Altitude can affect ambient temperatures, and in the high hills many lochs and reservoirs have seriously curtailed seasons because of low temperatures. Spring comes late in the hill country, and summer can be a brief affair. Whereas the lowland loch can be producing fish in March, on upland waters serious effort should be postponed until May at the earliest.

## In Conclusion

Being aware of weather conditions and their likely effects upon trout behaviour virtually guarantees improved results. I am always perplexed by anglers who stubbornly refuse to study the weather or look at a forecast before venturing out on the loch. In this game forewarned is forearmed, and information and understanding is worth fish in the boat.

*Headley's Rule of Thumb no. 4*: When the weather is poor and the sport is dire beyond belief, any change in conditions, regardless of what form that change takes, has to be for the better!

## TIPS AND TOOLS

If you find that a fly is attracting fish, but they are failing to take and just swirl or pluck at the fly, then you have two options: change the fly size, or move the fly to another location on the cast. Very often a pattern fished on the bob or tail will only attract fish but not supply a happy (to the fisherman) outcome. Swapping the flies around very often produces solid takes to the previously failing fly.

This is not a fail-safe rule but can give insight into a frustrating problem – fish coming short. If a fish jumps over a fly or 'head-and-tail's' it without taking I generally suspect the fly is too small; increasing the size (e.g. from a size 12 to a size 10) can often cure the problem. Conversely, in my experience, if the fly size is too large, fish will either ignore it or come short.

# 5 The Pick Of Scotland's Best Lochs

## The Orkney Lochs

Away in the far north, where the blue Atlantic plays footsie with the grey North Sea, lies a small archipelago known as Orkney. The origins of the name Orkney are lost in the mists of time. Some say the name stems from the Latin word 'orca', meaning whale, and relating to the resemblance of the low islands to a gathering of whales. Others maintain that the name comes from the Pictish word for pig, the tusked boar being the clan totem of the pre-Viking Orcadians (the place name Caithness is said to have similar roots in that these mainland Picts gathered under the banner of the cat). Personally I prefer the latter theory, but the resemblance of the islands to a pod of whales, low in the sea, is a strong one: all the Orkney islands, bar Hoy in the south, are very flat and low – which, if you remember Headley's Rule of Thumb no. 2, means shallow lochs. And the greenness of the islands, the victory of grass over heather, brings to mind Rule of Thumb no. 1, which tells us that such an environment should produce fertile lochs.

Orkney lochs are fertile and shallow. Their northerly latitude means that the waters are cold, but proximity to the North Atlantic Drift ensures a temperate climate of cool, wet summers and mild, blustery winters. The hills, composed of old sedimentary flagstone rocks, spew mildly alkaline, mineral-rich waters into the lochs, and, even where the waters are darkly peat stained, fertility and productivity is high. No ice in the winter, no drought in the summer, sweet water to swim in – this is trout heaven.

## Swannay

The first trout I ever caught was unceremoniously removed from Orkney's Swannay loch after it had gratefully accepted a worm that was attached to me via an extremely tired split-cane fly rod. This happened some 45 years ago and, though it should be a dim and distant memory, I could take you to the spot, tell you the wind direction and describe the weather of the day. That my career as a dyed-in-the-wool fly-fisherman, a glorifier of the artificial fly, should begin with a wriggling worm on one of Scotland's finest fly waters is testament to the fact that important events in one's life can have inauspicious and unlikely starts.

Anyone with a bit of highland loch experience who looks at Swannay could be forgiven for thinking: 'Small fish. Lots of them. Not much cop really.' Nothing could be further from the truth! I am a great lover of quality brown trout (not for me the glorification of the wonderful 'wee wild troot, four to the pound' – I like big fish), and that's why I'll always have a deep love of Swannay, even though she can be a dour old bitch at times.

This is the story of a stupendous day's fishing that I have told many times, but it bears repeating. My father and I set out from Kirkwall one foggy morning to fish Swannay. Foggy weather is not generally indicative of good sport, but neither of us was in the mood to call off the trip – not my Dad, who was at that time a Swannay addict, nor I, who was just a fishing addict, full stop. When we arrived at the Orkney Trout Fishing Association's boat launching site at the extreme southern end of the loch, visibility was down to somewhere in the region of a couple of dozen yards. Nothing daunted, we pushed out into it and set up a drift from the island to some indeterminate spot on the southern shore which the faint northerly breeze would select. Somewhere about half way between the island and the shore I had a gentle stopping take to my flies and, upon tightening into it, said, somewhat optimistically as it turned out, 'I've got one!'

'A good fish?' asked my father.

'Nothing special!' I answered 'About a pound or so by the feel of it!'

At that point the fish exploded out of the water about thirty feet in front of the boat.

'Goodness gracious me [or words to that effect]!' I gasped. 'He might be a couple of pounds.'

'More like three!' retorted my Dad, 'Don't lose him!'

By this time the rod I was using – a horrible little cut-down hollow-glass monstrosity – was starting to resemble a bicycle wheel, bent almost double as it was, and the fish was very much in charge. At every jump – and it was jumping quite a bit – another half-pound was added to its weight, and I must admit to a rising feeling of exhilaration, coupled with the mortal dread of impending doom. (Is this an emotion peculiar to fishermen, or is it felt by all humanity? The fish of a lifetime is hooked, and the over-riding feeling is misery born out of fear that the damned thing is going to get off! Is it better to have loved and lost than never to have loved at all?)

Anyway, the longer the fight went on the surer I became that disaster was just round the corner. I just couldn't cope with this airborne monster which spent a minute amount of time zipping through the water and a helluva lot more flying through the air. And then the gods of fishing took a hand in the affair: with a smirk and a chuckle they sent five-and-a-quarter pounds of seriously pissed-off trout out of the water like an Exocet missile … straight into the boat.

The ensuing chaos is hard to describe. I sat slumped, drained of all emotion, in a dazed and confused state, while my father chased the thrashing fish up and down the boat. By the time the monster was subdued the bottom of the boat was a-litter with water, sandwiches, tackle, sweat and slime. Of course, at the time we only knew it was a damned fine fish and had no real inkling of just how fine. The next few minutes were spent gazing at the brute, and interspersed with banal comments such as:

'That's a fine fish!'

'Yeah, pretty good! What do you think it weighs?'

'No idea!'

'Have a guess!'

'I dunno. Maybe … well, it could go as much as … dammit, I've no idea. Pretty big, though!'

'Yeah, pretty big! What do you think it weighs?' and so on.

After about quarter of an hour of this drivel, we finally got back to fishing, my father with expectation of something as big if not bigger, and I with a strange lack of enthusiasm that often follows the capture of a really good fish. A bit like post-coital blues, when you come to think of it!

The still-hidden sun was doing its level best to burn off the fog, and it had now taken on a pearly, luminescent quality which allowed us to decipher landmarks and locations. The breeze shifted from the north to a more easterly direction, and we set up a drift onto the knowe on the Heathery Shore. The knowe (pronounced *now*) in question was the remnants of a crannog or broch, dating back to the late Bronze/early Iron Age, and the shorelines of Orkney lochs are littered with such prehistoric sites. One of their attributes, apart from being excellent landmarks, is that they are invariably surrounded by a trench of deep water and, probably because of this, are a safe bet for a bigger than average fish. When we were a mere twenty or so yards from the north side of the knowe the Old Man hooked into another good fish, which had the good grace to stay in the water and behave in a civilized manner. It soon became obvious that this was a fitting partner to the one caught earlier, and I could tell that the same bitter-sweet feelings of anticipation and foreboding that I had experienced were in full flood at the other end of the boat. After all, when you've expended a whole lot of luck getting one really good fish safely in the boat, isn't Dame Fortune likely to take the rest of the day off? Odds on, I would say!

But it wasn't to be. My father had one overriding failing when playing a good fish: he always wanted it in the boat before it was good and ready. This time his foible worked in his favour. With the rod bent over in an extravagant hoop and the fish doing a passable imitation of a runaway train, he stuck the extended net into the water. With the careless self-sacrifice which would have been admired by a sake-soaked kamikaze pilot, the daft bugger (the trout, not my father) charged the net and got itself inextricably lodged in it. The term 'wild brown trout' suitably describes its antics as it then set about dismantling the landing net whilst my father swung the 'priest' at any part of the fish that he could identify amongst the buckling frame and water-logged net mesh. This trip was starting to take on a bizarre, surrealistic quality, and my father and I were decidedly punch-drunk from the blows of good fortune coming at us from every direction.

Then the sun came out, and the whole loch went dead. But that wasn't the end of the story. Just before the sun set, there was a brief midge hatch during which an impressive rise of trout took place. In those far-off days the general approach in a midge hatch was to cast standard traditional, big, bushy wet flies at rises and wonder why none of the trout was stupid enough to take hold. I did, however, snag one of the brutes, which, when laid beside the two taken earlier in the day, looked like a stickleback. In fact, it weighed 2½ lb, and the total basket weight for the three fish was 12½ lb: the first going 5 lb 5 ounces, and the second 4¾ lb. A day to remember, I think you'll agree.

So was born my long-lasting love affair with the Swannay loch. In subsequent trips I managed, with luck and a dash of skill born out of understanding, to take a whole list of specimen brown trout from what is arguably the finest fly-fishing loch to be found anywhere in Scotland. Swannay is a fisherman's loch, in that almost any technique can and will work on her at the correct time. Nowhere have I experienced dry-fly fishing of such a high quality. Conversely sunk-line fishing with traditional patterns or selected nymphs can produce baskets of wild fish that would make the most jaded angler drool like a baby. Give me a May or June day with a soft and light south-westerly, a high overcast and that weird tension in the air that is always present before a good hatch, and, wherever I am or whatever I'm doing, I immediately think of Swannay and its big and beautiful brown trout.

## Stenness

A couple of years ago Norman Irvine and I were drifting about in the top end of Stenness (Redland Bay to be precise) trying to track down some big-fish holding areas. We knew the fish were 'packed up' and not spread out as usual or in their normal haunts. They were a bugger to find, and we weren't having a lot of luck hunting them down.

Norman nosed the boat into a drift that would run us along the shore from Arion to Craya, a drift that was inches deep and stuffed full of bladder wrack and boulders. Not one of our favourite slots and frequently disappointing, this specific area had a reputation as a big fish haunt and was a favourite wading venue for our good friend Benny Norquoy, who had a long string of quality Stenness trout to his name. Shallow water drifting in Stenness is a real pain but obligatory,

I'm afraid. It's a pain because of the weed. Stenness is stuffed with weed. Real weed this, not like your soft southern weed. On the negative side it is hook-snagging, line-breaking, boat-drift-stopping stuff; on the positive side it's full of scrumptious fish food and provides shelter and ambush cover for lovely big brown trout.

On this drift there is a shelving ridge of rock which juts out at right-angles to the shoreline, gradually sloping away to nothing in a southerly direction. This ridge creates a tight, one- or two-cast holding spot in the comparatively deep water to its north, and a fifty-yard area of good water in the lee of the shelf to the south. As we drifted towards the ridge we could hear the weed rubbing against the keel of the boat and knew that if the fish were here we were right on top of them.

The first indication of anything out of the ordinary was a muffled '!!*#@?!?' from the other end of the boat. Norman's rod was bucking like a branded stallion, and there was a watery whoosh and clatter as a sodding great fish erupted out of the water. One of the biggest brown trout I've ever seen was literally hanging in the air a matter of feet from the gunnels of the boat, and I swear to this day that I actually saw the size 12 fly stuck in the maw of the fish immediately before it sprang loose to come hurtling back to the boat. The splash of re-entry rocked the boat and the silence was deafening. I couldn't speak because the circuitry between gob and brain had become temporarily disconnected (and the fact that my lower jaw seemed welded to my chest didn't help); Norman couldn't say much because what *do* you say when you've just let slip the heaviest fish you've ever hooked in a lifetime's fly-fishing. ('Let slip' is perhaps harsh, though. Such a fish is either well-hooked or not. If not, there isn't a whole lot you can do about it, and if it is, then all being well, he's yours to do with what you will.) We did find another pod of fish later in the day – good fish – and we took a few, but there was a subdued atmosphere in the boat as our minds continually flicked back to that amazing encounter below Craya, and what might have been.

I have no problem admitting that I am in the minority, and that some think I am mad because I list the Stenness loch as one of my favourite lochs. But, although I've had more blank days than successes, some of my most exciting fishy adventures have taken place there. I lived for twenty-odd years by the side of this magnificent water, and over those years it crept into my heart and bedded down there like a Labrador in front of a fire. When the wind gets up and blows hard and the waves get a nice creamy top to them then, wherever I am, if I'm not on Stenness I wonder why not!

Stenness fish are unique. OK, almost every loch that remains relatively unabused by the compulsive stockers can boast a race of fish which in some way are different to all others, whether in coloration, shape, behaviour or environment. But how many can say their fish are unique on all four counts, plus another couple on top. Stenness can!

If you remember my deliberations on dynamic and integrated populations you will also remember that my example was the Harray/Stenness/Scapa Flow system. In this system Stenness does very well, in that it takes population overflow from Harray, and all the sea-run fish heading from Scapa Flow to the Harray spawning burns, have to pass through it. Because Stenness has largely lost all its spawning resource, apart from the vitally important Workies Burn in the extreme south-eastern end, it does not carry a great head of fish and relies on Harray overspill. However the loch's feeding potential is immense, and what trout there are grow very fast and, potentially, very big.

As if that wasn't enough the critical factor which adds quality to this unique trout environment is that it is a brackish-water loch. Every fortnight spring tides push a great slug of rich saline water up from Scapa Flow, which boosts the basic, background productivity. The loch abounds with saltwater-tolerant copepods and crustaceans, and the shallow water teems with stickleback fry. Add to this pure saltwater species such as butterfish, juvenile saithe, then a sprinkling of freshwater food forms such as gammarus species and common eels, plus a few salt-tolerant insect species, and we end up with a virtual protein soup which offers the relatively small head of fish a tremendous potential for growth.

At the beginning of the last century a Stenness trout was taken on a line set for flounders: it weighed a staggering 29¼ lb. Tate Reagan, a taxonomist who specialised in defining and describing distinct fish species in the UK, was convinced that trout from this loch were a race apart and classified them as *Salmo trutta orcadensis*. Given that Stenness is part of a dynamic and integrated system now relying heavily on

Harray spawning burns for its recruitment, there is room for doubt as to whether this conviction is tenable. But there is little doubt that trout from this loch are beautiful, finely formed fish which have about them a certain distinct look which probably stems from nutrition and environment rather than from any genetic source.

The topographical layout of the loch also adds to its unique nature, in that Stenness, unlike its near neighbour Harray and almost every other loch in Orkney, is very much a shoreline drift water. There are very few offshore shallows – a sprinkling in the Voy–Redland areas, plus one or two at the Brodgar end, but everywhere else requires that boats bump the stones. Not that the offshore water is by any means deep: fourteen feet is about as deep as it gets. However, Stenness trout like very shallow water and, as far as the big trout are concerned, the less covering their backs the happier they are. On occasions high winds can produce free-swimming blooms of mud-dwelling copepods, and then good fish can be found in open water taking full advantage of the unexpected windfall, but the smart angler looking for a monster always fishes in inches rather than feet of water.

Although sea trout, and the occasional salmon, frequent this loch, brown trout are the prize. I haven't found better browns anywhere in a lifetime of hunting. A typical Stenness brownie of about 2 lb will have a tiny head, massive shoulders and a body girth which will explain why they fight till they die. Their coloration varies somewhat but, returning to the typical fish, they are dark purple-brown on top fading through pewter to stark white underneath, with a good splattering of coal chunks and fragments of ruby to set off the whole colour scheme. The belly fins are always a wondrous shade of dark amber, and there are electric blue highlights on the gill covers. Occasionally a fish turns up which is very brown, almost khaki-coloured, with buttery flanks and so beautiful that it brings tears to the eyes. I remember Norman taking a fish like this out of Seum's Bay, a 4 lb vision of beauty I would have given almost anything to have caught.

And then there are the 'sea trout' as opposed to the sea trout. Confused? You will be! At any given time of the season, with a bit of luck, it is possible to find what are ostensibly sea trout but which I suspect to be resident Stenness fish with a pelagic habit. Sea trout do run the loch, and in large numbers in the appropriate season, but these green-backed, silvery fish which masquerade as sea trout are probably resident trout with deceptive colouration, making a good living hunting down the zooplankton shoals which are constant feature of the loch. I have long suspected that these shoals of 2–3 lb fish were not sea-run fish but there was no proof of my belief, until the commercial salmon industry, resident in Scapa Flow, started exporting sea lice. It suddenly became easy to differentiate sea trout from resident Stenness fish – all Scapa-sojourning-fish carried varying amounts of fin damage consistent with sea-louse attack, and none of the Stenness residents, regardless of coloration were so marked. The worst of the sea-louse-inflicted damage took place during the immediate post-smolt stage of development, and, regardless of how long after that period the fish was examined, residual scar tissue on the fins would always reveal where the fish had spent its juvenile years. (Of course, because Stenness is an extension of the sea, it is an arguable point that trout do not have to leave the loch to become true sea trout. After all, 'sea troutishness' is only an attitude of mind and/or lifestyle choice and at the end of the day means a whole lot more to anglers than it ever did to trout.)

Whether the angler is mooching about in the knee-deep water, kicking the crabs at the Brig o' Brodgar in a March blizzard, looking for that first fish of the season, or bouncing from wave top to wave top off the Ness of Redland in a summer gale hunting down the plankton feeders, Stenness is one of the most fascinating lochs to fish. I know of nowhere like it – where every rule of fishing is either stood on its head, or blindfolded, spun round a few times and then sent off in the wrong direction. It is the living proof of the tenet that anglers with open minds catch fish, those with closed minds struggle.

Oh, by the way, whilst I lived by the side of Stenness there was an experiment I fully intended to carry out but never started. I had this theory that all the biggest trout in the loch largely fed on fish, and the fish of their preference were eels and butterfish. Almost without exception, investigations showed that big fish stomachs contained eels subjected to varying degrees of the digestion. My plan was to fish at night/early morning with long fur-strip lures – Minkies or Zonkers – in appropriate colours (olive-green or dirty orange) in areas where the bigger fish were most often seen – Voy Shallows, Redland, Ness of Seatter, Brig o' Waithe and Brig o' Brodgar – over a period of, say, a couple of weeks. The preferred eel size for these fish was somewhere in the 9–12 in. range, so lures would probably have to match this size. This wasn't either going to be pretty fishing nor very productive, I'd guess, but, if the patterns were acceptable and the technique worked, then a small number of fish would be caught and they would be big fish. A specimen/ferox-hunter type approach would be essential and the temptation to slip on a few standard patterns would have to be resisted at all costs, but the rewards would be high. Maybe someday someone will try. If so I wish them all the best. This lucky person may discover that there is a whole class of Stenness fish waiting to be caught.

## The Machair Lochs of South Uist

We look at the Scottish landscape and think what we see has been there since time began, and, for large slices of it, this would be a reasonably accurate assessment. After all, there are rock formations in the far north-west Highlands which were formed long before life appeared on this planet. But in the Western Isles, along the Atlantic shoreline, is a strip of land bearing lochs of indescribable beauty that were formed in the relatively recent past. This is the machair land of the Isles, famed for wild flowers, rare birds and some of the finest wild trout fishing to be found anywhere.

Whenever someone asks me where he/she should go to find the finest fishing in Scotland, South Uist always springs to mind. The machair lochs, though fragile environments needful of protection and care, offer a very fine class of trout fishing for those who like quality and quantity. Their secret lies in the machair land. *Machair* is the Gaelic name for this land born of the sea, an accumulation of shell sand deposited over hundreds of years by the tidal streams that ply the western seaboards of the Isles, all bound together by a thin top layer of soil and grassland. Shell-sand is basically a very, very large volume of crushed sea shells, and is built out of the same chemical compound, calcium carbonate, that predominates in chalk and limestone. Though not particularly soluble, shell sand will quickly neutralise any acidity in water, producing slightly alkaline water with a very high level of dissolved minerals.

Because the machair land is ancient sand dune, and the lochs lie in the dips and hollows which are a natural feature of such links land, the lochs are very shallow. And because the North Atlantic Drift washes up the western seaboard of the Isles, bringing damp, mild air all the way from the Gulf of Mexico, summers and winters are soft and mild, with none of the harsh extremes which can compromise the life quality of humans or trout. All these factors – climate, soil pH, waters which are shallow, mineral rich and alkaline, plus a high degree of control and protection – produce some of the best fishing this country has to offer.

Studying a map of the west side of South Uist can leave anyone wondering if they are looking at the sea with lumps in, or very, very wet land. It is a staggering fact that though the Western Isles have only a tad over one per cent of the land mass of the UK, fifteen per cent of the freshwater surface area can be found there! This is not only machair land, it is also loch land with almost every combination of aquatic features imaginable. There are big, wide-open, virtually featureless waters like Bee. Then there is mighty Druidibeg that has enough features for a dozen lochs. There are big puddles and tiny lochans all over the place. And every splash of water, regardless of size seems to contains trout. But there are a handful which can seriously claim to offer the finest fly-fishing in the western hemisphere – Stilligarry, Grogarry, West Ollay, and Bornish.

## Stilligarry

I love Stilligarry. I think I'll call my next Labrador puppy 'Stilligarry'; even better, I'll spell it in the old Gaelic way, Stadhlaigearraidh. (Pretentious? Moi?) Stilligarry is another dour old bitch of a loch which, like a certain little girl, when good is very, very good, and when bad is bloomin' atrocious! I've been on her, wondering who killed all the fish, when, as if by magic, she has 'switched on' and some of the finest trout anyone ever saw have started frolicking about in the waves like carefree kittens. No other brown trout loch that I know of beats Stilligarry at the old 'switch on/switch off' trick, but big, well-fed trout have their own agendas which are mysteries unfathomable by mere humans.

Stilligary trout come in two colour schemes: standard hunter-style with big red spots, buttery golden flanks and brown backs; and the typical grazer-style green-backs, whose silver flanks show a distinct lack of red spots. The hunter-style fish are to be found near the shorelines and/or rocks, mostly in the northern and eastern areas, and the silvery grazers are almost exclusively found across the open water in the south and west. (In Chapter 1 we discussed the grazer/hunter forms of brown trout and why they took up differing colour/camouflage schemes.) The only surprising factor in all this is that Stilligarry is much smaller than most other lochs which show this sort of population split, but it is a perfect example nonetheless.

Almost all my favourite Stilligarry recollections involve very windy weather. OK, South Uist is a very windy place, but surely I should have been entitled to more than one reasonable day in six. That one really good fishing day, with high cloudbase, a dash of filtered sunshine and a light easterly breeze, wasn't even a day, it was only about an hour-and-a-half. I had been up in South Harris prospecting what was supposed to be an early run of salmon and sea trout into a loch system there, and had arranged to take the CalMac ferry from North Uist to the Mainland. This gave me 3½ hours to kill between the ferry arriving from Leverburgh and the Lochmaddy departure. A very good friend of mine, Keith Dunbar, had a party fishing out of the Grogarry Lodge on South Uist and asked me to kill the waiting time with them on a loch of my choice.

Fishing is supposed to be a relaxing sport, but it isn't if you have to make a frenetic hour-long dash to the loch and another one back to the ferry terminal, jamming in a couple of hasty drifts in the middle. Trying to rig up your fly rod and make up a cast as you're trotting from the car to the loch side doesn't help either, but I was getting a crack at Stilligarry, and that's worth a whole lot of sacrifice. Billy Felton, one of the UK's finest ghillies (or should I say 'guides'?) was waiting with his guest at the boat noust*. I literally threw myself and gear into the boat

---

* noust/noost: literally nest; generally naturally formed boat mooring station where boats can be partially or fully drawn from the water. (Orkney/Shetland dialect.)

as Billy backed out into deep water, shook hands all round, ate a hurried sandwich, and when I looked up we were at the head of the drift. In a 'no time to fanny about' situation like this there is only one strategy: floating line, three reliable 'banker' wets, keep your head down and your eyes open, and go for it. I stuck on a Green Peter Muddler on the top, a Fluorescent Soldier Palmer in the middle and a Silver Invicta on the point. On the first drift I took two cracking 1 lb-plus fish on the Muddler, and on the second, as the boat skirted the short point on the southern shore, a superb 2 lb-plus fish on the Silver Invicta. And that was it; I had 75 minutes to get back up to Lochmaddy and check in, or I was going to be stuck in the Isles overnight. As I walked back to the car I had this bizarre vision of the fishless guest turning to Billy and, pointing to my retreating back, asking 'Who was that masked man?'

Another, briefer, vignette which wanders back and forth across my memory is of a very windy day on Stilligarry when Bob Carnill and I were drifting onto the islands in front of a very brisk south-westerly, which had ambitions to be a screaming gale. We hadn't being doing too well. Fish were seen, and fish moved, but I don't recall anything of importance coming to the side of the boat. But on the last drift, when the brisk breeze realized its full potential and the loch had decided to join us in the boat, a fish in the region of plus or minus 5 lb swam through a wave desperately trying to eat the Black Worm Fly I had on the point. Although, at the height of the storm, Stilligarry had 'switched on', we couldn't stay. To have remained out trying to catch that fish of a lifetime would have led to a disaster – and no fish, no matter how big, is worth that! But the vision of that wonderful fish with all fins bristling and blood in its eye, sliding through the wave, will stay with me for ever.

## Bornish

No one should be more surprised than I that, out of all the machair lochs of South Uist, I should select Bornish to discuss. Why? Because, in my opinion, Bornish doesn't really fish like a machair loch. Unlike its neighbours, it lacks the irregularity of shoreline or the myriad rocks and tiny islets which makes even a short drift a mass of opportunities.

Bornish is very regular of feature, has almost a geometrical uniformity and lacks a good 'machair edge'. (A 'machair edge' is the drop-off between the shallow margins and the relatively deep loch proper; it is easily identified by the sudden colour change from the light-coloured sandy marginal strip to the deep brown of the deeps. The quality and quantity of fish which lie along this drop-off is staggering, and to wade the margins dropping a fly just beyond the machair edge is one of the finest and most exciting prospects for a machair loch fisherman.) As Bornish has a poor 'edge', not well defined, most of the boat drifts are through open water, which is not standard on machair waters, where drifts are generally set to include as many visible features as possible.

Nor does Bornish have that same 'low stock density – high average individual size' characteristic that one comes to expect from a typical machair loch. But what it does – better than any loch of comparable size or configuration – is to offer masses of sport and lots of fish, and not small fish either! I really can't remember a trip out on Bornish when there weren't plenty of fish on the 'go'. My penultimate trip out on it was with Iain Muir and Colin 'Puck' Kirkpatrick (the latter supplied the photographs for this book). We had planned an evening trip to get some 'fish played against the sunset' shots, but we arrived just in time for the mother and father of all caenis hatches. It was one of those hatches where one has to tie a handkerchief over one's nose and mouth to stop the little buggers crawling in, and to stop one's lungs getting clogged with insect mass. It seemed as if every fish in the loch was 'up' and feeding, and 50-metre-wide shoals of fish were intercepting the boat in a regular procession. This went on from early evening until the last glimmer of light faded in the west, and not one fish came to the boat or was hooked. It happens! One day you come across half-a-dozen fish and you catch every one of them, and the next day you see a thousand and retire defeated, not to mention 'skunked'!

However, the following day Iain and I set out again in less than auspicious circumstances. At about midnight the previous night, as we were berthing the boat after our fruitless foray amongst the Caenis-feeders, a gale had sprung up from nowhere. This, added to some residual turbulence from an earlier blow, turned the loch water into something resembling oxtail soup, which glinted evilly in the strong sunlight. Turbid water is the curse of the machair loch fisher, for the fish don't like it at all and rarely co-operate with the angler when the water is too thick to drink, too thin to plough. Still, we only had a couple of days amongst the machair lochs, so we had to make the best of it, and at least that sudden gale had quickly fallen away, leaving us with a fair breeze.

While we were doing some set-up shots of boats and anglers against a backdrop of machair scenery Iain, posing for the camera whilst fishing in about ten inches of water, hooked, played and landed a nice 1 lb-plus Bornish fish. This was out of the blue, unscripted and a surprise to everyone including the fish, so we set about fishing with a fair degree of hope.

Standard gear at any time on these shallow lochs must be a floating line, but by the time we'd done our first drift proper, I was beginning to doubt the wisdom of sticking to standard tactics. The water was as thick as guts and I had severe reservations about whether the fish could see our just-sub-surface offerings. Although it pains me to do so on lochs of this type and quality, if I was going to get a fish then I would have to look to the sinking line, and the line of choice was a Wet Cel 2. This is not a bottom-dredging line but it was capable of dropping the flies down to a level where they could at least be seen by the fish. Well, I suppose there would be little point to this story if the tactic had failed, but of course it worked very well indeed – much to the disgust of certain of the locals who believe that using anything other than a floater is an admission of failure. Iain soon got the message and changed to a sinking line, and we finished the day with five for 8½ lb, not one over 2 lb and not one under 1½ lb. As nice a basket of wild fish as you could hope for in very difficult conditions.

Bornish is, arguably, the finest fly water in Scotland. But if it has a flaw it is that it can be a touch too co-operative at times and lacks the degree of challenge that its near neighbours offer. However, most people would class this as a positive quality, and who am I to argue. It's just that a day's fishing on Bee, Stilligary, Grogarry or West Ollay may see you 'skunked', but on the other hand you might just come home with something that will be peering at you from a glass case for the rest of your life.

# The Sea Trout and Salmon Lochs of the Western Isles

During the past three decades we have witnessed such a decline of our migratory salmonid species that some very dire predictions have been made, along the lines of total wipe-out and extinction. Such a calamitous conclusion to this downward spiral has not, as yet, occurred, and there are subtle signs that despite commercial and industrial threats, sea trout stocks are making something of a comeback. I doubt whether we can hope to see a return to the glory days of the past, when trout from the sea thronged every estuary and threw themselves up virtually every freshwater stream. But perhaps the worst is behind us.

One of my favourite books is Hamish Stuart's *The Book of the Sea Trout* (1917), which details the observations and experiences of one of the most accomplished and deep-thinking anglers this country has ever produced. Stuart died at sea in 1914 whilst endeavouring to recuperate from disease, and it never ceases to amaze me that a book written almost a century ago is, in very large part, relevant to our present situation. Many of the techniques that he discusses are unchanged to this day. Does that reflect his great insight and wisdom or the lack of advance and development in this branch of fishing?

Almost all Stuart's sea trout fishing was done on the West Coast or in the Western Isles, areas I have a passing knowledge of, and it is a very exciting experience to fish lochs of which he wrote, and cast flies to marks and rocks which he describes in his book. I only wish I could catch fish as big as the ones he regularly extracted from these same waters.

## Loch Fada

In his book, Stuart says that the finest sea trout loch in Scotland is Loch Roag, and its only serious rival is its sister loch, Loch Fada. Far be it from me to argue with the great man, but I feel that the reverse is now true; Fada would be my first choice and Roag my second. Roag, being a brackish water, can be tricky in the extreme, and on occasion I've spent very frustrating hours on it with hosts of fish, fresh off the tide, leaping all over the place but not one of them taking even the slightest interest in the fly. But it must be said that every sea trout heading for Fada, and that is a substantial number, must do so via Roag, unless of course they have a bus pass!

I must admit I love Fada very much. It somehow encapsulates the very essence of the Scottish sea-trout loch. It is not big, the water is dark and mysterious, there are some exciting wave-washed boulders which just reek of big fish, the burn mouth looks like it was designed by a 'fishophile', and the fish always tend to be where they should be, where they were last year and where they'll be next year, too! That's not to say it is an easy venue, because it most certainly is not! Every fish you take from Fada will be hard-earned. Like any other sea trout and salmon water the marks can be fished over hard all day without sign of fin or scale, only for the whole place to go ballistic for a brief spell, then shut down just as quickly.

Fada is shaped like a long-legged Y, the axis being north-west–south-east. My favourite areas are every last square inch of East Bay, the peninsula point and the mouth of West Bay. The burn mouth has only ever given me one very black sea trout and one very red salmon. But I like that too! On so many lochs of this type the fishing centres round the burn mouth, and the angler's confidence decreases in direct proportion to the distance away from it.

But, oh, that East Bay – what memories it holds for me! A couple of years back I was fishing there with Neil Patterson, under the close supervision of ghillie *extraordinaire*, Billy Felton, when the record Fada sea trout was brought into our boat. OK, you've guessed it, it was not caught by me but by that tarry swine Patterson! We were on a drift from the west shore into the south end of East Bay, and had just entered the latter when Neil was almost dragged from the boat by 10 pounds of fighting fury. I can be as magnanimous and noble as the next man in the face of a boat partner's success but there was a distinct shade of green to my homely features that day, I can tell you!

Some of my recollections are less spectacular but equally memo-rable. For instance, there was the time when I hooked a powerful little fish just as the boat ran aground on the east side of the island. Nothing Billy or anyone else could do seemed capable of extricating the boat from the obstruction, and I just couldn't get control over the fish either.

So what was my brilliant solution to both problems? Stepping out of the boat into what I thought would be about 18 inches of water, thus lightening the load and allowing it to drift clear. The problem was that the boat was lodged on the top of a very big boulder, and I stepped into five feet of water. My feet hit the bottom and a split-second later they were back in the boat, the immersion being so brief that I hardly got wet. I didn't think this occurrence the slightest bit funny, but I was in a minority of one (again!). I got the fish though!

John Kennedy has long talked of the South Uist's October sea-trout run and bemoaned the fact that so few regular guests are around to witness this regular event. I was lucky enough to witness a part of this run one bleak October afternoon when Ian Kennedy and I were berthing the boat after spending a very tough day on Fada. We had just emptied the boat of all the gear, broken down the rods and were about to set off for the car when a bright, sparkly sea trout of about 2–2½ lb jumped just off the transom of the boat. We stood and looked at the spot, thinking 'Sod's Law! We've just spent the whole day for one rather the worse-for-wear fish, and then a fresh one damn near jumps in the boat at the end of the day!' But then there was another … and another … and, look! there's another one down there! Never in the field of sea trout angling has tackle been resurrected in less time. I can't quite remember how many we caught but it was a few, and they were some of the finest, fittest, plumpest October sea trout I've ever taken out of fresh water. It was also the perfect way to end a season.

## North Harris Estate/Amhuinnsuidhe

There are few places which, when mentioned in a company of anglers, would create a total silence as every ear was tuned in to listen. Grimersta is one and Amhuinnsuidhe is another. The North Harris Estate is famed as a sea trout fishery and, although not perhaps sharing the South Uist lochs' predisposition for massive size, it makes up for this shortfall in offering masses of fish to fish-hungry rods. The sheer volume of fish which run this system beggars belief and is not matched by any other rival system. Amhuinnsuidhe Castle is a magnificent fishing lodge, sitting at the head of a little sea loch called Loch

Leosavay on North Harris. From there blessed anglers sally forth to fish some of the finest sea trout lochs that the gods of fishing saw fit to create.

Surprisingly, save for Loch Voshimid, the names of the other lochs on this system are not widely known. Who has heard of either Ulladale or Scourst before visiting the estate? Even I, for whom the name Amhuinnsuidhe rang like a stroked crystal glass, was unaware that such wonderful fishing venues existed until the summer of 2003. Iain Muir and I arrived at Amhuinnsuidhe Castle late on the Wednesday afternoon to discover, to our horror, that we had been expected that morning and that our only chance to fish the famed Loch Voshimid had disappeared like snow off a roof. (This was not good news when the only loch on the system that was known to us was, of course, Voshimid.) But a visit to the tackle room went a long way towards calming our fears and raising our hopes. By reading the list of specimen sea trout etched into the very plaster on the walls, it became obvious that, though Voshimid was prolific beyond the dreams of the most acquisitive angler, Scourst was the loch capable of throwing out the really big fish, and Ulladale was no mean venue either. We were due to fish Ulladale the following morning and Scourst the day after. Some brief inquires of other guests produced the information that to reach Ulladale required a brisk walk. These words would come back to haunt me half way up a mountain on the following day!

I served my fishing apprenticeship on an island which the gods use as a billiard table, where anglers drive to the very edge of the loch, trip getting out of the car and fall straight into a boat, so walking/hiking to a loch for a spot of fishing is somewhat alien to me. Of course, Muir had spent virtually all his life in Wester Ross, where there all the flat land is kept in a museum for curious folk to come and peer at and popping out for a bucket of coal involves strapping on hiking boots, so he revelled in the perpendicular path to the loch. Innes, our ghillie, and Muir literally bounded up the path like a pair of red deer stags on a promise, and I was left panting and gasping in their dust. Well, not dust exactly, as there was a fine highland mist pushing in front of a strong westerly blow, and the cloud base was some hundreds of feet below us by the time we reached the

summit. If I had had a spare breath I would have been cursing everything: my testosterone-loaded companions (who, it must be said were
carrying most of my gear by this time); the humorous swine who had
described the 9 kilometre 'yomp' as a 'brisk walk'; my parents for
having produced me; my breakfast (varyious portions of dead pig
which seemed determined to part company with me at every step);
and whoever had selected and constructed the path, for not making
it wide enough for some form of wheeled transport. As I grabbed a
couple of lungfuls of breath at the side of Loch Aiseabhat (literal
translation 'Loch of the Coronary'), the halfway point, and admired
the angels mobbing the eagles *below* us, I remember thinking 'This
Ulladale had better be good!'

Leaving the Loch of the Coronary, we started to descend and
another thought struck me: 'Goodness gracious me, this is steep! And
I'm going to have to climb back up here in a few hours time!' The only
consolation was that I didn't think I was going to live that long! We
eventually arrived at the edge of Ulladale, and I had a small celebration
in the shape of a cup of tea. (I was celebrating the fact that I hadn't had
to be carried the last kilometre and had completed the hike on my own
two wobbly feet!) To welcome us to our destination a salmon leapt in
the mouth of the burn and a sea trout flipped over a wave a couple of
dozen yards offshore. You can't say fairer than that!

No outboard motors are permitted on the North Harris Estate, but
the lochs are of only modest size, none longer than say a half-mile, so
this is no handicap in a moderate breeze. The excellent estate ghillies
are more than capable of rowing the boats back to the head of the wind
all day. But the wind which curled round Sròn Uladal and sent horrible
black scud across the face of the loch was by no means a moderate
breeze. It may not have been gale force, but it had ambitions in that
direction, and Innes, wisely, suggested that we put off boat launching
until we had exploited the wading potential and/or the wind had
decreased.

Iain set off for a very tempting and attractive series of rocky points
and small islands in the general direction of the outflow burn. Having
witnessed my last few faltering steps to the fishing hut before total
collapse, he rightly assumed I wouldn't be going far and left me the
short length of sandy beach surrounding the burn mouth. The wind

was pushing in on the shoreline and as I had only a pair of short knee-length boots with which to brave the waves anything more than covering the margins was out. As it turned out this wasn't a problem. Whilst tackling up Innes and I had spotted a number of salmon cruising just behind the breaking waves, and I suspected that the spateing burn had got them 'up on the fin' and unable to resist the clean, unsullied aromas of the water fresh off the hillside they were taking it in turns to 'buzz' the burn mouth. After a few casts a fish showed some fifty feet downwind of me, and heading in my direction. I cast out in an interceptory fashion and was treated to a great bulging rise to the Kate McLaren Muddler on the bob. Thinking that there was no more to come from the brute, I turned to Innes and said "Did you see ...?', when suddenly the rod was almost wrenched out of my hand and the fight was on! When fresh-run salmon get excited by a spate they fight like the very devil! This one, a nice summer fish of about 7 lb, went berserk, tail-walking and cartwheeling through the waves, never going further than thirty yards from my immersed feet. I like to think that I can be an instrument of natural selection, so the harder and more spectacularly a fish fights, then the more likely I am to return it, on the principle that it is a good thing for such fish to pass on these characteristics to the next generation. So I really leant into this fish and bullied him to Innes' waiting net, where he was quickly divested off the hook and returned forthwith, to go and sulk some-where deep in the loch and reconsider his decision to break his fast for just one more succulent offering.

Well, so far so good! Half-an-hour's fishing and my first Harris salmon caught and successfully released. Could it get better than this? Why, yes it could! I was back in the water no more than fifteen minutes when a slow draw to the tail fly, a Peter Ross, developed into a hard, head-shaking take which numbed my arm. An even better fish than the first one lunged out of the water and my 10-foot rod was slammed down to the horizontal as the reel screamed in protest at the speed of departing line. Gaining some semblance of control over this fish which had one aim in mind – reaching the far shore – was impossible. All I could do was let it have its head and hope that backing knots would successfully navigate past rod eyes, that there was enough backing on the rapidly emptying spool, and that the fish was well hooked. (All the potential obstacles were safely overcome although in the backing line department it was a close-run thing!)

Having to tow 45 yards of floating fly line and God knows how much backing is a serious restraint on any fish, and this one was no exception. He returned to my feet like a well trained dog. But once the resistance was reduced, he decided he could manage a few more rounds, and started whipping up and down the shoreline, with more head-shaking thrown in to further tire my already aching arm and shoulder. Innes put paid to those shenanigans, however, by being in the right place at the right time, intercepting one of his shallow water runs with an adroitly positioned net. Again we decided that a battler like this one deserved his freedom, so Innes slipped him back to the cold comfort of the loch. His pocket balance registered this fish at just over 10 lb which made it my heaviest loch salmon in fifteen years of endeavour.

Within a further thirty minutes I was into yet another fish: a sprightly whippet of a grilse that led me a spirited dance before submitting grudgingly to the irresistible resistance of rod and line. As I subdued this little 5-pounder Iain appeared over the bank, back from his fishless wanderings in the nether reaches of Ulladale. I think he was a bit nonplussed that I, having barely moved my feet, had snagged three salmon whilst he had stumbled, slipped, slithered and trudged around half-a-mile of loch shore for but one abortive offer. My suggestion that the walk would have done him good brought forth a stream of old Anglo-Saxon words that would have made Chaucer proud. Some people are just grouches, and that's a fact!

Innes and I ate a hurried lunch while Iain made a couple of unsuccessful passes through the same water in which I had experienced such good fortune, then we jumped to the erroneous and optimistic conclusion that the wind had dropped and it was now time to go afloat. This gave us a chance to fish the weather shore, the classic area at the tail of the wind where perceived wisdom would have it that crashing wave and gathering spume meant suicidal fish. As Innes manfully fought wind and wave, I managed four sea trout and a handful of finnock from the offshore deeps and comprehensively failed to set a hook in the jaw of a salmon that, in an effort to get caught, did everything short of throwing itself in the boat. After two perambulations round the loch,

Innes was done; I reckon his arms had gained a few inches given his heroic exertions on the oars like a hero for the best part of the afternoon. Anyway, it was time for a brief rest and a dram before facing the hell that was the climb back to the car.

When I reached the summit, and after a few minutes of gagging and retching, I looked back down the valley to Ulladale. As the sun glanced through the broken clouds and the loch blinked up at us, perched on the crag, I had a strange feeling of impermanence, as if a landscape that had existed unchanged for tens of thousands of years had been totally unaware of our presence. I don't often get all poetic and airy-fairy when I'm fishing, and certainly not when almost hanging by my fingernails to the side of a mountain, but there was something about that day, that landscape of loch, bog, burn and rock – the indestructibility of it all – that stirred the soul and refreshed the spirit. I thought 'It is as if we were never there at all!' I didn't mention this to Iain and Innes because neither was in earshot, and anyway they would have called me a big girl's blouse and thrown rocks at my head, but it was a hell of a day and one that will live in the mind's eye for many years to come.

## Grimersta

Now and again in this business I come across places that seem to be lost in a fold of time; the world moves on and leaves these places untouched by, and oblivious to, change. Grimersta is a classic example. I have suggested that there were fishing places that must be referred to in a whisper because the very mention of their name causes heads to turn and conversations to falter. Grimersta is a classic example. And there are places where, like many of my colleagues, I dreamed of rinsing out a few flies, but never thought the day would ever dawn. Grimersta is a classic example. One of the great things about compiling this labour of love is that it has provided me with chances to do things which had seemed totally unattainable.

When I received an invitation from the Grimersta syndicate to go and experience one of this country's most prolific salmon fisheries, I almost passed away with excitement. I was fully aware of the historical records set on this system of lochs and short rivers. This is where summer salmon fishing reaches a zenith that other systems can only dream about. If summer salmon fishing was a country then Grimersta would be its capital city.

For example, during a prolonged dry spell in the summer of 1888 a vast head of fish gathered in the sea waiting to run the system. Weeks later, with no appreciable river flow to allow fish up the system, fish started to die in the sea. A plan was devised by which the fish could be saved: the exit stream from Loch Langabhat was deepened and a temporary dam was created at the exit stream on the lowest loch on the system. When the water level in this loch had risen by a foot, the dam was removed and thousands of salmon ran the river on the artificial spate thus created. A certain Mr Naylor then proceeded to take a record catch of salmon to his own rod. I will now let Mr Naylor finish the story in his own words:

> Two days after we let down the water I got 31 in the first loch, but for the next few days the weather was bright and calm, and not many fish were got by any of us; but on August 27 the rod which fished the first loch got 36. Next day I got 54. The rod on that beat the following day got 46, and the next day I had it I got 45. The total take for the three rods for the last six days of August was 333 salmon and 71 sea trout. All the fish were fairly caught with fly.

A hundred salmon in two days fish simply beggars belief. I don't know whether they fished single-handed rods in those days, but I do know it would have taken a very fit individual to have fished all day with the tackle of that time, never mind the brute strength required to haul fifty-odd salmon to the boat. We simply don't have yardsticks by which to comprehend the magnitude of the task and the scale of the accomplishment. Even if we do, for a moment, forget the sheer fishing ability necessary to hook, play and boat this incredible number of fish, the stamina and endurance it must have taken make it an outstanding achievement in the annals of field sport. This was the fly-fishing equivalent of the first successful attempt on the North Face of the Eiger.

Something that strikes me about Mr Naylor's record is that, whilst the 54 salmon averaging 5·8 lb he took to his own rod is well-known and lauded, but there is very little no mention of the 12 sea trout averaging 6 lb that he also caught on that fateful day. So his actual total catch was 66 fish averaging 5¾ lb per fish in one day, to one rod. This means, of course, 66 fish × 10 minutes per fish (roughly) = 660 minutes = 11 hours attached to fish! I'll bet when St Peter saw him coming, he thought 'Oh bugger! He'll be wanting my job!'

Sadly sea trout of the quality experienced by Naylor are no longer a feature of the system, and, as sea trout were poorly and rarely recorded in the game accounts of this fishery, it is not possible to identify when the decline began. Perhaps it is part of the same population collapse that has affected so many other systems in the past few decades. What I do know is that in late July 2003, when I was there, the rods took but a few sea trout, the best being a modest 2½ lb fish, and in the whole 2002 season only 68 were recorded.

But enough of sea trout. Grimersta is a grilse fishery par excellence, and in that same 2002 season 551 salmon were taken, and the 2000–2002 three-year average was 553. We are all probably aware that 2003 saw a national grilse run collapse of almost unprecedented scale. Due to the singular lack of rainfall in late June, July and August fish were unable to access many systems, but a revival starting in September saw Grimersta achieve an acceptable 250, plus or minus a few, by the season's closing date on 15 October. For one of the most prolific grilse systems in the UK this was somewhat of a disappointment, but plenty of evidence points to this being a blip rather than a source of deep concern. Time will tell.

The Grimersta Lodge, a modest sprawl of white buildings tucked into a hillside, is situated at the head of the giant sea loch East Roag on the island of Lewis. Sporting gents and their families have been coming here for well over a hundred years for the sole purpose of enjoying superb loch fishing for salmon in very comfortable conditions. Well … as comfortable as you can be with a hundred million midgie eyes watching your every move from the surrounding vegetation.

There has been a determined effort by the syndicate to stop time in this isolated neck of the woods, and to a great extent, it has succeeded. There are some marvellous traditions at Grimersta, which seem to be a direct result of the peculiar conditions of life in the Western Isles. Because anything vaguely resembling pleasurable activity on the

Sabbath is strictly prohibited by the indigenous religious organisations (and, until very recently, that included travel to or from the island), a Grimersta fishing week starts on a Thursday and ends on a Wednesday. Sunday, of course, is a no-fishing day, so for the lodge guests the day of rest has a special routine. It goes something like this. Wake up late and have a sumptuous cooked breakfast, which (to all intents and purposes, is a funeral pyre for a couple of pigs); sit round in a stupefied state for a couple of hours, attempting to read a book/paper, or grunt in a Neanderthal fashion at your fellow guests. Then go in for a lunch which appears to commemorate the recent demise of an Aberdeen Angus which had been beaten to death with an assortment of fresh vegetables; return to bed and sleep the afternoon away while your digestive system desperately tries to clear the backlog. Rise, drink tea, and wander about aimlessly in a token exercise sort of a way, before a mercifully light evening meal (which in our case involved some perfectly prepared marine crustaceans washed down with some excellent wines, sloshed about in a 'no tomorrow' sort of fashion). Then retire for the night, desperately trying not to think of the medical implications of what you have just experienced. Sunday at Grimersta may be a no-fishing day, but that doesn't mean that anyone has to be miserable!

Other evidence of time warp is obvious in the style of fishing that the guests enjoy. Not for Grimersta the common regime of boat drifting at right angles to the wind, with a rod at either end of the boat fishing the drift in a 'hostage to fortune' manner. This does not suit the ghillies at all – and on Grimersta water Grimersta ghillies are one step down from God! If two guests are in the boat they sit side by side in the stern of the boat, casting over the transom whilst the ghillie carefully and subtly manoeuvres the boat onto known salmon lies. Should a fish be moved but not hooked, the ghillie will pull the boat upwind from the lie and then back down onto it again (one abortive go at a fish before the boat rushes over the lie is not for Grimersta ghillies). This system also means that if a fish is moved, retried and still refuses to properly co-operate, the boat can be steered away from the lie so as not to disturb it, and the fish can be tried again later in the day. This routine (though taking a bit of getting used to), has a whole load of plus points, but it absolutely requires two things:

a) some semblance of casting ability by the rods, otherwise a whole host of recurring and god-awful 'fankles' are inevitable, and b) a robust ghillie with arms like Garth! The best loch salmon fishing inevitably takes place in windy weather – flat calms are anathema in this business – so two rods thrashing the water to a foam, shoulder to shoulder, requires a system under which only one line is in the air at any given time, and the windy weather means that the ghillie is rowing virtually all day! Mind you, this method of ghillieing, systematic and methodical covering of each and every possible lie, does go a long way towards explaining why so many salmon are caught on the Grimersta system.

I have continually used the term 'Grimersta system' rather than loch names, because the system is looked upon almost as a long river with four massive pools: Lochs One to Four. Loch One contains Beats 1 and 2 (Beat 2 containing the famous and highly productive First Stream); Loch Two is not fished by Grimersta guests but is leased to local angling clubs; Loch Three is Beat 3; and Loch Four is the massive Beat 4, the only beat to allow trolling on a restricted section of the loch. The stream from the exit of Loch One to the sea is divided into sections and alone accounts for a very high proportion of the annual catch, especially at modest water levels.

Iain Muir and I visited in late July during a settled period of weather which didn't have 'loadsa fish' written all over it, but this had never curbed our enthusiasm before. And, anyway, we were on Grimersta, and magic happens at Grimersta! To show us the ropes Jason, the head ghillie, took us out on Beat One on the first day and hope and optimism were high, I must say. There was a good overcast and a freshish south-westerly breeze as we set out, and these conditions held for the rest of the day. I thought conditions were pretty good for a salmon, but Jason reminded us that to get the best out of the Grimersta salmon required nothing short of a screaming gale.

We expected magic at the Pentacle, and visited the Pyramid. We made a point of fishing hard at Mackay's Point, and were present at The Barricade. We returned fishless from Fish Bay, and expected Lever Pier to raise our catch rate. We moved fish – lots of fish; we just couldn't stick a hook in one. I have never spent so much time in a boat bringing so many salmon to the fly without actually hooking one of

221

them. But, although frustrating, it was only unusual in scale. Salmon are moody, tricksy creatures at the best of times, and attempting to understand them is beyond the hopes and competence of mere humans. Salmon and bizarre behaviour go together like happy-hour and hangover, and we shouldn't ever be surprised by their strange sense of humour, but I got the distinct impression that at times Jason was close to wrenching the rod out of my hand and consigning me to the oars.

On the following day we were given the roving boat and Robert the ghillie. The roving boat wanders between Beats 1 and 2, but defers to those allocated either named beat. This is a system that must work very well when large numbers of fish are present, because the temptation will always be for Beat 1 rods to take to the lower river and Beat 2 rods to man the First Stream. This scenario did not apply, however, and we spent the day being extremely courteous and doffing our collective cap to those with first call.

We did catch a fish, though, and it went something like this. The wind, such as it was (and that wasn't much), had set in from a northerly direction, but a high overcast blotted out any sun, which was a factor on the positive side. We jumped in the boat at Pierre Alphen's Jetty and set up a drift to Lever Pier on the west side of the loch. There was little evidence of much action other than a distant splash from a big fish on the southerly end of the island at the top end of the loch. Because of the previous day's experiences, and because of the poor wind, our hopes weren't unduly high. Wind is conducive to salmon sport on lochs, and there just didn't seem enough on this particular day. But as we drew level with the Lever Pier a salmon savaged my bob fly in a ferocious take which seemed to display sheer aggression rather than appetite. Salmon takes are often like this – one moment you are fishing away, admiring the tweety birds, or discussing world politics or what's for dinner, and the next you are playing a fish. It takes a fair amount of rummaging about in the memory banks to actually recall what happened in between. For all the slow, deliberate takes, or the acrobatic and graceful head-and-tail rises that I have experienced there has been an equal or possibly greater number of 'Wham! Bam! Thank you ma'am!' takes. This was most definitely one of the latter type.

Desperately requiring a few hooked salmon action shots for my portfolio, I immediately handed the rod to Iain who, it shames me to admit, looked at me as if I had gone mad! This was not typical Headley behaviour, I must admit. Mumbling something like 'Here, take it! Must get some shots!', I scrambled up to the bow of the boat and clicked away like a death-watch beetle on speed, whilst Robert pulled the boat – and fish – away from other potential lies, and Iain chuntered and swore as the fish powered back and forth across our wake in an obviously disgruntled state.

I am always faced with a dilemma when on these fishing trips far from home: whether or not to kill fish. I love to eat wild salmon – but not that commercially reared muck – and I have my own cold-smoker at the back of the house, the sole purpose of which is to process the odd salmon and big trout. But the hassle of freezing fish, remembering to take them home (I've left innumerable fish to languish at the bottom of hotel freezers all over this great country of ours) and keeping them frozen throughout the return journey sometimes seems just too much bother, so I often return them. This nice fresh fish of 6–7 lb got a second chance. I just hope he didn't throw it away by trying a second helping of Grimersta Muddler.

That brings me neatly round to Grimersta fly patterns, which is a story in itself. Grimersta salmon love muddlers, and the standard set-up is a Grimersta Muddler – vast amounts of deer hair, a wing of golden pheasant cock, centre tail, and an appropriately coloured tinsel body – on the bob, with a double Silver Stoat on the point. Some traditionally minded or long-serving rods fish Ransome's Blue Elver as a top-dropper candidate, but most stick to giant muddlers. A two-fly rig is standard. In a good wave a size 8 muddler with a size 12 Silver Stoat is recommended, decreasing in size with any lessening in wind speed. It should be noted that the above hook sizes refer to salmon hooks rather than trout, so if you are tying on trout hooks a close approximation would be size 10 on the point and size 6 on the bob.) Those used to loch salmon and sea trout elsewhere may lift an eyebrow at the construction of a Grimersta cast, but in its defence I must say that this rig would have been ditched long ago if it didn't work. Nowhere else that I know has such a short list of preferred patterns to the exclusion of all others, and Grimersta's attachment to the Blue Elver in particular has been a source of wonder and debate for as long as I can remember. It is only in this corner of Lewis that gigantic muddlers and 3-in.-long streamer-winged patterns are first line of attack, but the catch statistics of the fishery underline their effectiveness, so who am I to argue? I did try standard tactics with big, bushy Bumbles and outsized trout flies, but whenever I did the ghillie would mutter under his breath and the fish would be equally disgusted, so I did what I was told ... and caught a salmon. There can be little doubt that the water-disrupting properties of the muddler have a strong attraction for salmon, but that wouldn't explain the historical passion for Blue Elvers. Perhaps if sea trout were a more regular feature of the catch then the approach may have changed. Who's to say?

The greatest achievement of the syndicate and staff is that they have brought together the best of old tradition and modern practice and produced a fishery with assured longevity – provided wild salmon survive. And it is to the credit of the Grimersta syndicate that it manages to peacefully co-exist in a community where memories of the bad old days are still fresh, and where the image of 'toff's fishing' does not necessarily bring a smile to the lips of a native. It interacts well with the local community, is mindful of its social responsibilities and still successfully tackles the uphill task of remaining commercially viable in a very competitive market.

Grimersta gives a false impression of being one of those 'dead men's shoes' operations that impoverished chaps like myself can only dream about, like the archetypal dirty kid with his nose pressed against the glass. But that isn't a true reflection. Places within the let become available reasonably regularly, and even syndicate places occur from time to time. The present policy of the estate is to allow casual visitors the chance to sample the wondrous fishing that is Grimersta. If you are in the area and want to treat yourself, call the estate office and ask; you will most likely be pleasantly surprised, as I am assured no one is turned away if at all possible. You may not get the best beat on the system, but even a second-division beat on a system which throws out 550 salmon per year is well worth a visit.

I don't know whether I'll ever have the good fortune to return to Grimersta. I hope I do. Perhaps if I built my own Tardis ...

# The Limestone Lochs of Durness

In the extreme north-western corner of the Scottish mainland, in the county of Sutherland, is the small village of Durness. And surrounding the village, in a cordon of sorts, are some of the finest trout lochs in Scotland. Some of you will know the area better as Cape Wrath and the lochs – Borralaidh, Caladail, Croispol and Lanlish are often known as the Cape Wrath Lochs – but this is misleading as the lochs are actually some distance from the Cape.

Sutherland is a county of heather, crags, bogs, salmon, sea trout, red deer and grouse, and not the place one would normally expect the finest brown trout in the UK. But there is a secret, not immediately obvious to the eye, which accounts for such an anomaly. The main geology of the far north-west is seriously old rock, igneous in nature, which has been processed and reprocessed repeatedly since the Earth cooled down enough to become a planet. If you've ever left something in a corner of the oven, ignored and forgotten, and recooked it a few dozen times you'll get an inkling of just how hard the Sutherland rocks are. You could drop an asteroid on the Sutherland hills and, apart from a nasty scuff mark and the audible evidence of ricochet as the asteroid rebounded into space, no-one would be any the wiser. We are talking hard!

In the midst of this unrelenting granite and basalt, though, there is a strip, an intrusion, of limestone. From a geological perspective, limestone is a soft and soluble sedimentary rock which is alkaline by nature. Water running from typical highland sources will be slightly acid, and, coming into contact with the limestone, will have the same effect on it as does a hot knife on butter. The result is water which is somewhat alkaline, high in dissolved minerals and a perfect medium in which to grow trout and the invertebrates that they love to eat. Other evidence of this reaction between acid and alkali are rivers and streams which run underground and vast holes in the lochs where the water has gnawed its way through the living bedrock of the lochs. The most dramatic example of the latter being the inky-black Abyss to the north of the island in Borralaidh (pronounced Boralee).

## Borralaidh

I haven't caught a lot of fish in Borralaidh. It is not a loch where hours spent are frenetic and filled with screaming reels and the splatter of fish thrashing on the surface. It is a hard water in the way most good fish waters are, and it can be desperately unproductive at times. Borralaidh fish are not as prolific as those on Croispol, not as accessible as those on Lanlish, nor as co-operative as those of Calladail. But, for all that, I love it with a passion, and it may just be my favourite place to wave a fly rod.

Borralaidh is not a big loch by national standards, but is the biggest of the Durness lochs and achieves a reasonable 120 acres, give or take. It sits down in a hole of its own creation, where the surface water has eaten its way towards the centre of the earth through the limestone deposits. The eastern and northern ends are ringed in by cliff face, there are some high slopes to the westward, and the only lowish ground is on the southern approach. Oh, and if you want to gloat, a reasonable argument could be made that this is another contravention of Headley's Rule of Thumb no. 2, in that the bulk of the loch is very shallow. But, in my own defence, there are two very deep holes in the loch – a trench to the south of the island and the previously mentioned abyss to the north. I feel duty bound to describe the Abyss; scientifically, the hole to the north of the island perhaps does not merit the name, but if you have ever drifted the gin clear waters of Borralaidh, across the pinkish-white marl bottom and over the lip of the black waters of the pit, then you'll agree that Abyss is the only name that does it credit. I suppose it is the contrast. One minute you can see the corixa and shrimp scuttling across the bottom in six feet of water, then.... nothing! Drop off! Nothing to see but blackness! But there is a lingering suspicion that many eyes are looking up, and not necessarily friendly eyes, either!

I've always resisted what my wife always referred to as 'cry of the curlew' school of romantic claptrap fishing journalism. You know the sort of stuff 'We fished all day and caught nothing, but what made it all worthwhile was the cry of the curlew, the wild flowers nodding on the grassy banks, blah, blah, yawn, and blah!' Hogwash, balderdash and a load of old bollocks! Fine for blue-rinsed spinsters to read over their morning coffee, or office-bound urbanites who have a Beatrix Potter view of the countryside, but not for seekers after wisdom like ourselves! For all that, though, I've always thought of Borralaidh as a loch of mystery. What does swim at the bottom of the Borralaidh abyss? Are there subterranean connections to the other lochs? What is the relationship between the char and the trout?

A few years ago, after a hard days plugging away on Borralaidh for damn all result, Jimmy Ireland and I retired to the hotel with plans for a return match after dinner. The evening conditions were perfect: warm, softening southerly breeze, high overcast and the promise of a midge hatch. In the far north-west all too often early summer evenings can be bitter, nasty, brutish and short, but this was an exception. Getting back to the lochside by about 9 p.m., we cast off from the moorings and did a long drift from the shallows out to the South Deeps. Lots of fish spend their daylight hours deep in this trench, venturing out when conditions are right and there's some reasonable expectation of a good dinner. But nothing broke the surface ripple over the south, nor disturbed the waters of the Channel (between the island and the east shore) which, lacking any ripple at all, was too calm for productive fishing effort, and the west and north side of the island were, as far as we could ascertain, similarly devoid of life. However, there was an expectation of something pending; the tension in the air was nearly tangible.

Then, a very light smirr of drizzle swept over the loch, midge started to hatch and a myriad tiny, dimply rises splattered across the surface of the water directly over the Abyss. I'd never seen anything like this before. I knew that what I was seeing weren't the rises of trout. What could they be? I was fishing a pair of midge-imitating patterns on a very long leader so as not to spook fish in such a fine ripple. The take, when it came, was a jarring rattle totally unlike the surging thump a trout would impart in such conditions. It was my first arctic char, a long, lean, silvery fish which had more of the herring about it than any similarity with trout. And, just as I took another one, a massive fish rolled over on the surface some distance away from the boat. In the dim light all that was visible was the silhouette and an impression of massive bulk. We kicked in the electric outboard and headed in the general direction of the fish. What we

227

hoped to do when we got there is open to question, but like moths to a candle, the attraction was too strong to resist. Just as we arrived in the area of the first rise, another fish of similar dimensions broke surface fifty yards away, slap-bang in the middle of a shoal of dimpling char.

Some years before this experience I had sent a visiting friend out to fish a trophy fish loch in Orkney with instructions to fish right into the dark. He returned the next day to admonish me for sending him to a loch which had seals in it but no trout. It took me some time to convince him that what he had seen were trout, rolling on the surface. I now knew how he felt. Jimmy and I were sitting in a boat on a loch with a virtually mirror-flat surface and every so often a great, black back would arc up and over, and all we could do was just sit and gape in awe.

There had always been talk of monster trout living in the Abyss. Divers, carrying out survey work in the deeps for biodiversity studies had reported seeing immense fish, and anglers in the old days would put on a Phantom Minnow, or suchlike, and troll it back to the head of the drift, occasionally catching trout of up to double figures. But that was all it had appeared to be – just talk! Now I was seeing the truth behind the stories. The big boys had followed up the char shoals, and we watched in fascination as they picked off the 12-oz char in studied, effortless fashion. Jimmy and I, with our tackle geared for modest-sized fish, were just an irritant to these fish, mere jackals hovering around the lion pride after the kill. Of course we never so much as got a chance to cover one of these leviathans – when we moved to an area where they were working they would then shift to the area we had just left. They knew we were there, but, like a dog with a bone, they didn't want anybody too close as they went about their business. And then, after about three-quarters of an hour of activity, a cool breeze ruffled the surface, and … they were gone!

We fished our way back to the moorings, more out of a sense of duty than in any hope or expectation. Jimmy did catch a decent trout of about a 1½ lb but after what we'd seen it was difficult to get excited about it. Many since have thought this story a typical fisherman's tale, and I can hardly blame them. To see one massive trout is easily accepted; to see a shoal of fish, any one of which would be the fish of a lifetime, stretches credibility. But it is that night and that experience which keeps me returning to Borralaidh in hope of a rerun. I still wouldn't expect to catch one but I would be more than happy just to be a spectator once again.

A few people have told me of their somewhat dubious efforts to effectively fish the Abyss. Small, dead fish have been lowered into the depths, and saltwater jigs have been bounced over the bottom of the pit, but no one has succeeded in removing one of the inhabitants. My old friend, Keith Dunbar, has explored the hole with a 'fish-finder', and fish show up throughout the area, but differentiating between shoals of char and individual big fish would require more sensitive, sophisticated equipment. The Abyss is a mystery, and long may it remain so.

General trout fishing in Borralaidh can be good, but blanks outnumber successful days. Some of its regular visitors are concerned about stock levels, but this is an ever-present worry for those who find the fishing unbearably unproductive and hark back to the glory days of the past. A couple of years ago I went up and sat on the cliffs on the east side on a quiet, mild evening on a sort of 'recce'. As the corncrakes (yes, more than one!) called from the island, I watched the rise start in the South Deeps, and there seemed to be plenty of fish on the move. I don't believe that there is a stock problem on Borralaidh. What I think is actually happening is that the general, national, reduction in aquatic insect life and the associated decrease in hatches means that surface feeding is not so common among Borralaidh trout as it was in the past. I do know that in recent years, during daylight hours, my catch rates with intermediate and full sinking lines have vastly exceeded any success on the traditional floating line. Fishing down through the Channel and out into the fringes of the South Deeps with a Wet Cel 2 or a Fast Glass has rarely let me down, and the floater is put aside until there is strong evidence that it is needed, and that doesn't come often.

But, if the conditions are appropriate, then dry fly is always a likely option on all the Durness lochs. These pernickety, well-fed fish do seem to have a soft spot for something vulnerable, trapped in the surface film and, as always, the bigger the fish the stronger the susceptibility. Maybe a foot-long floating fry might just tempt one of the monsters from the Abyss. (No, on second thoughts, I think I'll give that a miss if you don't mind!)

## The Caithness Lochs

Caithness shares many visual and geological similarities with my home county of Orkney. This is mainly due to the fact that they both sit on the same geological rock formations, old alluvial deposits from a time, many millions of years ago, when this part of modern-day Scotland was the bottom of a lake. The muds and sand that made up the bed of this ancient lake now show themselves as old sandstone deposits, known colloquially as Caithness Flags, rocks which are slightly alkaline. Lochs based on these deposits are rich and productive and, if not quite the trout paradise on earth that limestone produces, then not miles removed from it either. Other beneficial aspects, closely linked, that these rocks formations provide are gently undulating land-scapes and shallow lochs.

Because the whole of the county lies in the weather shadow of the Sutherland hills to the west, Caithness has a microclimate all of its own, which can be blessing and a curse, depending upon perspective. It is arguably one of the driest counties in Scotland solely due to the Sutherland hills bleeding the air dry of rain before it reaches the lands further east. This effect, although a curse to the salmon fisherman, produces settled conditions which favour trout fishing. But the down-side is that the county is often plagued with cool north-easterlies coming in off the North Sea, even when the rest of the country is enjoying winds originating from the Atlantic. I suppose there must be some sort of back-draught created by the Sutherland Hills which causes localised wind change in the area, because often I would phone friends in Caithness who would complain of the northerly or easterly winds whilst balmy south-westerlies were blowing round my house in Orkney.

The best known of the many lochs of this region are Watten, Heilan and St John's but there are many others. For example, Thurso Fisheries controls many fine trout lochs on the Ulbster Estate that, if located in any other region of Scotland, would be widely praised and much frequented.

Regardless of wind direction, though, Caithness trout are fine specimens. The Heilan trout can stand comparison with any, being a fast-growing strain which regularly produces fish approaching double figures. St John's Loch trout are also of a high average weight, growing fat on Scotland's most northerly mayfly population. But both these lochs are hellishly prone to turbidity, which can put them out of action for days and, occasionally, weeks, and even when the lochs are clear the inhabitants can be difficult to extract. Heilan is predominantly an evening loch, but not just any evening. The locals wait for fine, mild, calm evenings before venturing out. St John's Loch has a reputation for dourness, and its trout only seem to get excited when the mayfly is about. But arguably the finest loch in Caithness has no such problems. Watten trout are magnificent and co-operative, and it has always been a mystery to me why it is not more widely known.

## Loch Watten

There is a persistent myth continually cropping up that Watten trout descend from an infusion of Loch Leven trout introduced in the past. I suspect that this is total balderdash. Why? Because isn't it strange that all the lochs in Scotland (and some elsewhere) that have fine, fit silvery trout were all stocked from Leven. Why were waters where the trout are black, lean and ugly not given an injection of Leven stock?

In the bad old days, when our Victorian/Edwardian grandfathers thought that they could always improve on nature, there was always some interfering sod rushing around the countryside with a bucket of Leven fry. Leven fish set a standard to which all other trout should strive to attain. And our forefathers thought that the strong genetic traits of Leven fish would displace the poor alternatives in other lochs. What they failed to understand is that trout are pretty much a product of their environment. If the indigenous fish were not fine, fit and silvery there were good environmental reasons for that, and dumping in a bucket of better stuff was not going to make much difference in the long term. This is a point I've made already in this book, but it bears repeating – taking trout with fat, silvery parents and dumping them in a loch where the indigenous fish are lean and black will result in the stocked fish being, in the long term, lean and black; reverse the process and introduce lean and black fish into waters producing fat and silvery fish, and the introductions will become fat and silvery. Genetics will not overcome poor environment. So Watten trout are fine, fat and silvery because Watten is a fine loch with good water qualities and plenty of food, not because of some alien introduction in the dim and distant past.

It is a sad admission to make, but I, like so many of my countrymen, have not paid this loch the attention it deserves. On the basis of a handful of visits, I firmly believe that Watten is one of the finest venues for traditional-style loch fishing to be found anywhere in the UK. It is shallow and productive, with a very healthy population of trout ranging from takeable size to fine specimens in the 4–5 lb range. Very occasionally the odd salmon is captured, a vagrant from the Wick River, but that would be a minor distraction from some of the most co-operative, free-rising trout that it has been my pleasure to encounter.

Many years ago Harray was, like Watten, full of fish that wanted nothing more than to impale themselves on traditional flies fished off a floating line. But those days are gone, and the love I had for the Orkney loch, born out of the sheer excitement of rising dozens of fish in a day, from gin clear water, is now reserved for Watten.

Watten is controlled by the riparian owners whose land encompasses the loch and who impose restrictions which suit themselves. For example the loch opens later and closes earlier than almost all others in Scotland, opening day being 1 May and closing day 30 September. Some of the locals must be frustrated by the late opening, as many lochs of this type and in similar latitudes can provide some of their best fishing in April. However the closing date should pose few disappointments, as brown trout in Scotland are well past their best by October. Watten isn't a particularly large loch, but it makes up for lack of size by being capable of producing fish from almost every square inch. Shoreline drifts and open water drifts offer varying opportunities, depending upon the mood of the fish. This is unusual in a Scottish loch although not unique (Boardhouse in Orkney, Caladail in Sutherland and Bornish in South Uist offer similar trout prospects). But it does pose problems for the angler in that, more often than not, the feeding regime of the shoreline fish may well differ markedly from that of the

THE PICK OF SCOTLAND'S BEST LOCHS

open-water feeders, requiring at least different fly patterns, if not a radical change in technique.

A very welcome aspect of fishing the loch is that visiting and local anglers will invariably make contact with Hugo Ross. Hugo is the tackle dealer in Wick and runs a very efficient and user-friendly fishing service on most of the Caithness lochs. He has boats for hire at either end of Watten, and his local knowledge and enthusiasm for fishing ensure that the visiting angler is very well served indeed. His shop contains great arrays of flies specifically designed and suited for local loch fishing, and patterns such as Hugo's Olive, Watten Warrior and Dirty Weeker are his answers to fly-fishing problems posed by Watten.

Whenever I have ventured out on Watten it has been under Hugo's surveillance, and we've had some spectacular trips. My last visit, a couple of years ago, accompanied by my good friend Colin Kirkpatrick (a wizard with a camera) took place at the end of June, a prime time for Watten. Our expectations were high, and, though the first two days were hampered by strong winds, the last day dawned fair and we enjoyed fishing the like of which I hadn't seen in twenty-odd years. We met up with Hugo, bright and early, at the moorings at the east end of the loch, and almost as soon as we got adrift we were surrounded by rising trout. Caenis, olives, a few sedges and plenty of midge were disporting themselves on the surface of the water, and the fish were taking full advantage. I simply love to fish dries for wild brown trout, and think it the finest way to fish bar none. Seeing a neb appear as your delicate dry is sucked from sight – or the more full-blooded but rarer engulfing-head-and tail rise – is, as far as I'm concerned, the ultimate thrill in fly-fishing, especially when it's done by a fit two-pounder or better.

I did snag a couple on the dries in the opening salvos but something was telling me that dry-fly tactics were not the definitive answer to the question 'How can I fill this boat with fish?' We drifted on towards Watten's solitary island, and the rises changed from the sip-sip of the above-surface feeders to the heavy bulging rises of what I took to be midge-feeders. Midge, in their hatching process, have a vulnerable stage in which they hang suspended from the surface film as they attempt to split the pupal shuck. Trout know this and, rather than chasing the lively ascending pupae, specialize in cruising about just sub-surface, engulfing the suspended pre-hatch pupae. The rise form created by this feeding process is a big bulging up-thrust of water which does not break the surface film, and it is very indicative of fish feeding on midge. Unfortunately, it does not rule out trout feeding on other creatures similarly located just below the surface.

I tried a few dedicated midge patterns and techniques and was bewildered when no response was forthcoming. I could see the midge on the water and in the air, but the trout, of which there were growing numbers showing, were definitely not feeding on them. What was going on?

Colin solved the puzzle which, once laid bare, had a rather obvious explanation. He took a fighting 1½-lb 'terrier' which led him a merry dance before succumbing to the irresistible pressure of 3½ oz. of carbon fibre. In the interests of science, and because I just had to know what was going on down below, this one was for the chop! The fact that it had fallen victim to a Green Peter Sedgehog should have added another piece to the jigsaw, but the whole picture was forthcoming from the first dip of the marrow spoon. The bottom half of the spoon – the early morning feeding – showed Caenis nymphs and midge pupae, but the upper half – the contemporaneous stuff – was all freshwater shrimp. Of course! The effects of the previous two days' winds had been to bring the shrimp out on a feeding/mating spree, and when in this mode they love to swim about just under the surface film. That explained the 'pseudo-midge-bulge' rise forms which had me totally perplexed. The trout were sailing about in a virtual smorgasbord of nutritious food items and selecting out the high-swimming shrimp. Once we knew the tactics and preferred food items it was simply a matter of switching flies, sticking to the rocky shallows and getting stuck in!

We ended up with a fine catch of fish ranging from 1 lb to 2 lb with the odd better fish missed or dropped! It was a fantastic day – not simple and straightforward, but testing and challenging in its way – and full of sport, with lots of trout on show. It took me back to those well-remembered days on Harray when I was learning my trade and the shallows were full of shrimp-bashing trout. The memories of that Watten day are bitter-sweet. It was wonderful to experience something I thought I had lost forever, but it also reminded me of waters and forms of fishing that we have lost. Harray, the last loch that had shown me similar sport, with a similar excellence of trout and water quality, is now diminished, and that made me fearful for the future of Watten. How easy it is to stand by and let our best lochs decline. How difficult it is to get them back once they have gone!

## Loch Leven

Do you remember me saying that I was in the minority by stating my love for Stenness? Imagine how small a group I number myself amongst by freely stating that I still love Loch Leven. Being in love with Leven (or the Loch, as it is referred to, in a superior sort of way round the Central Belt) is a bit like being in love with Adolf Hitler: the object of your love may be fundamentally flawed, a shadow of its former lovable self, the destroyer of many a hope and aspiration, despised by many, and you can't divulge your secret passion to just anyone – but that's love for you!

When I started this long-standing love affair, Leven was a brown-trout-only loch. Not any more, however. In a failed effort to boost the punters' flagging enthusiasm for the loch, and in a misguided attempt to rectify a perceived lack of stock, Leven Fisheries, aided and abetted by Scottish Natural Heritage, introduced the first stockings of rainbow trout in 1993. The fishery management team decided to adopt the classic Scottish response in dealing with any fishery problem – they threw fish at it. It is an endemic fault of Scottish fishery management to think that the solution to any problem can be found within the confines of a hatchery. Leven has proved to me, and to a growing band of like-minded souls, that stocking with alien species is the ultimate aquatic vandalism and rarely addresses the fundamental problems. It is equivalent to putting a sticking plaster on a broken leg; the option to face the real problems and deal with them in a responsible and envi-ronmentally friendly manner never seems to occur to these people.

The Leven experiment with rainbow trout – which has, as I write, almost brought the loch to its economic knees – is a stark lesson to us all: simply throwing fish at an environmental or ecological problem very rarely solves it. Leven was a world-class commercial wild trout fishery. It is now a gigantic put-and-take pond, and not even a very good one. Its future as a trout fishery is under serious threat, and I despair of it ever regaining its position as the finest wild trout fishery in the world. (In Chapter 7 I will detail my views on the problems that will face all freshwater fisheries in the future.)

I was born in Fife and lived there until I was seven. My father taught in a school a stone's throw from the banks of Leven and fished it regularly back then. I suppose I must have listened to his stories when he returned from the Loch, because I certainly grew up with a Pavlovian response to the word 'Leven': like the famous dogs I found my mouth watering at the mention of the name. Back in the 1960s and 1970s Leven was the flagship water, the Mecca, paradise on earth for all loch fishers, and everyone wanted to fish there. My chance came in the early 1980s, and I was taken out by Ken Bell, a weel-kent face in the Pier Bar and drifts south of St Serf's. I suppose I was very lucky in that our allotted July evening was just about perfect. As I remember it, there was a good fresh breeze from the east which gradually diminished as the hours past. There had also been a heavy hatch of buzzer during the afternoon, and I was stunned not only by the number of midge shucks in the water but also by their immense individual size. This was my first introduction to the famous 'curly bums' of the Loch, and how I grew to love these beautiful, big dusty-grey chironomids!

Ken and I had a bit of a wander round the loch at first because, as he told me, the best of the fishing would come with sunset and there was nothing to lose by having a wee reconnoitre. My first Leven fish – yes, I remember it as if it was yesterday – was a cracking silvery-sided, black-spotted beauty from a deepwater drift on to the Burleigh Sands. He, or probably she, thought that my Woodcock and Mixed was irresistible, and it was a double thrill to take my first Leven brownie on a traditional Leven pattern. The next fish was not quite so traditional-minded but no less welcome for all that; totally unlike the first, it was a spectacular yellow-bellied individual that was lurking in some very shallow water beside the Scart. The Scart is an islet about halfway between Castle Island and the Burleigh Sands and a famous mark for good-quality browns. I know this fish was lurking in shallow water, because about 90 seconds before I hooked him we had been aground on the sides of the Scart, but he had ignored the muffled curses and oar-banging required to refloat the boat, and had snaffled my size 12

Loch Ordie like a good 'un. Probably never seen a good Orkney fly before – certainly never saw another!

After that memory gets a bit hazy – not because of any ingested stimulants, you understand, but because the curly bums decided this was a perfect evening for a hatch. By this time we were off the east point of St Serf's Island and planning to drift all the way home to the pier, the light of which was just starting to twinkle in the distance as the evening light faded. Fish were rising all round the boat, and I was getting just a little bit excited by it all. The situation where, with the fly line in the air, one must choose which of half a dozen rising fish within casting distance to cover, is the sort of problem we should all face at least once a week! (If we did, then I might just learn how to solve it!) I generally find that I loose my cool, and things pan out something like this: I am covering a nice fish when twenty feet to the left another, even better, fish moves. So I attempt to cover this new fish only to discover that the first fish has taken the fly – and then decides to spit it out just as I get some sort of handle on what is happening. The next five minutes are spent getting the loops of fly line from around my neck and untangling my leader, during which time a squadron of record-breakers have wallowed about in front of the boat in a lewd and lascivious fashion only to disappear once I'm 'back in the water'! This scenario, with variations, continues until the hatch eventually peters out and I look round to discover that I've caught but one fish, and that's the smallest one seen all evening!

Well, I must have been blessed on that drift from St Serf's. I can't remember exactly how many fish actually came to the boat, but eight or nine seems about right. I know I was doubly blessed because most of them fell to my rod, and Ken was slightly miffed that Leven would show a rank newcomer such a good time while treating him so shabbily. One of the interesting lessons I learnt that night, and one which I have to keep reminding myself of, is that I stuck to my normal Orcadian fly selection. Flies, indeed, that had been catching well for me on fishing trips at home immediately prior to my Leven outing. Over the years I have often witnessed this phenomenon of successful flies, flavour of the moment on one water, being gladly accepted on another miles, if not counties, away. Whether this suggests universal compatibility between trout and all trout flies, or whether confidence is nine-tenths of successful fly selection, I wouldn't like to say, but I recommend the concept to you – stick to your favourites; it is simply amazing how often in the wrong place at the wrong time they can work miracles! (I remember a strange day on Blythfield Reservoir in deepest, darkest England when the only fly worth a damn was a Goat's Toe! Strange but true!) I must say that Ken had raised an eyebrow or two at the flies I attached to my cast but the results vindicated the selection, and, as I said to him, 'Orkney flies travel well!'

I've had many other wonderful experiences on Leven but the best, the ultimate session, was the one in which I won the Scottish National Fly-Fishing Championship. (It may seem a tad immodest to talk of this, but so many interesting things happened that evening that it would be selfish not to share them.) In those pre-rainbow days the National was fished in the evening, because that suited the indigenous brown trout of Leven, which really gave of their best at this time of day. We left the pier with a penetrating drizzle being pushed in front of a brisk south-westerly and, having done very well there a week before, I suggested we fish the area around Cardine Bay. This turned out not to have been the wisest choice, because by the time we got a few dozen yards off the shore the wind was pushing up a good wave and causing our boat to pitch and yaw in an uncomfortable and distressing manner. My boat partner and I decided that shelter was the thing, so we instructed our boatman to take us to Factor's Pier, an area of water which should provide shelter in that particular direction of wind.

Upon our arrival, soaked like a trio of 'drookit dugs' (why do Leven boatmen think it a hoot to travel across a big wind with the wave hitting the boat at an acute angle to the beam, so that, contrary to good boating practice, the water joins the punters inside the boat?), I noticed that the wind was starting to drop away. Although the desire to return to my preferred area in Cardine Bay was strong we collectively decided that the time loss couldn't be justified, so we set up a drift to take us from the Factor's Pier to the Scart.

Things started quietly, but as I was checking my leader for tangles by lifting the cast out of the water, fly by fly, a trout launched itself out of the water and took my middle fly which was suspended about 24 in. above the surface at the time. On boating this fish I thought 'Bloody hell! That was lucky!', little realizing how much more luck was waiting in the pipeline. (This penchant Leven trout have for taking flies which are out of the water is something I've witnessed on a number of occasions on this loch, and nowhere else to anything like the same extent. I once had a fish of somewhere between four and five pounds attempt the same trick in the Horseshoe, just to the north of St Serf's, in a day of flat calm and brilliant sunshine, and many of my colleagues tell similar stories.)

Anyway, back to that fateful night. As the drift neared its end, about fifty yards or so beyond the Scart, I saw a fish head-and-tail some distance in front of the boat. It was a long way downwind, and I had serious doubts whether I could reach it, but a rising fish on Leven must be covered! The hard part on The Loch is not to get the sods to take, it is to get them up close enough to take. A rising fish has done the hard part; all the angler has to do is get a fairly acceptable fly across his nose, and two times out of three the response will be positive. I stripped off a good length of line and, after a couple of false casts to build up line speed, shot the lot, hoping it would arrive just in front of where the fish had risen. This was the fly-fishing equivalent of the 'double top' shot in darts. Everything seemed to happen according to plan, because when I gave the first pull everything went tight and he was on! This was Leven luck of a high order (I began to wonder if I should sneak ashore and buy a lottery ticket!). I now had two good fish in the bag and it wasn't 8.00 p.m. yet. The best was still to come.

I knew that there was a strong possibility of a good 'rise' of fish and fly in the area between the Reed Bower and the Kelston Strip if things panned out. There had been one the previous evening, and there was every reason to believe that a repeat performance was most definitely on the cards. We got into place at about 9.00 pm, and within minutes we were in amongst fish. The moderating south-westerly was now no more than a breeze which pushed us nicely from the deeps towards the shallow shores around the Bower. Big, juicy grey midge were popping up everywhere, sedges were scuttling about over and across the ripple, and the odd, occasional sound of a heavy fish slurping some tasty tit-bit on the surface could be heard over the lap-lap of wavelets hitting the side of the boat.

In practice and experience immediately prior to the National I had learnt that to strike a fish visibly moving to the flies was a guaranteed way to miss or subsequently lose the fish. The technique was to ignore all visual evidence and wait for the weight of the fish to 'grow' on the line. By the time the fish was felt in the hand he was already well-hooked and the chances of loss were minimal. This is a lesson which I gladly pass on to novices on Leven – when fishing with a line which will show the 'take' as a water disturbance on the surface, never strike until you actually feel the weight of the fish. The sinking-line equivalent technique is to give any fish a damned good clout when you first feel him. I have lost a power of fish on The Loch by assuming that the powerful take on a sinking line is an automatic hook-up. If in doubt, smack him one!

Drifting between the mid-point between the Kelston and the Bower, onto the Bower, I took another six fish by chucking a good long line, keeping my rod point down, pulling long sweeps of line back to the hand, ignoring the swirls and boils at the flies and waiting until the resistance at the end of the line wouldn't allow me to pull any more. It wasn't, perhaps, a pretty technique, but by all the gods it was effective! My compatriot at the other end of the boat was a traditional-minded soul who short-lined all night with his top-dropper fly never in the water. He moved three times as many fish as I did, struck at every offer, and put nary a fish in the boat. I showed him what I was doing and talked him through it, but he could only stick it for a couple of casts and then he'd be back to his own ways, bib-bob-bobbing along, with the inevitable result. I took in eight fish for somewhere in the region of 13½ lb – not one fish was under 1½ lb and not one over 2 lb – and one of the best baskets of Leven brownies it has been my pleasure to catch.

I don't know if we'll ever see these days again. I must admit to harbouring serious doubts about the long-term, and short-term, well-being of the loch as a trout fishery. It would be a great to think that our children may have a chance to fish the finest wild trout fishery in the world. But when I down a pint poured for me by Elvis in the Pier Bar is about the time I'll start believing that Leven will return to the glory days of the past. I hope I'm wrong, but I doubt that too!*

## TIPS AND TOOLS

Many anglers bedevilled by total lack of wind and tempted by the sight of the occasional rise of a feeding trout will resort, in desperation, to dry fly. There is no more hopeless scenario in which to try dry fly. Calm water has a very high surface tension, and, regardless of what you do to hide it, your leader will almost inevitably float in the surface film like a stick of wood. Fish will not generally accept a fly which is attached to said 'stick'! On balance, I'd rather fish dry fly in a howling gale than a flat calm and would certainly expect more action in the former. The best resort in a flat calm is to slip the flies below the surface on an intermediate or sinking line and fish them slow. If, to add insult to injury, the sun is bright, increase the sink rate of your line.

When covering a rising brown trout, little will be lost by chucking the flies directly at the dying rise form. Those who regularly fish for rainbow trout get into the habit of chucking ahead of the rise to intercept the moving fish. If we remember that brown trout tend to be territorial and feed in a vertical direction, it becomes obvious that the fish is unlikely to be far from the rise form he has just made, and probably directly below it. Occasionally, such as when feeding on adult insects in a calm, or virtual calm, wild brownies may roam around in a circle or ellipse, as if tied to a tether, mopping up food items. The centre of this area will be home, and the limited direction of travel will fast become evident to the angler, who should react accordingly.

When the loch is 'dead', and nothing or very little is happening, any weather or condition change, even one ostensibly for the worse, can only be an improvement.

* Since writing these words, Leven Fisheries have decided to terminate the policy of rainbow trout stocking in Leven. I, and many like-minded souls, applaud this action, and sincerely hope that their new strategy will be vindicated and return Leven to its status as the Mecca of trout fishing.

# 6 Loch Silver

Every fly-fisherman has a stack of memories that he rummages through in the depths of winter when fishing is far away. Some of my most cherished reminiscences involve big, silvery fish arching over a bob fly tripped across a lifting wave, and the grossly exaggerated curve that a 10-lb salmon can put in a single-handed trout rod when it decides it would really rather be somewhere else – fast! Way out west (and very occasionally east) amongst the rocks and crags of the Highlands and Islands, are some wonderful lochs which take runs of salmon and sea trout. This is where dreams are made, but such dreams that very few now have the inclination or aptitude to enjoy. Ah, what fools these mortals be!

Thirty years ago almost every fly-fisherman in the UK had the ability, tackle and experience to participate in what is now regarded as an esoteric branch of the sport. Modern stillwater anglers are ill-equipped to catch salmon and sea trout from lochs. The tactics and techniques learnt from big reservoirs, small commercial fisheries and rivers and streams will not greatly help you conquer the lochs. On the contrary, the deeply traditional techniques which score on the migratory fish lochs of the far west are very much akin to the short-lining practices of our fathers, the stock-in-trade tactics of the wild-trout fishers of the Highland lochs and the typical top-of-the-water skills essential on the big loughs/lakes of Ireland. If you don't know how to keep a top dropper fly furrowing across the wave tops without the benefit of liberal coatings of floatant and your reaction to a heavily-hackled size 8 wet fly is one of horror and disbelief, then your chances of success are greatly reduced.

Having spent some time and words describing my own favourite locations for this branch of fly-fishing in the previous chapter, what I want to do here is discuss the similarities and differences from brown trout loch fishing, and how we can all improve our chances in an arena where the fly-fisherman's ability to control his luck are limited.

## Silvery Fish Are Where You Find Them!

The prospectors of the Gold Rush era had an expression 'Gold is where you find it'. What they probably meant is the only sure way to find gold was to ... find it; there were no rules or guaranteed shortcuts, and gold was a product of its environment. Sea trout and salmon loch systems are very much like that, very much the product of the specific, individual environmental conditions which apply to the region in which they exist.

In Chapter 1 we discussed the environment immediately after the last Ice Age, when trout and salmon colonised (or possibly recolonised) this country we call Scotland. We drew a picture of a ravaged landscape with rushing torrents, glacial moraines, screes and boulders, thin soils and low-level fertility, which suited the migratory fish that left the shallow seas to explore a virgin landscape of lochs, streams and rivers.

Great tracts of north-western Scotland would appear not to have changed much in the ten thousand years since the ice slipped away northwards. Ron Greer in his excellent work, *Ferox Trout and Arctic Charr* (1995), describes the climate of northern Scotland as subarctic. I have, believe it or not, visited the Arctic Circle in December (it was some years ago, admittedly, and had nothing at all to do with fly-fishing), but my somewhat blurred recollections lead me to believe that even a Laplander would be shocked and flabbergasted by the chill factor of a January easterly blowing across the moors of Caithness. The south of England may well expect summer temperatures approaching 100°F, but I have just returned from a July visit to Harris in the Western Isles and can assure you that there was more need of a down-filled parka than factor-50 sunblock.

Trout and salmon are subarctic creatures. They require cool water temperatures and are not dismayed by low water fertility, and these conditions they find aplenty in the far north-west. And, because migratory salmonids get almost all their nutritional requirements from the sea, it is a matter of total indifference to them that their preferred freshwater habitats are the wet, nutritional equivalent of the Atacama Desert. There are valid theories, which maintain that sea life is essential for large salmonids, because if they stayed in the waters of their birth they would, of necessity, start to cannibalise their own offspring. In other words, salmon and sea trout go to sea in order to protect future generations. Whilst I think this is a misreading of the actual facts, it does help get a handle on the true scenario. It is now generally accepted that what we see is a strong case of niche environment exploitation. No other fish species desire this environment so there are no slavering predators looking for an easy meal of parr, whether salmon or sea trout. What small quantities of food are available are more than enough to give juvenile salmonids a good start and then send them off to the rich marine feeding grounds with a positive attitude towards taking advantage of suitable available food sources.

Watching a three-inch salmon parr struggling to engulf a three-quarter-inch sedge fly, one begins to realise not only that low fertility is a matter of degree but also that an opportunistic and optimistic attitude towards food can get a small fish a long way.

Let's have a round up. Sea trout and salmon spend part of their lives in a marine environment for a variety of reasons, but one of the most important is that the sea's fertility allows them the potential for growth and early maturity that their freshwater nursery is incapable of providing. Some of the best loch systems for migratory fish occur along the West Coast of Scotland and in the Western Isles. The geological type most common in this region is peat bog and hard, insoluble metamorphic rock, so the lochs are largely devoid of the dissolved minerals and nutrients capable of maintaining healthy, self-sufficient populations of large, stay-at-home fish. The brown trout populations are, by and large, stunted and long-lived; the typical four-ounce trout can be older than the child that catches it. In search of fertility to enable large volumes of healthy eggs to be formed in her ovaries, the typical hen sea trout has taken the obvious option in going to sea. And the bulk of West Coast sea trout *are* female; the male fish, which the angler may discount as a pitiful brownie, can and often does stay at home in fresh water, because the low-level fertility in the lochs and streams does enable them to produce enough milt to fertilise the eggs of the returning female. The individual egg is a treasure chest of stored nutrition for the earliest stages of the growing juvenile, whereas the individual sperm requires very little back-up nutrition to fuel its short-lived function. So, when you are on a known sea trout loch please be courteous to the humble brownie which engulfs your fly. He might be the father of that ten-pound bar of silver you hope to catch in five years time.

Salmon, of course, have their own agenda and are also products of infertile waters but must be viewed from an alternative perspective. Young salmon in their freshwater habitat are voracious predators but also a valuable food source for larger predators. The infertile habitats in which they thrive have enough food to allow the tiny parr to mature but don't encourage the presence of predators. This is niche exploitation in spades. No other rivals are competing with the salmon juveniles for their environment and, although it is an unspeakably harsh place at times, in what to all intents is sub-arctic Britain, this ecological nursery which the salmon has claimed for its own is more than capable of instigating the fabulous runs of salmon and grilse which flood into such loch systems as Grimersta.

## Migratory Fish Runs

Most fisheries which take runs of salmon and sea trout expect their fish to start arriving somewhere about the end of June, all other things being equal. Some notable exceptions do occur but they are very much in the minority. On balance, and in my experience, salmon/grilse runs commence late June and are largely over by the end of August, whereas sea trout runs start slowly in June, are going about flat out in August, and gradually taper off to a finish at the end of September. This is broad-brush stroke stuff, doesn't take into consideration external factors, such as rainfall and tidal movements, and should be used as a general guide.

The Howmore system in South Uist, for example, falls in with the general pattern and expects its sea trout fishing to start getting under way sometime around the first week in July. However, it also takes a good late run of sea trout in late September/early October in a more or less regular fashion. I know this to be true not only because it is common knowledge amongst the fishery staff but also because I once witnessed with my own eyes a flood of shiny, clean sea trout move up from Loch Roag into Loch Fada one October afternoon. Watching these fish fan out across the gun-metal grey waters of Fada in the fading light of an autum sky, the odd leaping fish showing the dispersal, is a memory that I treasure. At the other end of the scale Grimersta takes a desultory spring run of salmon with low but improving numbers of fish probably entering the river from April, until the grilse runs fill the system in late June/early July.

All the rules are there to be broken, though, and, as any regular loch sea trout or salmon fisher will tell you, the calendar is a poor guide to being in the right place at the right time. It is the practice of visiting fishers in the West, endorsed by estates/fisheries, to take the same week year after year in the hunt for salmon and sea trout. Such a regime probably means that the angler will get it right about one year in four. That doesn't mean that three years out of four will necessarily be awful, but it does mean that the fourth year will probably be spectacular, with the lucky fisherman wandering around with that far-away, glazed, slightly dazed, look which only comes from catching more fish than is good for him!

It is a truism that the big heads of fish generally arrive at the burn/river mouth to coincide with the spring tides. These occur twice a month, always a couple of days after either the new moon or the full moon, and are the highest tides of the month; the new moon spring high tides tend to be bigger than the full moon springs. If you can arrange it (i.e. you've got a direct line to the Almighty), what you want is lots of rain coinciding with a new moon spring tide somewhere about a day before you start fishing in the last week in July. If you are fishing for a week, Monday to Saturday, another small freshet or mini-spate about Wednesday will probably provide you with the fishing trip of your, or anyone else's, lifetime. That is the dream. The reality is that you may get one, two or all of the above elements, but lack the essential catalyst which makes it all come together. For example, I have had all the above and sat out on a glassy calm surface for a whole week getting eaten alive by the dreaded midge, burnt to a crisp by the sun, mocked by jumping fish which refuse to look at a single offering, and all the time praying desperately for some semblance of wind which wouldn't disappear within minutes of arriving. Although it has never happened to me, I have heard of others who had the perfect set of conditions and timings and the fish have, for reasons of their own, simply not arrived home from the sea. Couple all this with the fact that your intended quarry is not a feeding fish (salmon and, to a lesser extent, sea trout do not feed in fresh water) and you may begin to see why I talk about a successful hit rate being about one trip in four.

## Salmon and Sea Trout Behaviour in Lochs

Salmon and sea trout, being saltwater fish, prefer to acclimatise to fresh water before entering it. This basically means that a fish which has regulated its kidney function to expel salt and protect bodily fluids as a priority must now reprogram it to save salt and expel water. This does in some way happen in the estuary (if there is one) and will be well under way in that first run up the burn/river. How this affects the fish's response to the angler and his flies I know not, but there is little doubt that salmon, particularly, upon arriving in the loch require a good twenty-four hours to settle down before looking for a nice fly to gnaw on. Of course, this may be because the fish requires a few hours to select a good lie from which to observe the passing world. I don't know (and I am wary of anyone who claims 20/20 insight into this behavioural quirk).

Sea trout, on the other hand, hold to their shoals upon entering fresh water and seem reasonably eager to have a go at flies almost straight away. As their sojourn in the loch continues the shoaling instinct fades, the fish become dispersed and less likely to take. Big sea trout seem to adopt the behavioural instincts of salmon and, unlike their smaller brethren, seem quite happy in shallow water. It is a never-ending source of amazement to me that large sea trout and salmon prefer a mere teaspoon of loch water covering their backs. Smaller sea trout are often found in the deeps, but their bigger brothers and cousins inhabit incredibly shallow water almost all of the time. Many years ago I fished a South Uist loch called East Ollay with Captain John Kennedy, Fishery Manager for the South Uist estate. John was, and is, probably one of Scotland's finest exponents of the art of catching salmon and sea trout from the shore (he is also very, very good from a boat). On this particular day there was just too much wind from the south to comfortably fish from the boat, so we waded. In disbelief I watched John taking a salmon from a lie so close to dry land that, whilst his dropper fly was in the water, his point fly was as likely to catch a rabbit as a fish. And that's not much of an exaggeration! There was a boulder jutting out of the water less than a metre from the rock shore-line and John threw his flies into the gap and hooked his fish. I later went to that spot and measured the depth of water – and to this day I can't understand why the salmon's dorsal fin wasn't sticking out above the surface. (Maybe it was, and John saw it and made the cast! Who knows? – Captain John no doubt, but he's not telling!) I've said it before and I'll say it again: salmon will lie in water that would make a stickleback nervous!

However, I have never known even big sea trout to lie in water quite that shallow, although the best fish seem always to be closely associated with a shoreline, an offshore reef or boulder. Smaller sea trout seem quite happy in open water and to form relatively close-knit shoals over water that can be comparatively deep and devoid of any obvious mark. All this is most bizarre when one considers that, to all intents and purposes, in salt water salmon are fish of the wide open spaces and deep waters (although the bulk of their feeding will be at or near the surface), while sea trout are shallow-water roamers and feeders, rarely if ever venturing far from coastal waters and intertidal zones. They are most contrary brutes and hard to fathom.

As their time in freshwater increases sea trout quietly disappear from view, and the next we will see of them will be in the spawning burns during the close season. Salmon, on the other hand, will have a second run at the flies late in the season when they become sexually mature and aggressive (cock fish more so than hens); like the sea trout, though, they will be most likely caught when they are freshly in and thereafter, until the hormones kick in, become daily less likely to co-operate with the fisherman.

There is one caveat to all this, however. When the feeder burns are in spate both species are likely to come nosing into the outflows in a sort of rehearsal for the real thing which will happen in the winter months. A burn in spate will be regularly visited by fish from all over the loch and the angler who wants some action would be well-advised to do the same. If truth be told, the bulk of the fish that have their noses jammed into the outflows of spating burns, especially in the late months of the season, will probably be quite stale, but amongst them will be a few bright fish worthy of the effort.

In *The Art of Sea Trout Fishing* (1963), Charles McLaren reckoned that sea trout upon entering a loch had well-delineated travel routes through it, and, if you knew their location (the routes and, by defini- tion, the fish), you could have exemplary sport by focusing on specific areas of the route which were prime taking spots. This, like so much information about precise sea trout and salmon behaviour within a system, is only available from ghillies nowadays. We, as anglers, gener- ally don't have the ability, time or money to get to know a system well enough to be able to work these things out for ourselves. I suspect that McLaren's theory is valid (after all who in their right mind is going to argue with the great man), for we can recognise it in fragmented form; our ghillies know open-water places/lies where fish are caught regu- larly or where fish seem to gather and, conversely, other locations best avoided, and this tends to back up the 'travel route' theory. Further to that, I also believe that when fish for some reason or other get active they go for 'roam abouts' in the same way we would go for a walk with a dog of an evening. I am convinced that salmon in a loch behave this way and suspect, with less evidence, that sea trout probably do the same. My principal evidence for this hypothesis is that there are defi- nite 'jumping places' where salmon throw themselves skyward in a manner liable to get an angler's juices running. That fish are rarely, if ever, caught in these spots and that when active in this way are some- times caught in well delineated spots, at varying distances from the 'jumping spots', tends to indicate not only that travelling is being undertaken but that there is a specific 'roam about' route/routes well known to the fish of that system.

It is an overworked axiom that salmon and sea trout are best sought at the tail of the wind. In my mind's eye I see big, silvery fish arching over well-worked bob flies in the turmoil of wind and wave that exists on the weather shore.* However, when the wind is at its barely fishable worst (say about Force 6–7 or between 25 and 35 mph) the weather shore can be deserted, or fish still holding there are unwilling to take any interest in the fisherman's flies. I have seen this set of circumstances many times and wondered over it, but on a recent trip to the Western Isles I witnessed this in definitive form over a succession of very windy days. At the head of the wind, where there was a substantial ripple, fish were moved but not often caught. As we progressed down the wind there was an optimum point where fewer fish came to the fly but those that did generally came in a very positive manner. From this optimum point to the end of the drift on the weather shore no or very few fish were seen and none caught. The only exception to this rule was in the shelter of islands. If there was an island on the drift – no matter how far down the drift and regardless of wind speed and wave height – fish, both salmon and sea trout, could be expected in the short length of sheltered water in the lee of the island.

Here's an example. We had drifted out of the best of the water and were fairly racing down the wind, almost leaping from wave top to wave top. The only sounds above the wind were the swish-swish of lines being cast, the cursing of Dave, our ghillie, plus the grinding of his teeth as he fought to control the boat. There was a small islet on my side of the drift and Dave steered the boat so that I could get a cast onto the rocks on the upwind end of it. No response. I cast the flies along the shore of the islet as we passed it. Again, no response. Just as we arrived at the sheltered downwind end of the wave thrashed island I saw a salmon head-and-tail slap-bang in the centre of the sheltered water. A long cast just got the flies across his face and he arched magnificently over the flies … but to no avail – whether due to his failing or mine, I do not know. However, I thought to try him again and chucked the flies out to the fading turmoil of his 'rise'. By this time we

---

* Before we go any further, let's get one definition more or less straight – to a fisherman the lee shore is where the wind is blowing from and the weather shore where the wind is blowing to. The yachtsman has it the other way round, and we tend to laugh at each other's usage. I'm sorry, but I don't make the rules – that's just the way it is.

had pushed further down the drift, so the cast had to be made slightly more across the near-gale than I would normally like. The outcome was that the flies landed some 4–6ft downwind of the salmon's lie, and I promptly hooked and landed a 2½-lb sea trout. The image that immediately sprang to my mind was that here we had a collection of fish sheltering from the unwelcome gale in the lee of the island just as a bus queue, on a day of driving rain, piles in behind the rather overweight gentleman in the overcoat. On the run down to the island we had seen nothing, and after departing its idyllic shores we saw nary fin nor scale; just the two fish were encountered, within a few feet of each other, in the lee of the island.

Nevertheless, salmon and sea trout do like a good wave, and, generally speaking, such conditions are liable to produce rather than detract from potential sport. The sort of wind that produces what I refer to as a 'lifting wave' is best. A lifting wave is one which has a well-defined crest and trough formation and tends to produce some froth. Winds with a touch of west and south in them are most likely to produce a lifting wave, whilst winds from the other side of the compass tend to generate a 'flattening wave' which has no crest height and appears like a demented ripple, sometimes referred to as a 'cat's-paws' or 'scud'. Scud is not good, and seems to deter fish from being surface active, if active at all.

Perfect conditions for this type of fishing are hard to categorise, and I have known good fish come in every possible combination of weather types, even in flat calms. But the typical good top-of-the-water day with a high overcast, a mild south-west wind of, say, 15–20 mph would be my choice, if choice were ever an option. And then I would expect my fish to be found towards the tail of the wind.

As an aside to the matter of tail-of-the-wind turbulence, a fishing friend of mine who indulged himself in a bit of sub-aqua diving once remarked to me that he was astonished that fish seemed to be perfectly happy in the chaotic water of a weather shore. He said he had been in just such locations when immersed and had inevitably become quickly disorientated and nauseous. But then, we are not fish, and our physiological processes are not designed to be of use under water.

## Tactics for Salmon and Sea Trout

Where sea trout and salmon are found together in a loch, tactics tend to favour the species which predominates. For example, at Grimersta, which is almost exclusively a salmon system, boat fishing techniques are virtually indistinguishable from grilse tactics on a river. Salmon patterns such as small double Silver Stoats, Jeannies, etc., are mandatory point flies, and the only trout-style fly which is in any way encouraged is an outsize muddler on the top and only dropper.

Just around the corner, at Amhuinnsuidhe, which is possibly the finest, most prolific sea trout system still remaining to us, big, bushy traditional trout flies in appropriate sizes are routinely and successfully used for both the salmon and sea trout. If you speak to the ghillies at Grimersta they will tell you that their salmon don't like big trout flies, and when used such flies don't do well. Unfortunately, on my one and only visit to this hallowed fishing ground there were not enough fish in the system to carry out any sort of valid examination of this hypothesis, but it does clash with the practice and theory on almost every other fishery of its type (except, notably, Lough Beltra in Ireland).

So, we have established that there may be some adaptation required in fishing tactics for salmon and sea trout, respectively. Of course, we do appreciate that, as described above, the two species have slightly differing behavioural tendencies when they enter freshwater lochs. But how does this affect our attempts to catch them? Salmon have a well-documented tendency to fill a system up from the top down. In simple language this means that the first fish enter at a trot, head as fast as they can for the headwaters, take up residence, and subsequent arrivals slot in behind them. All things being equal, in an imaginary river with three distinct runs, spring-run fish will locate themselves far upstream, grilse and summer salmon will invade the middle reaches, whilst the autumn fish will stock the lower beats. In a one-loch system, where there is a burn into the head of the loch (the spawning burn) and one out to the sea, things are not that simple and what tends to happen is that the first fish take up the best lies nearest the spawning burn, then the best lies in other parts are occupied, and the last arrivals have to make do the best they can. Pecking order will have a lot to do with individual fish location, and

I have little doubt that a heavy summer salmon will soon displace a grilse from a favoured lie.

In a multi-loch system the first arrivals will, water levels permitting, fill it from the top down. This will not happen within hours and may take some time, but the speed with which salmon will pervade the system can be breathtaking, with fresh sea-liced fish appearing dozens of miles inland within a day or so.

Sea trout movement in loch systems doesn't seem quite so well regimented, but their ability to diffuse throughout a system within a short period of time is well-known. The shoaling instinct is strong in fresh fish, and they move almost as an entity and go to areas where they intend to stay put until the spawning runs commence.

Salmon tend, as we have said, to adopt lies, but sea trout are generally found on drifts. Salmon lies can be marked to the inch; sea-trout holding areas are not so precise, and some movement within a reasonably well-defined area, due to external factors, is probable almost on a daily basis. For example, on Loch Dionard salmon adopt lies on the southern shore under the cliffs on the slopes of Foinaven, while sea trout tend to inhabit the bays off the northern shore. On Loch Roag I have most often encountered salmon along the northern (road) shore and amongst the rocks at the extreme western end of the loch. Roag sea trout hold to the main basin, off the southern shore, with the odd very good fish slumming it with the salmon amongst those western rocks. In general, sea trout prefer deeper water to salmon, and, although it is not uncommon to find the two species together, it is also not unusual to have a salmon side in a loch which is well differentiated from the sea trout side.

When hoping to snare a salmon, never underestimate the importance of lies in a loch. Good ghillies will know them almost as well as the fish themselves, and if an incumbent is removed from a favoured lie one day there is a very strong possibility that there will be a new tenant the next. But if salmon are generally easier to locate than sea trout, on the converse side, sea trout tend to take as soon as they hit fresh water, and this is probably because they won't seek out a lie as a prerequisite to taking.

We have already discussed weather and dwelt on the subject of wind and its effects. Let me say again, though, that salmon like a good wind and will take in wind speeds that discourage sea trout from coming to the fly. Light winds, particularly when fish are very fresh, can be fine, but flat calms are a disaster. The only guy I have ever known to catch more than the odd, lucky fish in a flat calm was my old mate Andy Wren. He stumbled upon a technique which could catch sea trout in the worst of all possible conditions – a bottle-glass flat calm – but I will save that little tale for the section on desperation tactics later in this chapter.

Very fresh sea trout can be made to take a dry fly in calm conditions, but they must be very fresh – maybe one day in. This is somewhat surprising since they probably rarely if ever eat an adult fly in the sea and presumably have no recent memories of having done so, but the behaviour of sea trout is totally beyond the comprehension of mere mortals, I'm afraid.

In many years of loch fishing for salmon and sea trout in flat calms I have caught some sea trout, but not many, and never a salmon. No doubt somebody out there has succeeded in what I consider a very difficult task, but I strongly doubt whether they could repeat the feat more than one time in a hundred. Moving swiftly on to other weather types, rain is good but better in the immediate past than the present. (On my way to the fishing there is nothing I like to see more than the burns running white on the hillsides.) Impending rain, especially if there is to be a deluge, can often make fish very active a day or so before the flood arrives, so that is worth looking out for. However, my experience tends to lead me to believe that, although much activity may be seen in the way of leaping and jumping, fish take best after the rain has fallen. Sunshine, if it is wall-to-wall, is generally bad, but if associated with a west or north-west wind and interspersed with high, fluffy clouds it can be bearable. Blue skies would never make me throw in the towel if all other weather factors were favourable.

A summary of weather and its effects would have it that what we consider to be good loch-fishing weather in general is good for our migratory salmonids but with an added bucketful of wind in generous proportions.

So, now we have a fairly good understanding (if such is possible) of most of the factors affecting the fish and their willingness, or lack of it, to co-operate with the angler. What can we do to tip the scales in our favour?

## Tackling the Job

From a tackle perspective we can do a lot. Rods traditionally preferred for this game are long (11 ft +) and limber with some backbone. This sort of length allows bob flies to be worked at a reasonable distance from the boat and does provide added leverage for bullying fish when they are close to the boat, a worthy consideration in a time when catch and release is a vital component in maintaining a sustainable and viable fishery. Because I have a shoulder almost totally wrecked by a lifetime wielding rod and shotgun (and the added leverage of the long rod defeats me never mind the fish), I plump for a 10-ft rod with an AFTM rating of 7. As long as I balance my leader and flies properly I can work a bob fly to my satisfaction.

Reels require a tad more consideration for this job than those selected for brown trout. Big sea trout, and to a lesser extent salmon, can seriously test the bearings, drag and line capacity of any reel. Sea trout can cover a very long distance in a short space of time, especially when they first feel the hook. Generally speaking, monofilament selection should carry enough forgiveness so that we should not expect a break-off, regardless of the breaking strain of the leader material. However, all may end in tears if the backing runs out, or the reel drag is inadequate or poorly set. I strongly advise the use of modern wide-arbor reels for this game, as they feed line easily and quickly, with minimal inertia, and are also capable of rapid line recovery when that sneaky fish decides to sprint back to the boat. The narrowness of the traditional small reel spool means that as every coil of line leaves the spool the inertia and resistance to spool revolution is incrementally increased, to the point where the coils of line trying to leave the reel are tiny and the inertia is colossal. Outcome? Potential break-off if the fish is moving away fast, and poor line recovery rate and chance of a snag-up or the hook falling out if the fish is coming towards the boat.

Leader material selection rarely presents a problem, but I can see a few looming up in the future. I fish bog-standard nylon monofilament of somewhere between 0.22 mm and 0.18 mm. Diameter of nylon is much more important than breaking strain, because the thickness/ diameter of the nylon should be geared to the requirements of fly size. We have discussed this before, but, big hooks break off small diameter nylon regardless of b.s., and small hooks do not act or swim properly when tethered to heavy nylon. Size 6 flies (a size rarely if ever required, except in a howling gale?) fit best on 0·22 mm nylon, size 8s about the same, size 10 flies like 0·20 mm (and, for the odd occasion when I fish dries, 0·18 mm). Many experts and ghillies in this field like the old-fashioned Maxima Chameleon. (You know the stuff – looks like tarry rope and has all the inbuilt memory of a fathom of barbed wire). I don't use it, because I believe that clear monofilament is less obvious to the fish, but the facts and practice seem to prove that fish don't object as much as I do. And it does carry flies well, is easy to knot and seems reliable enough. Make your own choice. I've already made mine.

Leader length depends upon how many flies you wish to fish. Ghillies often advise the use of a two-fly cast for a variety of reasons, amongst which are:

- fewer tangles in the wind speeds often encountered;
- fewer multiple hook-ups, which almost inevitably mean break-offs;
- fewer flies to catch in weed-beds, around which salmon and sea trout have a distressing tendency to lie;
- middle dropper flies rarely score;
- and (probably most important of all) fewer ghillies acquiring feathered earrings.

In my arrogance, I believe I am capable of avoiding these snags and almost always fish three flies, because I firmly believe that one can't fish a bob fly properly without the anchoring weight and resistance of two flies beneath the bob fly, both well buried beneath the surface film. I accept that the middle fly has a poor success rate when it comes to actually catching fish, but its use, as outlined above, is essential to the way I like to work the flies.

A two-fly cast should be no longer than, say, 12 ft; 5 ft from line attachment to first dropper, and then 7 ft more to point fly. A three-fly cast should be arranged thus: a 5-ft length to the top dropper, as above, and then two other 5-ft lengths from top to middle dropper and from middle dropper to point, producing a 15-ft leader in all. Dropper length should not exceed 6 in. or, if you are convinced you won't be changing your original selection of flies, I would advise maximum length of 4 inches. Dropper knots must be water knots, which in 0·22–0·18-mm monofilament can consist of three turns, four for the anally retentive. After a hard fight from a heavy fish, wisdom would suggest checking all knots for potential weakening, examining the whole length of the cast for any signs of fraying, and, for the nervous of nature, a whole leader reconstruction. If, after a tough and prolonged tussle with a heavy fish amongst the rocks and boulders, the leader fails on the next fish hooked, then you have no one to blame but yourself. Chances of the fish of a lifetime, by definition, don't come often enough to justify taking a cavalier attitude to one's end tackle.

It never ceases to amaze me that so many fly-fishermen will pay a king's ransom to get to the dream fishing location, plus hundreds of pounds for reels, rods, tackle bags and jackets, will avail themselves of the best fly lines that money can buy, and lots of them, but then go and finish off the ensemble with some of the tattiest, cheapest, self-destructing flies on the market. Eight out of ten fishermen's fly boxes are a damned disgrace when for less than a pound per fly those fishermen can buy quality stuff from people who not only know what a trout looks like but also probably spend a lot of their time fishing for them. Look at it this way: the fish don't give a tuppenny damn what you are wearing, or the make of your rod or reel, because they'll never see them, but they *will* see your flies, and will have to make up their minds whether they want to eat them or not. Flies are the only point of contact between a fisherman and his desired quarry. In the name of all that's wonderful, let us all put on the very best flies we can afford or tie.

Having got that out of the way what is the well-equipped angler going to tie on his cast to catch salmon and sea trout? Let's examine the ground rules:

1. Almost every loch system taking mixed runs of salmon and sea trout has its special favourite patterns, which we would be insane to ignore.
2. There are standard patterns which work almost everywhere.
3. By studying the preferred patterns of a specific fishery, the accomplished fly-tier can, and should, try a few adaptations and variations, if only for his own amusement. It works for me!
4. The degree of 'freshness' of the fish sought (how long in fresh water) can radically affect fly colour preference by fish, and therefore, fishermen.
5. Size does matter! Some fisheries like small flies and some prefer big ones.

The fisheries of the far west tend to have peat-stained water in their lochs. This has a profound effect upon pattern colour. Generally, the best colours for peaty water are strong, hard colours, such as black, red, orange, claret and silver. Some other systems can have gin-clear waters, and here muted colours, e.g. green, olive green, fiery-brown, golden olive and gold, can do well. But, if in doubt, always expect flies strongly favouring black, claret and silver to interest fish.

Every practitioner of this art will have his own favourites and I have mine, but there are flies which will appear in all but a very few boxes – Kate McLaren, Bibio, Black Pennell, Claret Bumble, Mallard/Grouse and Claret, Blue Zulu, Soldier Palmer, Teal Blue and Silver, Peter Ross, Goat's Toe and Butcher. Patterns which I can't do without and would add to the above include Kate McLaren Muddler, Peterson's Pennell, Gold Muddler, Green Peter Muddler, Clan Chief, Leggy Claret Bumble, Leggy Golden Olive Bumble and a Jungle Cock Bibio. Bit-part players are Bruiser, Doobry, Golden Olive French Partridge, Olive French Partridge and Katie Ross. Many people whose selections I respect would add some small salmon double patterns such as Assassin, Weasel, Silver Stoat and Stoat's Tail. Somewhere amongst this lot is a selection which should suit anyone.

Kingsmill Moore, a great sea trout fisher and fly pattern innovator, suggested that specific colours appealed to fresh-run fish, and that their attraction waned as fish became increasingly stale. His theory, with which I fully concur, promotes the idea that silver and blue are the best colours for very fresh fish, then moving through the olives and greens for those that have been some time in fresh water, until the only colours that stale fish would gladly accept (if they would accept any at all) would be black and claret. I would read into this statement that the old judge fished clear waters and I would add one proviso to his hypothesis: water colour and strength of ambient light will also influence the outcome. Black and claret work well in poor light regardless of water colour, blues and oranges work well in strong light regardless of water colour; and the muted shades perform in all levels of light but do require low levels of peat stain before they do their best work.

As regards pattern size, the old books talk of sizes 6 and 8 being standard, but nowadays, generally speaking, sizes 8 and 10 are more acceptable, with the odd size 12 in very calm conditions. Weather will have an impact on fly size choice, with the hook size preferred in light winds increasing incrementally with the wind speed until in a very strong wind size 8s become mandatory. Some still swear by size 6s, but I seriously believe that no one's catch rate is going to drop if they throw all their massive irons away. I also have a sneaking regard for the old adage that small waters favour small flies, and vice versa, but it doesn't seem to apply to this game: Loch Lomond is a massive water, and the regulars there prefer quite small wet flies in the size 10 to 12 range.

To test the waters, so to speak, I would advise putting a large fly on the top dropper with the smallest on the point – the big, preferably bushy, pattern on the top bringing fish 'in to the cast', where they may select something smaller following up. I have seen this work remarkably well, and often, for both salmon and sea trout. I know that many fishers are reluctant to have the heaviest hook at the top of the cast and the lightest on the point, since they wish to avoid tangles, but with reasonably robust nylon and conservative casting technique all should be well. Bearing in mind what I said earlier about leader material diameter and hook size, it is, of course, possible to make up compound casts with the material varied to suit the different sizes of fly on the cast, but I always compromise, erring on the finer side to suit the smallest fly. In this age of gossamer nylon that is strong enough to moor boats, break-offs in fish should not be a major worry.

## Short-Lining Technique

Short-lining is the traditional technique for presenting flies to sea trout and salmon, but one that on balance, I suspect, works better for sea trout than salmon. Having said that, though, I am continually faced with circumstances which make me doubt that observation. I am just back from a very successful trip to the Western Isles during which the only fish to come positively to a close-in worked bob fly was a grilse. All the sea trout (and there were a goodly number of them) came to a pulled fly at some distance from the boat.

So, what is short-lining and when is it best employed? Short-lining as a technique grew out of poor tackle that in bygone days was incapable of throwing a long line. In the bad old days, fishing close to the boat was unavoidable, and short-lining was a way of doing it very successfully. Here's how it's done. Enough line is thrown to allow about 3 or 4 sweeps of the left arm (if the angler is right-handed) to bring the top dropper fly up into the surface film when the rod is at an angle of, say, 50–60° to the horizontal. This will, of course, depend on wind strength – in a light wind the rod may have to be virtually perpendicular, and in a near gale the rod may be virtually horizontal! But let's say we have a nice fresh breeze. The cast is made, and the first handful of line is retrieved with the rod close to horizontal, the second with the rod starting to rise (at about 30°) and the third at the designated 50–60° angle. The rod is then maintained in this position whilst the fly is slowly retrieved with the left hand. Whilst the angle of the rod to the water surface is not varied much, the rod can be moved to left or right causing the flies to follow a similar course across the water in front of the boat. A successful variation of this technique is that, when the bob fly is played out and no longer capable of being held in the surface film, the middle fly can then get a short spell in a similar role and position. This is virtually impossible in a light breeze, but then the whole technique is built on the premise that there is a good wind blowing.

So, as you can see, short-lining is primarily about top-dropper work. The concept is that a nice, big, hairy bob fly is dragged through (not necessarily over) the surface film, creating a wake which, theoretically at least, is irresistible to our prey. The following flies, those on the middle dropper and point, fulfil a support role, in that if the fish is attracted to the bob fly but won't take for some reason, then it may succumb to something following on. This strategy is generally successful when done well; unfortunately, it is often not done well by people who find the practice is totally alien in their day-to-day fishing.

Let's break short-lining down into its constituent parts in an effort to understand what is going on and one's part in making it work. Firstly, it matters very little what type of line one employs – floating or fast sinker – because there will be little enough of it beyond the top eye to make much difference, although generally a floater or an inter-mediate is employed. If I was an avid short-liner, which I'm not, I'd always plump for an intermediate for reasons which will become apparent shortly.

The rod should be long. It is possible to short-line with a 10-ft rod but, unless there is a good, strong wind blowing, it will often mean that the flies are worked too close to the boat; an 11-ft rod, or even longer, is probably best, but the stature of the individual wielding the weapon has to be taken into consideration. Wielding an 11-ft rod in a gale can have seriously tiring effect upon the arm and shoulder. Short-lining involves maintaining the rod at the near vertical almost all the time, and the leverage effect exerted by a strong wind on a vertical rod over the course of a long day's fishing is cruel, unless you are a prop forward or a professional caber-tosser.

The number of flies on the cast is important: there should be three because, in order to control the wave-top-skimming top dropper candi-date, there must be weight below it to act as a drogue. Without this weight below, the top dropper will skate too rapidly across the water towards the lifting rod. And this is why I would choose an interme-diate, because it will help bury the mid and tail flies just that little bit deeper in the water and increase the drag-back quotient which will make the worked bob fly come alive.

As regards working the bob fly – which is intrinsic to the whole tech-nique – it is inadvisable to make it do anything fast. Even a bob fly held static in the surface film will attract, as it is, in effect, moving against the surface flow of water by remaining motionless in it. However, I prefer to give the fly movement roughly at right-angles to the wind and water direction and, if possible, always away from rather than towards the sun's position in the sky. I have discussed this earlier, and it works for salmon and sea trout as much as it does for brown trout, and for exactly the same reasons. (See Fig. 12 on p. 179.)

The appropriate response to a fish coming to the bob fly is critical in the pursuit of success. Salmon are harder than sea trout to deal with, as they tend to steadily, slowly and determinedly engulf the fly in a heart-stopping display of controlled aggression, during which the human ability for 'cock-up' is never more apparent. Sea trout, generally speaking, do everything quicker, and are either 'on or off' when the angler comes to respond. When the salmon comes up to a worked bob fly it is vital for the angler to remember that, unlike the trout, he will not have the fly securely in his maw until he is turned well down on the fly. Hence, any attempt to strike or tighten into the fish whilst any part of him is still visible above the water is likely to end with a total miss, a pluck, or a very short and disappointing struggle. It is hard not to respond in some way to a massive fish rearing up out of the water within a few feet of the boat, but my strongest advice would be to do nothing other than what attracted the fish (i.e. keeping the line taut) – or, indeed, nothing at all until the line does or does not go tight. Anything else you might do is extremely unlikely to hook the fish. If the salmon, after what seemed like a determined effort to commit hara-kiri, has obviously not taken the bob fly, then do not despair; on many occasions, in just such circumstances, the offending brute has redeemed itself by swallowing a following fly to the angler's joy and the ultimate downfall of the fish.

One of the biggest salmon I've ever encountered on a loch was missed by my total inability to follow my own advice. While being rowed across deep water on Loch Bharp in South Uist, from one prime area to the next, I was casually flicking the flies out on a short line and allowing them to come across the wave into the turmoil of the boat's wake. All the while I was chatting to the ghillie, with no expectation of any interruption to our conversation. Out of the corner of my eye I saw a fish rear out of the water in a much-exaggerated attempt to annihilate the tripping Goat's Toe. To my horror, and the disgust of the ghillie, I struck immediately – which produced the inevitable outcome. I put this inexcusable lack of control down to the fact that the sod (the fish, I hasten to add, not the ghillie) caught me totally unawares, eliciting not a knee-jerk but an arm-jerk reaction. Believe me, it is distressingly easily done!

Sea trout, as I have said, tend to be considerably more readily brought to a well worked bob fly, but can lack the 'blood-in-the-eye' determination of the salmon. It is possible to move fish after fish to the short-line technique without having any real opportunity to feel the weight of a single trout, and this seems to be the norm rather than the exception. But, as stated above, the saving grace of sea trout is that, when committed to the rise, they rarely allow the angler time to mess things up. They are not so prone to the graceful head-and-tail manoeuvre so loved by the salmon, but they have the ability to attack and engulf a bobbed fly without showing much or any part of their body above water. The speed of the attack generally means that the fisherman is aware of the fact that he has a fish 'on' just as the pictures of the rise are being displayed on the screen in his brain. Experience does suggest that the old saying that trout take the fly on the way up whilst salmon take on the way down is perfectly true. Most ghillies of my acquaintance advise an instantaneous reaction to a sea trout rise, should one be needed at all, and a delayed, or no, reaction to a salmon rise.

## Long-Lining

Most modern anglers who dabble a bit with migratory fish in lochs tend to be more comfortable with long-lining than short-lining, since the former is basically the same technique employed to take their brown or rainbow trout at home. And, whilst it may lack the skill and beauty of a well-worked bob fly technique, it is a very successful tactic for loch fish.

Most anglers like to think they are performing a compromise tactic by working the bob fly after hand-lining back thirty-odd feet of line, and, whilst this can work to an extent, experience shows that the bulk of long-lined fish are caught within the first five pulls of the line. Fish that have had a long look at a thick floating line being pulled over their heads are not overly inclined to calmly accept the flies which trail behind it. Long-lining is a means by which fish may be caught at a distance from the boat but not a means to extend the working length of a retrieve. To all intents and purposes, long-lining is just short-lining but at a distance and with no overt bob fly work (although there is a way round this shortcoming – read on!).

Long-liners almost always fish a floating line, although there is evidence to suggest that lines of varying sink-rate may help boost the basket on occasion. Floating lines make fishing in the seriously shallow loch water that salmon adore a simpler business. A drift amongst the salmon rocks followed by a sea trout drift over open, deeper water may suggest a line change to the exceptionally keen, especially when sea trout are not overly fresh and unwilling to come to the top, but in practice it is rarely done.

However, when on a sea-trout-only water, or when salmon are unwelcome due to staleness, I have no problem fishing lines which explore the depths when the light is harsh or the winds light or cold. It is always more pleasing to see the fish take on the surface but in conditions unlikely to bring fish to the top a sinking or intermediate line may be the only hope of a fish or two. Some years ago, when fishing Loch Roag with Keith Dunbar under the strict tutelage of Neilly Johnston the ghillie, we were faced with September conditions which would break the heart of those who go afloat on lochs – a cold, fresh north-easterly blowing out of a cloudless sky. Sunburn and frostbite are not unheard of in such conditions! We had worked damned hard with the usual tactics in all the best places and hadn't seen fin nor scale of a fish all day. In the late afternoon I thought 'To Hell with it! I'm going downstairs!' and stuck on a fast intermediate with a tandem Orange-Hackled Worm Fly on the point to add weight and increase the sink factor. This was not done with any great expectation of result, but when the standard techniques have been explored and found wanting all that's left is to try the obscure. The result: a handsome fish of just over the 4-lb mark to the Worm Fly, when all the smart money was on a blank! Just recently my boat partner of that day, Keith Dunbar, contacted me with the information that, in difficult conditions on a Western Isles loch, he had been sorting out a few sea trout on a Wet Cel 2 when nothing was forthcoming to the floater. As his week declined into high water temperatures and unremitting sunshine not even the use of the sinkers could turn a poor week into a good one. It must be said, however, that the best fish of his week (5 pound plus) fell to a Grouse and Claret on a floating line in bright sunshine. There are no answers, just questions!

As far as long-line technique is concerned, anyone who has fished lochs or reservoirs is well enough equipped, although it is advisable to moderate the distance you cast if you wish to hook the fast-taking sea trout. Retrieve speed for salmon should be moderate; for sea trout it can be stepped up a bit. Having said that, I have known salmon to hit a very fast fly indeed – but we aren't talking about a one-in-a-million occurrence here, but a workable, acceptable, reliable approach.

A ta tic that has been working for me over the past few seasons in a good wave situation is to employ semi-buoyant flies on top dropper and point, with a standard pattern in the middle (by semi-buoyant I mean muddlers). This season's favourites have been a Kate McLaren Muddler on the top dropper, a copper-bodied Grimersta-style muddler on the point, and whatever the freshness of the fish or the ambient light dictates in the middle. The use of the two muddlers top and bottom ensures that the top dropper, at least, kicks up quite a fuss in a good wave, and this added disturbance seems to pull fish to the cast in better than average numbers. Perhaps the fact that this style makes every fly fish high in the water is the key to success. Will it work next year? Who knows? Sea trout and salmon are contrary beasts, and it is not given to us to understand them! (See Fig. 13, p. 266) Update: I'm just back from a late September trip to Loch Lomond, where the above tactic boosted the offer rate by a factor of approximately three. My boat partner, Colin McCrory, fished a Claret Bumble on the bob and a double on the point in strict adherence to standard tactics, and I fished a similar bob fly but with a muddler on the point. My response (from the fish) rate was about three times better than Colin's, which I put down solely to the use of the semi-buoyant tail fly. Obviously, the top dropper fly needs to be something the fish will accept. On this Lomond trip they weren't partial to muddlers, hence the Bumble on the top dropper, and the tail fly was sacrificial – after all, if the tail fly makes the bob fly work better by a factor of three, then the tail fly is already doing more than enough, should it not take a fish all day.

standard tactics

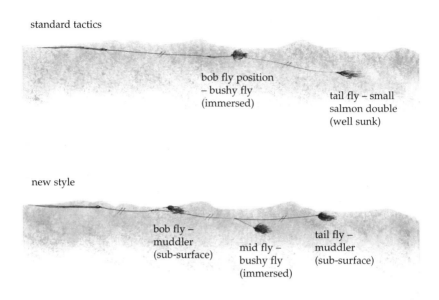

bob fly position
– bushy fly
(immersed)

tail fly – small
salmon double
(well sunk)

new style

bob fly –
muddler
(sub-surface)

mid fly –
bushy fly
(immersed)

tail fly –
muddler
(sub-surface)

*Fig. 13    Salmon and sea trout leader make-up*

# Minor Tactics

## Dapping

To classify dapping as a minor tactic may seem surprising, but that probably says more about me than about the technique. I really can't imagine anything more boring than a day's dapping. I have tried it but I never feel really involved in the process of fishing when the wind is doing almost all the work. It's a bit like trolling, where the angler sits like a statue waiting for the line to go tight. When I'm casting and retrieving flies I know that all my successes and failures stem from my own precise actions or inactions. And buggering about with damp blow-floss just does my head in! However, those who share my views may be quite happy to find themselves in a boat with someone who feels quite the opposite, as dapping can be a good way to bring fish up in the water, where they can then be successfully snared by the wet-fly fisherman. I have heard of this technique working, though I have never experienced it, for most of my sea trout fishing has taken place on the shallow lochs of the isles, where dapping has limited attraction for salmon and sea trout. The long, deep lochs of the mainland, such as Maree, Hope, Stack, Lomond, etc., where fish regularly lie in deep water, are the happy hunting grounds of the dapping fraternity.

This may seem a strange differentiation, but I believe I may have an insight into why there is a different reaction to the dapped fly in deep and shallow lochs. The dapped fly of yore was a great big, over-hackled monstrosity which had a greater resemblance to a dead blackbird than anything of the insect species. Fish lying at depth will likely have little ability to ascertain the actual size of the 'insect' being pulled across the surface, but they will definitely see it – and that is probably more than can be said for the standard wet fly, which probably comes and goes without being spotted. Imagine the scene: A deep-lying fish sees the dapped fly hovering over, or on, the surface film and comes rushing up to investigate. Upon closer inspection the fish realises that it would rather not tangle with this beast, which looks just about capable of reversing the process and eating it, so it swirls underneath it but does not take. When the wet fly appears in the same vicinity the fish, like any self-respecting bully, thinks 'I'm not picking on that big chap, but this wee shrimp over here is going to cop it!' OK, that doesn't account for the reasonably numerous occasions when the dap does take fish, but it does go some way towards explaining why dapping is known for occasionally sorting out the big boys in the salmon and sea trout world. The most successful dappers of my acquaintance who operate on the shallow lochs have always been anglers who have dramatically scaled down their flies or offered natural insects, such as crickets or daddy-long-legs. So, if you are a keen dapping enthusiast who knows of a loch with big sea trout and wouldn't mind me tagging along to flick wet flies at the leviathans that come up to, but fail to take, your flies, give me a call. I'll be with you before you can say 'Damn it! Missed another one!'

I will talk no more of dapping, because it is not a field of endeavour in which I am well versed, and with the gradual decline (and rapid decline in some cases) of the big, deep, mainland sea trout lochs it seems to be a dying art with very few modern practitioners. Perhaps the small signs of revival witnessed at Lomond, Stack and a few other notables may see a resurgence of interest in this ancient skill.

## Dry Fly

Now, dry fly, on the other hand, is a different kettle of fish, if you'll excuse the pun! Sea trout are such surface-active fish when they are 'on the go' that I feel that dry-fly techniques should be a worthwhile tactic. And, considering the basic premise of dapping technique, there would appear to be a strong attracting factor involved in a poor defenceless hairy object sitting in the surface film of water containing sea trout.

Surprisingly, whenever the topic of dry fly for sea trout comes up in the presence of ghillies and estate personnel, these knowledgeable and worthy chaps tend to mutter a bit, shuffle their feet and give the dry-fly protagonist the sort of looks generally reserved for inmates of cells where the walls are nicely padded and the jackets fasten up the back! And I suspect we are back to the percentages game. If the lochs of today were stuffed with fish, as they were at the beginning of the last century when a lot of experimental and innovative techniques were developed, then I'm sure that dry-fly tactics would feature more than they do at present. Why am I so confident? Dry-fly tactics and techniques for loch trout have become a major part of the sport; there are a lot of guys out there who are very good at it; and, most importantly of all, sea trout are not immune to the charms of a dry fly, even if they don't generally see one from one marine season to the next.

I have long had suspicions that dry-fly tactics would be worth a run-out on my favourite sea trout waters, but had never had the proper opportunity to give them a serious go until a very memorable day on Loch Fada, South Uist. Andy Wren and I had been patiently waiting for our Fada day to come around on the rota. Fada is a superb loch, home to massive sea trout, and the whole hotel knew that Loch Roag, just downstream of Fada, had just taken a big run of fresh fish up the Howmore Burn from the Atlantic, and their imminent arrival in Fada was eagerly awaited. Roag, unlike Fada, can often take a big run of fish and give nothing to the angler; some blame Roag's saltwater content, probably justly. However, fresh fish arriving in Fada can produce a bonanza for those lucky enough to have their visit coincide with the recent arrival of fish.

Neither Andy nor I were overly pleased to wake up to sunlight lancing through the bedroom curtains on our allotted Fada day. To find also that the sea bay below the Lochboisdale Hotel had only a few patches of slight ripple following each other in a desultory manner across the bay sent us out on the long road to Fada with more than a faint grudge against the gods of fishing. The portents were grim!

Pushing the boat out from its noust at the north-western end of the loch, our first drift was made from the point of the peninsula into the sandy bay on the north-eastern shore. I had rigged up with trout flies in deference to the light wind, and my bob fly was a greased-up Green Peter. As we inched closer to the sandy beach and ghosted up the side of the weed bed there, a fine sea trout of perhaps a pound and a half, and as fresh as paint, engulfed the Green Peter as it skated high and dry on the surface. Minutes later, on the very last cast of the drift in the lee of the weed bed, another similarly sized fish had a go but missed the fly. No response to the 'wet' flies but distinct interest to the one and only 'dry' one! Andy had neither moved fin nor scale.

Another similarly angled drift into the bay produced nothing and, as the sun climbed higher and brighter into the heavens, I began to think of delving a little deeper in search of more fish. I stuck on a fast intermediate line and slipped the greased-up 'Peter' to the point position in a compromise tactic designed to search the relative depths with the bob and middle flies whilst allowing the point fly to stay up for as long as possible. In contrast to what happens with a floater, the point position is the best for a greased-up fly on an intermediate or sinker, as the retrieve will be well under way before the sink rate of the line actually pulls the tail fly below the surface.

We were without a ghillie, and Andy is no boatman, so when drift-adjusting oar-work was required it was my responsibility. This involved chucking the flies as far from the boat as possible, putting the rod down and jumping up to give the oars a couple of good pulls to avoid running aground/straying too far from the shallow margins, and then rushing back to the rod again. During one of these enforced breaks in fishing, whilst the rod was out of my hands and the oars were in them, I heard an almighty splash from the front of the boat. I instinctively grabbed the rod and found myself into a very angry sea trout which had, with malice aforethought, eaten my Green Peter, which must have been innocently sitting up on the surface film, minding its own business.

Now, I'm no Einstein, but what grey matter I do possess was capable of putting the evidence together – three sea trout moved, all to floating flies – and shouting in my mental ear: 'Wake up! Smell the Gink! Get the bloody dry flies on! Now!' I won't bore you with a blow by blow account of the rest of the day. Sufficient to say that Andy and I, both fishing ginked-up Sedgehogs and Green Peters, managed a very respectable basket of fish in the sort of weather conditions that can make hardened loch sea trout and salmon fishers spontaneously burst into tears. Andy finished the day off with a cracking 4-lb-plus fish, and I had the gilt firmly wiped off my gingerbread by hooking my heaviest ever sea trout only to have the hook (not the leader, the *hook*!) break after a ferocious ten-minute struggle. All the fish were in mint condition, members of a run that had entered Roag a couple of days previously, and looked as though they had arrived in Fada only hours before us.

So, dries can work for *fresh* loch sea trout. The jury is still out on salmon, although, given the usefulness of dapping on lochs and adjusted dry-fly technique on summer rivers, I see no real reason why there shouldn't be a time and a place for loch salmon dry-fly tactics. You may have noted that I stressed 'fresh' in this paragraph's leading sentence. That is because I've only noted this or any similar technique being useful against very fresh fish. But fresh fish are much more accommodating to fishing technique in general than stale fish, and fresh sea trout are inclined to rise and show much more than freshwater conditioned fish – so who really knows? There is much room for experimentation, and a set of ground rules as regards suitable patterns and weather conditions needs to be established. However, most of us get only brief visits to the battlefield, and, faced with perfect conditions on a loch stuffed with fresh-run fish, to spend precious time dabbling with dries rather than standard wets may irritate the most even-tempered ghillie.

## Desperation Tactics

It is a given that you need wind for loch salmon and sea trout, and a fine corduroy ripple just doesn't qualify. So, what happens when there is none? Desperation tactics, that's what!

Here's an example of what I mean. Many years ago the erstwhile Andy and I were fishing Loch Dionard in Sutherland. Reputed to be one of the finest sea trout lochs in Scotland, in its heyday Dionard took tremendous runs of big fish. Like all lochs of its kind it is now in some-what straightened circumstances, and the runs are not what they were. But it is still one of the best mainland lochs and only seriously chal-lenged now by Isles lochs, and I have never visited it and come away fishless (which is more a reflection on the loch than my ability).

Andy and I had the Friday on the loch and, as we had elected to stay overnight in the bothy, we were entitled to fish the loch until the new rods arrived at about 10.00 am on the Saturday. The Friday had been wonderful, with a goodly number of sea trout coming to the fly, Andy's four-pounder being the best of a good bunch. But the Saturday morning dawned bright and calm after the wind and rain of the previous day. I admit I wasn't too keen to venture out, but Andy, faced with a winter in London, wanted to savour every single minute of Highland freedom and seemed quite happy to sit out and study his somewhat hirsute reflection on the unblemished surface of the loch. Anyway, to cut a long story short, Andy caught a couple of very nice fish in what would be considered by experts as absolutely hopeless conditions. How did he do it? Simple! He chucked out his flies and did nothing more than keep in touch with them as they slowly settled in the water. In the course of an hour or so, two fine sea trout swam along and ingested his flies and were caught!

The corollary to this story was that, some years later, I was on Loch Oscaig with Keith Dunbar, a native of those parts. I was telling him of this experience and, as we were plagued with similar conditions, Keith suggested I give it a go. Having been put on the spot, I tried to explain that I thought the key element in the reaction was a special fly of Andy's contrivance, but Keith would have none of it and browbeat me into trying to copy the experiment. With little confidence I chucked the flies out and let them sink, just keeping in touch with a slow figure-8. 'Gosh,' (or words to that effect) I said, 'I've got one!' And so I had. A modest little sea trout had engulfed a Golden Olive Bumble slowly sinking through the depths. On the next cast I missed a steady going-away take, and that was the end of the successful part of the experiment. We didn't get any more response to the technique, but as Oscaig sea trout are about as plentiful as hen's teeth, this was not surprising.

I don't know if either Keith or Andy have tried the technique since, but I haven't. I would suggest, however, that as a usable technique it is flawed. Firstly, it would require the total co-operation of a very broad-minded ghillie at the oars (or *not* at the oars) to take you to likely spots and allow you the time to experiment with a concept he would almost certainly consider ludicrous if not downright insane. And secondly, as the flat calm means that the boat is not moving, the angler must be 'over' fish, so if there are no fish under him then none will be liable to attack the fly. The technique worked on Dionard because it has a tremendous head of fish and the loch is small, and it worked on Oscaig because we were on one of a very few known hotspots (if such a word can be used in relation to Oscaig and its sea trout) and because of a dash of blind luck.

I haven't tried basic trout nymph tactics on becalmed sea trout but there is no good reason why a tactic that works for brown trout shouldn't succeed with their marine brothers and sisters. Another good friend, Eddie Maudling, who regularly visits Lough Currane in Ireland, says he has used such methods to good effect when, due to lack of wind, all else had failed.

## Wading

Virtually everything that has been said above is based on the principle that the angler will be afloat, and in a perfect world he always will be. Sea trout and salmon fishing in lochs is about one or two rods operating out of a (ideally) ghillied boat. But there are times when wind and weather conspire to make boats an ill-advised if not downright dangerous option. Let's face it, a good wave on a sea trout loch if extrapolated onto a southern reservoir would ensure that not a boat left the dock. I have been brought up and served my fly-fishing apprenticeship in a county where people only start commenting on the wind when it gets to gale force, so I have little difficulty fishing effectively in conditions which would terrify a reservoir angler. (This is not arrogance on my part, simply a statement of fact. It is the dreaded flat calms that pose me problems!) However, when the wind speed has reached a pitch that makes safely returning to the head of the wind a serious problem then it is time to moor the boat and take to the wellies.

Wading has its own problems. It is difficult to fish well when the wind is not only trying to blow the angler into the water but also provide him with new earrings, and when rocks arrange themselves into hurdles or pitfalls in front of him. Moreover, where the fish are lying may not be fishable water for the wading angler. That is the negative side. The positive side of wading is that the angler can fish the marginal water properly, in a methodical and precise manner, whereas the boat angler in similar conditions will get one cast into the area before the frisky wind whips him away to pastures new.

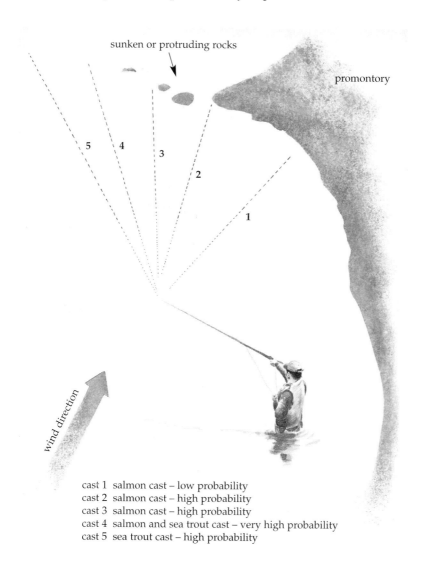

cast 1  salmon cast – low probability
cast 2  salmon cast – high probability
cast 3  salmon cast – high probability
cast 4  salmon and sea trout cast – very high probability
cast 5  sea trout cast – high probability

*Fig. 14  Wading technique for salmon and sea trout lochs*

THE LOCH FISHER'S BIBLE

The one overriding failing of the wading angler is that he often tends to fish too long a line, and I am no exception. I justify this bad practice by claiming that it allows me the cast over deeper water for a sea trout, and also that it allows the flies to cover fish which are unaware of my fumblings and stumblings many yards upwind. Unfortunately, neither argument holds much water. Recently, on a trip to the hallowed waters of the North Harris Estate, I was fishing Loch Scourst in just such a gale. Sharing the fishing with me was a relative newcomer to loch fishing, Paddy Lindsay. I had discovered a pod of sea trout which were just reach-able from dry land, given a long cast. I could cover them easily, because I was wearing chest waders, but Paddy had only knee boots and was struggling somewhat with the conditions. I took him up to this water I had discovered, and he promptly removed a 7-lb summer salmon from the very sheltered water at the head of the wind that I had omitted to fish because I could wade beyond it. Fishing is full of little lessons like this. The trick is to notice them as they flit past, take the lesson on board and, most importantly, not make the same mistake again.

The deep-wading angler can dismiss water which should be fished, but he will be able to fish the weather shore, which is beyond the capa-bilities of the welly-wearing angler. The ability to wade deep and fish shallow is not one to be missed, although I personally find it better in theory than in practice in the sort of wind-speeds which drive me from the boat.

Another important item of knowledge, hard learnt and worth passing on, is that just because you have fished a stretch, and fished it hard, for no result doesn't mean that a return visit might not provide the fish of a lifetime. In wild windy weather it would appear that sea trout and salmon will often desert their lies and roam about the loch, visiting likely areas (burn mouths, rocky bays, etc.) where a well-posi-tioned angler can reap rewards. But if you are not alone on the loch, don't be a water-hog! Allow your fellow anglers a go at a hot-spot. It will save you from drinking alone in the bar later and being omitted from the return trip next year.

Boating is almost all of loch fishing for migratory fish. It is a convivial way to fish and, if you are wise enough to take a ghillie with you and the weather is kind, then the whole loch becomes your play-ground; you can go where you will!

## Ghillies and Boatmen

To refer to a good West Coast or Isles ghillie as a 'boatman' is the ulti-mate insult and will ensure that its unfortunate perpetrator not only casts his fly into some of the most unproductive water in the loch, but will also be surreptitiously steered away from good lies and have any fish he is likely to hook knocked off in the netting process.

A 'ghillie' is probably a better angler on his waters than you will ever be and is worthy of your respect. Treat him properly, and he will work hard for you; offer him a dram; ask his advice; make him your friend and it will mean fish in the boat. Get on his wrong side and your chances of fish will diminish. I leave it to you to decide which is the smarter option. I once shared a boat with a rather arrogant and self-opinionated chap who seriously rubbed the ghillie up the wrong way. Retribution came late in the day when the idiot at the other end of the boat had his cherished hip flask (which the ghillie had not been offered the opportunity to sample) 'accidentally' knocked off the boat seat and into twenty feet of water by an injudicious oar stroke. As ye sow, so shall ye reap!

But nowadays ghillies are becoming a rare breed. It is a poorly paid job, the conditions and hours are unattractive and, although the bulk of clients are OK, there is always the odd exception. And when you can't get a ghillie you end up with a boatman. A boatman is the basic option: a chap who probably doesn't know the water intimately, or how to extract fish from it, and doesn't have a list of killing patterns to hand to improve your chances, but whose principal job is to operate the boat and make sure his clients don't drown. That's fine if the anglers are competent in the areas where the boatman isn't, but the combination of inexperienced anglers and a boatman is not a good one. When no fish are forthcoming to the obvious tactics, boatman and anglers tend to look at one another with an 'Er, what do we do now?' sort of look on their faces. Not good!

If you do come across a good ghillie on a water to which you wish to return, treat him right, book him for your return trip, and send him a Xmas card at the appropriate time. The odd bottle of amber nectar doesn't go amiss, either. In a world of diminishing fish and ghillies, a bit of forward thinking can help guarantee that you get your share of the former by virtue of the help and commitment of the latter.

## Catch and Release

People are acquisitive animals, and there is most definitely something about big, silvery fish which triggers this response in spades. We find it easy to return salmon and sea trout when they are not in the prime of condition, but when they are fresh from the sea the most conscientious of us can lose perspective.

I have little doubt that sporting/angling pressure on sea trout or salmon numbers will neither doom nor save the species. Fly-fishing is a perfect conservation tool, in that it is a very poor means of taking an effective toll on a run of fish; for every fish taken on fly many, for a variety of reasons, carry on regardless. Look at it this way, if there were so few fish left that the removal of even one would endanger species survival, would any of us actually venture forth with any hope of catching at all? I sincerely doubt it. For sporting fishing to have any meaningful result requires good numbers of fish present. If we can catch one in ten we would be doing well (or badly, depending on perspective!).

Given a law of diminishing returns and the capability of a pair of fish to produce thousands of fertilised eggs, catching enough fish to threaten ultimate survival is highly unlikely. But what an enlightened approach to individual fish does do is to produce a climate where the whole species is likely to be protected. In the bad old days when a caught fish was a dead fish regardless of any consideration, we never worried about the safety of a whole species. The fish would go on and be there tomorrow in just as prolific a quantity as yesterday and today. We no longer feel that way; we have seen the writing on the (hatchery) wall. There are a lot less fish today than yesterday, and who knows about tomorrow?

To return a sea trout or salmon probably won't matter a jot to the ultimate survival of the species, but it engenders a proper attitude that enables game anglers, with heads held high and feet firmly braced on the moral high ground, to claim to have the best interests of our prey species at heart. The non-fishing public needs to know that we are not savage, slavering brutes who think the only good fish is a dead fish. And if *we* don't look after the species, who will?

Some West Coast and Isles estates impose a limit on their guests, hoping to restrict the number of slain fish per week per guest. I have my doubts about such a system as I know from previous experience that limits fast become requirements. Being allowed to keep but two sea trout per day often evolves into the *necessity* to kill two sea trout per day, and that surely is not in the spirit of sporting angling.

Ghillies are often not helpful in such a situation. Ghillies are proud men and like their colleagues to know how good their guests are under their supervision, and this competitive spirit often produces a lot more dead fish than is necessary. On balance, ghillies are not greatly in favour of catch and release, although there are notable exceptions. In the best of all worlds the ghillie actively encourages the guest to return fish, but is capable of knowing when one or two are permissible.

Unfortunately sea trout and, to a lesser extent perhaps, salmon, are extremely tableworthy fish, and, as the last of the real hunter/gatherers, we should take a fish home occasionally. I'll go further. I believe it is our duty to take and eat a fish on a regular basis, just to remind ourselves that (a) there is a historical bond between fishermen and fish, we are the hunters, they are the prey, and (b) fish are not playthings, and the best reason we can give for interfering in their lives is to secure quality food for ourselves. Part of my justification for catching fish is that I will kill one from time to time and enjoy eating it. I fail to understand those to whom the death of a fish is anathema (I suspect this comes from a coarse fishing tradition), who won't eat a single mouthful of their prey, but who are quite happy to play a fish to the point of exhaustion before releasing it without a backward glance as they move off in pursuit of the next 'plaything'. I like to take a good fish home for my smoke-house. Home, cold-smoked sea trout is one of the finest foodstuffs to grace the table and is an essential part of the Xmas revelries. I'd hate to come to a day when such an indulgence was forbidden me. However, I suspect that the legions of tree-huggers, augmented by reinforcements from the mandatory catch and release brigade, are hurrying this sad day in my general direction.

All the catch and release in the world will not save our sea trout and salmon so long as other factors continue to push both species towards oblivion. However, a proper spirit of respect for a worthy opponent and a strong desire on the part of all of us to ensure that our children won't grow up in a land devoid of their beauty and grace just *may* produce an environment in which all the protection required arrives naturally.

---

## TIPS AND TOOLS

Take marks when finding a spot or drift to which you may wish to return. It never ceases to amaze me how many people, who should know better, find themselves incapable of repeating a drift accurately. The best means of taking a mark is to draw two imaginary straight lines: one down the wind with the boat being at one end, a spot in the middle distance being the middle of the line and some feature such as a house or rock on a hill in the far distance being the end. Create a similar line at right angles to the boat drift, and you will have precise relocation marks which you can use again and again.

Many people select monofilament by breaking strain which they judge appropriate to the weight/size of the fish they hope to catch. A better criterion for leader material selection would be to match monofilament diameter to hook size. Big flies on light leaders don't fish properly and are prone to snapping off, given even very careful casting. Conversely, it is extremely frustrating to try and thread small hook eyes with heavy monofilament, and the subsequent offering will neither fish well nor look right!

When using a half-blood knot to attach flies to leader material, do not pull on the leader to tighten the knot. Instead pull on the waste end and then trim it flush at the end of the knotting process. Whilst marginally wasteful of leader material this manoeuvre prevents kinking immediately in front of the fly which is unsightly, can prevent the fly fishing on an even keel, and will deter fish.

# 7 The Future

## The Means Justify the Ends?

It is to the undying shame of the Scottish people that wild fish in Scotland are in a precarious situation. The future of the species – salmon, sea trout and brown trout – hangs in the balance.

Just as was the case with the (now extinct) American passenger pigeon, no one from previous generations could have foreseen that the limitless numbers that then made up our native species could have been so drastically reduced in such a short period of time.

To put things into perspective, brown trout are not doing too badly in Scotland as a whole, but in the urbanised Central Belt wild loch trout are virtually extinct. The Highland Boundary Line not only delineates geological change it provides a demarcation line above which wild loch trout flourish and below which virtually no truly wild loch trout, worthy of the name, exist. Surprisingly, the Central Belt has some of the finest river brown trout in the UK, if not Europe, though this state of affairs is due to factors which do not apply to loch trout. It may be imagined that the difficulties of wild loch trout in the Central Belt region is due to water problems, such as abstraction, pollution or change of use, but that would not be even near the mark. The major source of the dilemma is Scotland's fishing club system and the individual angler's changing expectation of a day's fishing.

However, before we enter the tortuous world of club fishing and its ramifications on wild trout, let's have a look at what we are prepared to lose across the board.

It is not a secret that the political view of future economic and development trends in Scotland foresees little growth in traditional industries and much emphasis on light industry and the expansion of the service sector. The effect of this upon land use will have a tremendous impact upon the rural economy and the future of our sport. At the moment Whitehall and Holyrood seem to have little understanding of rural needs or the desire to address the aspirations or lifestyle of country people. What drives people like me to the verge of gibbering insanity is that there seems to be no one in either governing body who realises that urban health requires rural well-being, or that to impose urban solutions to rural problems is like driving a square peg into a round hole with a 5-lb hammer.

Take salmon farming, for example. It seems to matter not a whit that, for the past few decades, the message has not got through to the faceless bureaucrats that one wild salmon caught by a visiting angler is the financial equivalent of a thousand fish reared in a cage. The argument that commercial fish farming supplies jobs in disadvantaged rural areas does not hold water. The same economically deprived areas are the ones capable of producing tourism euros, pounds and dollars through the provision of sport angling. The presence of commercial fish farms in these areas not only decimates the raw material capable of supporting fishing tourism, it also reduces the general tourism appeal by destroying what the visitor found attractive in the first place – the unspoilt scenery, and the impression of wilderness and isolation. To see vast sea lochs bespattered with cages and the shorelines polluted by the detritus associated with them saddens the heart of all people who put quality of life before a few grubby banknotes.

But what about the jobs? So long as the big multi-nationals fight to keep the production costs of cage-reared salmon as low as humanly possible, the better to fight off competition, then so long are rock bottom wages, under-manned fish farms, non-local labour and low investment in the local economy facts of life. In a nutshell, the jobs, such as they are, are not capable of supporting the rural environment where the salmon and sea trout used to run. The term 'Scottish salmon' used to be synonymous with a rare, luxury, epicurean delight. Now the proud King of Fish has been relegated to a cheap, low-quality commodity food, stacked high, on special offer in every supermarket in the land. The internet hums with messages from all over the world telling us of the inherent dangers of eating this stuff on a regular basis. We have sold our wild fish birthright for a mess of cage-reared muck!

The alternative future for these marginal areas – a future without uncontrolled aquatic vandalism, where the only resources are those that nature supplies – lies in environmentally sustainable development. But commercial aquaculture is not even remotely environmentally sustainable; it destroys more life than it produces. Many of our sea lochs are denuded of life through the pollution effects of uneaten fish food; and marine food-chains are smashed to pieces by the wholesale use of destructive chemicals and the industrial-scale harvesting of sandeels to produce food pellets. Gross pollution of the waters of the West Coast brought about by enrichment effects of salmon farming results in massive algal blooms and shellfish poisonous to humans for the bulk of the year. Just like Frankenstein, we have, with the best possible intentions, invented a monster which now has run amok, leaving devastation in its wake.

There is hope in the form of recent legislation – the Water Environment and Water Services (Scotland) Act 2003 – which may see some sort of quango control imposed on an industry which seems unable to control itself. But, being somewhat of a cynic, I never underestimate the ability of the unscrupulous to find ways round any legislation, especially legislation devised and constructed by an executive that appears to have no understanding of matters rural.

I suspect history will deal harshly with us over the long-term environmental damage done to some of our most fragile habitats. That we have stood by and watched as sea trout and wild salmon stocks have plummeted to levels from which they seemed unlikely to recover is unforgivable. The natural resources of this land belong to every one of us, and for the people of Scotland to allow business interests to destroy them is a sad reflection of how little value we put on them.

But, in the end, never underestimate the ability of Nature to bounce back from even the most debilitating attack. In recent months I have seen some signs that sea trout stocks may, in the face of dire and lethal harassment, be rallying. However, such areas of recovery are still greatly outnumbered by river/loch systems which, once famous for their sea trout runs, have not had a fish come up from the sea for many years now, and have neither hope nor expectation of any change in the near future.

Reading the memoirs of our sea-trout-hunting ancestors may make the mouth water, but it doesn't provide a true perspective. Few writers put pen to paper to describe anything other than the good or best days and rarely draw attention to the many poor results or disastrous seasons. Sea trout stocks are, I suspect, prone to cyclical fluctuations regardless of environmental conditions and external pressures, but there is a strong likelihood that the negative effects of the latter can accentuate declines and reduce recovery. If it is natural for sea trout stocks to undergo cyclical declines, the worst-case scenario is as follows: if such a dip in the cycle coincided with detrimental external pressures, then localised extinctions could be a distinct possibility. And that, I think, is what we have experienced in the last few decades.

I would not like to think that I am letting anyone off the hook with what I've said above. I think that, for example, the short-sighted, self-serving, poorly structured and unmonitored actions of the commercial salmon industry has, perhaps unintentionally, managed to eradicate all the wild migratory species in its areas of operation. And when you hold a 12-oz. immature sea trout in your hands with only the sorry remnants of fins left with which to make its way in the water, and you know that the fin damage you are seeing is a direct result of government-supported salmon aquaculture; when you know that whole races of wild fish are jeopardised to provide cheap food of dubious quality which few want – then rage against the system is the logical outcome.

And then there is climate change posing new threats. To listen to the experts, we will either be burned beyond repair or frozen to death; drowned or live in a desert; see Mediterranean summers or the return of the Ice Age. Who knows? Probably no one for certain. But I suspect change is on the way, and change that probably won't be for the better. Sea trout and salmon, particularly, are very prone to climactic change. They spend their juvenile years in some of the harshest environments this country has to offer, and any appreciable change in climate is likely to render marginal niches such as these uninhabitable. Brown trout are more adaptable and will probably survive throughout their range, but where other detrimental factors apply, climate change may just be the final straw that sees threatened trout stocks slip into terminal decline. If the real rabid gloom-and-doom prophets have the right of it, and massive climate change is on the way, we will all have more pressing concerns to deal with than decline in trout stocks.

Time will tell. But whilst the jury is still out, let each and every one of us do all in our power to be part of the solution and not part of the problem.

## The Club System and Its Impact on Wild Trout

Due to water access problems for the common working chap in previous centuries, the angling club system offered the trout fisher his best, and sometimes only, means of securing affordable fishing. Clubs could lease trout waters and run them for the benefit of their members, or they could purchase fishing on desirable waters on a daily basis. Towards the end of the twentieth century both mechanisms threatened wild trout.

Clubs leasing waters wanted, understandably, to supply their members with good fishing. 'Good fishing', in a climate of commercial put-and-take fisheries, tends to imply numbers and size to the man in the street, and if the sporting qualities of the average fish must be sacrificed to achieve these ends then so be it. Good, hard-fighting wild brown trout of 1 lb plus are scorned by anglers who can visit the put-and-takes and expect 2 lb plus rainbows as standard and double-figure fish as an off-chance. To keep their members and afford to renew leases, clubs were pressurised into stocking already self-sufficient wild trout waters with reared fish of an acceptable size and ease of capture. Modern-day anglers are, on average, not prepared to accept the vagaries of wild fish; blanks days are an abomination, and when they occur the fishing proprietor is perceived to be taking money under false pretences. To many modern anglers buying an angling ticket or permit is tantamount to purchasing fish. Having worked on a commercial put-and-take fishery, I am well acquainted with the angler who puts down his money and states 'I'll have two/three/four fish, please!' What he means, of course, is 'I would like to purchase the opportunity to attempt to capture two/three/four fish, if you'd be so kind!' But the implication is there: we no longer pay for the privilege of fishing a water with, perhaps, the added bonus of a fish or two for dinner; we pay for fish (and it doesn't seem to matter whether these fish have any attractive features, such as fins or the ability to pull your 'string' a bit). Just as long as we get our limit of fish! Fish have become a commodity that we purchase like newspapers or chocolate bars.

### The Folly of Stocking Where None Is Needed …

But why should this have compromised the existence of wild trout. Well, the theory is quite simple, and it goes like this. Put rainbow trout or 'stockie' brown trout amongst an indigenous self-sustaining wild brown trout population, and the introduced fish will totally disrupt the natural balance of the environment. In effect, nine times out of ten, the stocked fish will outcompete the residents and push them away from areas of good feeding (i.e. the surface layers). On many waters this is a death sentence to wild brown trout because the depths, to which they inevitably retreat, are not capable of sustaining a healthy trout population.

If we accept that hatchery-reared rainbow trout are relentless 'protein hoovers', then it is not difficult to understand why our more diffident, circumspect indigenous fish should be so intimidated by them. Their feeding routines are totally different, and although rainbow are not required to feed continuously – most trout can do without food for long periods, measured in weeks at a time – their rearing-unit origins encourage them to do so. Wild trout generally tend to be binge feeders, waiting for times of plenty (hatches, etc.) to do some serious feeding, and generally going without in periods of relative famine. Introducing avaricious gluttons such as rainbow trout to such a scenario creates ecological upheaval.

Stock browns are strange creatures, too. One would assume that upon release they would quickly adopt natural behaviour and blend in with their wild cousins. That they do not suggests that the time spent swimming in endless circles in tanks, awaiting the inevitable so-many-times-a-day dinner bell has totally changed their behavioural instincts for the worse. Introducing such habit-adapted fish into environments where indigenous fish are struggling to provide sporting populations is a recipe for disaster. If the water is not capable of providing large numbers of sizeable wild fish enough to satisfy the angler, then pouring in thousands of grown-on 1–2-lb stock brown trout is only going to exacerbate the problem. One would have thought that this would have been obvious to anyone. Of course, if the bodies in charge of introductions and stocking do not care that their work is likely to doom the indigenous wild population, then understanding the consequences of their actions probably won't deter them one iota.

## The Cyclical Nature of Natural Stock Recruitment

Twenty-first century Man loves order and conformity. He pops along to his supermarket and expects to find that his fruit bears no blemish, the potatoes are nice, round and easily peeled, the pork chops are all the same size with a minimum of nasty fat, and the wine tastes the same this year as it did last, and the year before that. Modern man hates chaos and uncertainty. But, unfortunately, nature contains a large slice of chaos in its make-up, and that, I suppose, is why we have been battling it for the last few hundred years. Look around and most of what you see is Man's attempts to force nature in directions which suits humanity.

At the start of every new season the form the fishing will take over the next eight months is hidden from us. Those of us who indulge in wild fishing tend to accept the fact that what we may face can range from sublime to bloody awful. That's just the way it is – or, at least, should be. We *should* experience great years and hellish ones. The troughs and peaks *should* exist and not be ironed out in one long, tedious, mediocre sameness. After all, how can you appreciate a perfect season unless you have first-hand knowledge of the alternative?

But, alas, it is not in modern man's nature to accept the poor seasons:

they must all be perfect. I hear it all the time as I travel thither and yon. 'Bloody awful season! They should put some effin' fish in that loch!' That's why it is possible to find perfectly good, self-sustaining waters into which lorry-loads of fish are regularly injected by well-meaning people who don't have a clue what they are attempting to do or of its ramifications.

Wild lochs are, by their very nature, cyclical in stock levels. Some years are very good, some are OK, and some are just abysmal. That is the nature of the beast. Trout have good spawning years (which will, all other things being equal, produce a series of years afterwards during which stock levels will be high), probably followed by a few poor seasons until the next bumper spawning season comes along.

I used to watch Boardhouse Loch in Orkney go through this routine. The funny thing about it was that, from a close-up perspective, it looked as though the year-to-year stock levels were all over the place, but if you stepped back and took the long view it was actually very well-ordered. It went something like this:

*year one* – poor fishing year but good spawning year with the burns stuffed with quality fish (this was only identifiable in retrospect);

*year two* – hordes of undersized fish appearing from mid-season onwards; poor spawning year due to high proportion of immature fish in stock;

*year three* – bumper quantities of 10-in. fish (generally regarded as a poor year with no quality);

*year four* – great season with lots of fish averaging close to the pound mark; poor spawning due to high proportion of immature fish in stock;

*year five* – connoisseur's year and a big fish year (low quantity, high quality);

*year six* – poor fishing year but good spawning year with the burns stuffed with quality fish.

Boardhouse had a five-year cycle. This wasn't clockwork, you understand (there were many variables), but it was possible to see a pattern forming in the changing production of trout from season to season.

Boardhouse was lucky, in that in its poor years anglers would fish any one of the other superb Orkney lochs. But if it had been the best (or only) loch in an area where fishermen imposed a high level of demand and of expectation, then it is not hard to see impatience with the natural cycle arising. The likely outcome would be that in, say, year two man could step in and try to iron out the bumps by pumping in some grown-on stock to improve the quality, or in year five he could return to dump in some fingerlings to boost stock levels.

Interference of this nature will totally stop the natural rhythm and lead to any number of possible outcomes, none of them satisfactory to anyone. I have seen such impatient meddling with the natural rhythms of lochs all over Scotland, with the inevitable destruction of natural stock. The most common outcome is that the natural stock declines to such an extent that artificial stocking becomes essential if the loch is going to provide attractive (?) fishing for the angler. It is an easy thing to smash an eggshell, but it is beyond the hand of man to restore it to its original form. Similarly, it is all too easy to rush in to stock a self-sustaining water. The hard part comes in resurrecting the loch once its natural stock has crashed due to man's interference.

If we want to distance ourselves from the ongoing destruction and reduction of our wild trout loch stock, we have to start taking the long view. Hatchery men must hold their hand until they understand the natural rhythms of the loch they wish to help, and intercede only when the potential damage brought about by their intervention can be judged to be outweighed by the potential benefits. Anglers can help by taking the bad seasons 'on the chin', so to speak, and endeavouring to understand that the poor seasons are an investment, and that the rewards of patience will be better seasons.

Where the hand of Man *is* welcome in giving the loch's self-sustain-ability a leg-up is in habitat enhancement. Spawning burns can always do with a nip here and a tuck there. Spawning gravels respond well to a good rake in the months before the spawners arrive. Banks will be improved by a bit of shoring-up here and a touch of flow improvement there. Cattle-drinking places should be fenced off, so that bankside erosion is controlled. Bushes can be encouraged in strategically impor-tant locations to protect and preserve juvenile fish stock. Impediments in the streams can be removed to aid access.

But this work is endless and labour intensive, and relies on willing hands. How much easier it would be to back up a lorry load of tank-reared stockies to the loch edge and dump them in. Instant gratification is the thing. Ah well, stock in haste and repent at leisure!

## The Great Leven Debacle

Many waters in the Central Belt or closely related areas see potentially viable (self-sustaining) waters stocked with hatchery fish on a yearly basis, if not more often. Loch Leven is a prime example. Leven has, for hundreds of years, produced vast quantities of wild brown trout to the extent that at one time it was commercially netted. But, due to industrial, domestic and agricultural pollution of criminal proportions throughout the later half of the twentieth century, the water quality finally reached its nadir in the final decade of the century. Algal blooms on a life-threatening scale menaced all life within their reach, trout died in vast quantities, and the loch was closed for fishing and all other human activity. For years, the management of the fishery had, every year, introduced a smattering of wild brown trout of Leven origin, raised in its own hatchery, back into the loch. This had probably had little or no impact upon total stock densities in the loch, but we will never know because there seems to have been no practical marking of hatchery fish to provide a percentage of total catch figures. A friend and workmate of mine once said that stocking without science is simply vandalism – and he is one of the country's leading fishery scientists and biologists, and expert on stocking practice, we can assume he knows what he is talking about. But stocking without science has become the rule rather than the exception. Clubs with leases on waters, be they loch or river, regularly stock with grown-on fish without the slightest understanding of potential repercussions. Even worse, stocking becomes a habit, in that it takes place whether it is required or not.

Leven and its rainbow trout are a prime example. There never was a time when indigenous trout populations in the loch required the boost delivered by stocking; even after the massive fish death of 1992, fishery biologists reassured the loch management that more than enough wild fish remained alive to support the fishery. The introduction of stock rainbows never had anything to do with providing enough fish for fishing demand, what the management of the loch intended to do was to stabilise the financial standing of their enterprise by luring anglers back to the loch with the attraction of rainbow trout. In this they have failed. This failure has come about because there never were enough rainbow trout introduced to make it a properly stocked water, and what 'stockies' were introduced destroyed the natural brown trout fishery. If you'll excuse the pun, the stock of the loch has become devalued in the eyes of all concerned – brown trout catches have plummeted, and the rainbows failed to make up the deficit – and discriminating anglers are leaving in droves. The stocking policy has failed spectacularly, both in terms of the indigenous fish population and in economic terms.

As I write, there are strong rumours that the Leven rainbow trout experiment is over, and that the management is now returning to a policy of stocking with native Leven trout only. For this new plan to work will require determination from Leven Fisheries, goodwill, understanding and forbearance from the customers, and patience from both. The brown trout will not necessarily respond overnight, and many that enjoyed Leven as a rainbow fishery of sorts will be keen to see this new experiment fail. We Scottish fishermen are very often our own worst enemies and are quick to condemn and criticise those who sit at the controls of our sport. We expect infallibility in others but tolerance for our own fallibility in return. That does not bode well for this new phase in the Great Leven Experiment.

That I, and many other like-minded souls, would like to see Leven returned to a wild-trout-only fishery is no secret. We know the problems associated with the introduction of grown-on stock fish into an already self-sustaining fishery. I, therefore, suspect that the management plan to stock with large numbers of fish from its own hatchery is flawed. In any event, it is obvious from any perspective that the rainbows must go.

I would also like to see Leven cease to be an economic football. I firmly believe that a fishery as important as Leven, culturally as well historically, should not be in the hands of private individuals. If the principal interest of management is not in the fish or the fishery *per se*, but in the profit and loss accounts at the end of the financial year, then the long-term outlook is bleak. I would suggest that Leven's only real hope in an uncertain future is to belong to the nation. Unfortunately, I wouldn't entrust the welfare of a puddle at the side of the road to the current crop of bureaucrats at Holyrood. There seems to be no safe way out for Leven, and I suspect things may get a whole lot worse before they get better.

## A Whipped Dog With No Teeth

Scottish Natural Heritage (SNH), as a management partner of Loch Leven, has a major say in the management policy. This organisation is keen to see the loch maintained as a fishery, because this fulfils many of its requirements. But considering the somewhat dubious role of the SNH in supporting the continuation of the rainbow trout debacle, not too much faith should be put in its management ability, its under-standing of the biological dynamics of a successful fishery, or its resistance to political or economic pressure.

And consider this. Loch Leven is a Site of Special Scientific Interest (SSSI). There is a prime management rule for any SSSI: no alien species will be introduced for any reason. This is a *sine qua non*; without it there is no point in designating any area as an SSSI. Do you begin to see my point? Yep! You guessed it. What are rainbow trout, by any definition an alien species, doing swimming about in a loch which is a SSSI and, as such, is part managed by SNH? SNH, as the custodian of our valu-able SSSI resource, has totally betrayed what little trust and credibility it had by rubber-stamping rainbow trout introduction into Loch Leven. Many years ago, when lamenting the demise of the Nature Conservancy Council (Scotland) and concerned about the effectiveness of its politically acceptable replacement, Scottish Natural Heritage, I described the latter as a dog with no teeth. I now am prepared to go further and call it a whipped dog with no teeth. The part it played in the demise of Loch Leven as fishery, cultural icon, world famous and important natural site, is a national disgrace.

If SNH policy formation is going to be dependent upon the vagaries, whims and prejudice of party politics, then I believe the welfare of the Scottish environment is in unsafe hands. The late, lamented NCC (Scotland) was unwise enough to challenge Conservative Party policy, as it applied to the rural environment, and paid the ultimate price. Short-term political aims and long-term environmental welfare can only coexist to the detriment of the latter; the Common Agricultural Policy and Fishery Policy show that to be an unarguable truth. And yet Green politics lack grassroots popular support, so we seem to be in an impasse.

Are there signs of change? To be honest, not much, but we live ever in hope!

## Wild Trout Welfare and Sustainability

A dynamic system is a construct in which everything is interlinked, and what affects one aspect has knock-on effects on all the others. What we call nature is a classic example. Elsewhere I have called it a jigsaw, but it more closely resembles a house of cards, each integral part dependent and reliant upon the other. What was constructed largely in the absence of man is not responding well to his influence on the dynamic process, and we are witness to this effect today. Diminishing migratory runs, destruction of habitat, eradication of species and climate change all point to the fact that where man is not actively supportive of nature he is ultimately destructive. There appears to be no middle ground. Scottish wild trout populations and their preferred habitat are prime examples of this perception.

The Orkney lochs could serve as a model for the elements required for perfect trout habitat. They are shallow, with very little water deeper than twelve feet. The loch waters are, by and large, on the alkaline side of the pH scale. They contain many dissolved minerals and salts, essential for invertebrate life support. The underlying rock formations of flagstone are excellent for buffering the waters from the effects of any acidic rain. And many of the lochs have a good network of tributary burns that provide excellent and extensive spawning facilities.

From a climatic perspective, the short summer, counterbalanced by extended day length and cool summer temperatures, ensure that trout feed hard and long right through the optimum part of the fishing season. The mild winters allow fish to quickly regain fitness after the rigours of the spawning burn (it is not unusual to see trout taking advantage of a windfall midge hatch in the brief daylight hours of a mild midwinter day). The windy nature of the summer climate ensures that the shallow loch waters get well oxygenated on a regular basis, pretty much when necessary. And long droughts or intense heat waves are great rarities.

All this is very positive, but there are negative aspects. The wind working upon shallow water can cause intense turbidity, turning many of the lochs into muddy puddles after a period of gales. (The presence of material that creates the potential for destructive turbidity can be a product of unnatural land use within the catchment area.) The northern latitude of the islands means that summers are short and winters long, cutting valuable fishing time at either end of the season; whereas Ireland can provide excellent boat fishing as early as February, Orkney boats rarely emerge from their winter lairs until mid-April, and are sneaking back under cover by mid-September.

The fertility of the lochs is a by-product of land fertility, and land use practice in Orkney can have a profound effect on its lochs. The fertility of the waters can be turned from a benefit into a curse by the interaction of agricultural and domestic effluent. Excessive weed and algal production has been a worrying aspect of ecological upheaval brought on by changes in land use. Intensive agriculture is a vitally important aspect of the local economy but it impacts strongly on the lochs and trout habitat. The important spawning burns are frequently threatened by side effects of bad agricultural practice – burns are often canalized to improve drainage; water courses have a history of being used to remove unwanted, polluting, animal by-products (and this hellish practice still goes on); spawning gravels can become impacted and clogged with silt as a direct product of land tillage; the use of burns as watering places for cattle can lead not only to habitat destruction but also to direct pollution from animal faeces, creating many imbalances in these fragile environments.

Intensive agriculture and top-quality trout fishing habitats make incompatible bedfellows. It is a sad fact of life that modern agricultural practice is severely affected by the harsh economic climate that applies to almost all modern day rural activity. Many vital decisions,

made in the offices of bank managers, have major impacts upon
environmental issues. A state of impending financial ruin is not one
conducive to best environmental practice in the countryside. And
nowhere is this sad state of affairs more obvious than on the Harray
loch.

Harray is, or perhaps was, one of Scotland's finest trout waters, and
the effects of agricultural practice on this fine trout water have been
profound. OK, let's be fair, the problems that Harray has faced can also
be laid, in part, at the door of domestic effluent disposal techniques
within the catchment area. But the drive for early growth and maxi-
mization of harvest has seen an exponential increase in fertilizer use,
both chemical and organic. That this has been a major factor in habitat
attrition within the Harray catchment area cannot be denied or
ignored. But it is a testament to the resilience of nature that regardless
of the ongoing environmental damage, Harray is still a very fine fly
water.

When I first fished Harray, way back in the early 1960s, trout
production was colossal. Baskets of thirties and forties to a single rod
in a day were relatively common. It must be said that individual size
was not much to write home about, but the sporting potential of the
loch was unsurpassed by any water in the UK or Ireland. This happy
state of affairs continued up until the great Canadian Pond Weed
disaster of the mid-1980s. Then some strange things happened. As the
pondweed clogged the loch and forced fish into the diminishing clear
areas the catch rates soared, then, when the weed died off, the
massive release of nutrients from rotting weed created rampant algal
blooms, and the catch rates dropped like a stone. By the early to
middle 1990s, as the wild pendulum-like swings of water quality
started to stabilize somewhat, some very fine fish were appearing in
baskets throughout the season. Before the 1980s a 2-lb fish was
worthy of note, and fish over 3 lb were, like honest men in parlia-
ment, thin on the ground. The late 1990s put an end to all that, and
2-lb-plus fish were appearing with boring regularity, while the
average size jumped from a low of ten ounces to a present-day high
of fourteen. Add all this to the 2003 reports of staggering water
quality, the like of which has not been seen on Harray for twenty
years, and the best seasonal catch in living memory, and it is possible

to think that Harray's worst days are behind it, and it is once again the finest trout loch in Scotland.

## And in Conclusion

So what do you expect from me? A happy pat on the back and a murmured 'I'm sure it'll all turn out for the best!' Remember, I am a cynic. In the world of fishing, fishery management and national and local government, I have seen the best that man can do and the worst. The worst has always been more spectacular and long-lasting.

But I am one of that rare breed – the cynical optimist. I know that nature will inevitably win. It may be after man has joined the dinosaurs as archaeological oddities, but the day will come when everything we have destroyed will be resurrected. Grass will grow through concrete, wild flowers flourish on refuse dumps, and the bright silvery fish of tomorrow will run the dead streams of today. Brown trout will regain the waters lost to their transatlantic cousins. And the inert, poisoned and polluted stanks that offend us so, will one day sparkle in the sunshine of a new dawn.

And how far off is that new dawn? Well, that will depend on what we do today. My favourite little homily is 'Today is the first day of the rest of your life!' I don't know about you, but that strikes me as being quite appropriate.

A' the best!

## TIPS AND TOOLS

It is a responsibility of all anglers to do what they can to protect their own interests. There should be no excuse for anyone to be unaware that there are people in our society who are opposed to angling and anglers. Lack of respect for the environment, fish and other animals which inhabit the watery world of loch and river only supplies these people with the ammunition they require to mobilize the community at large against sport fishing.

Every single one of us has the potential to destroy or enhance our sport. Keep these few rules and we will make friends and lose enemies:

- Only kill fish that you, family or friends will eat, and return carefully those that are surplus to requirements.
- Dispose of litter thoughtfully. Take your rubbish home if there are no convenient litter bins.
- Waste monofilament nylon is very destructive to wildlife as well as being unsightly. At worst cut it into very short lengths before disposing of it. Much better, however, to take it home and put it in the bin.
- Always remember that each and every one of us is an ambassador for our sport, and that the many will be judged on the actions of the individual.

# Bibliography and Suggested Reading

Bridgett, R.C., *Loch Fishing in Theory and Practice* (Herbert Jenkins, 1924)

Frost, W.E. and Brown, M.E., *The Trout* (Collins, 1967)

Goddard, John, *Trout Fly Recognition* (A & C Black, 1966)

Greer, Ron, *Ferox Trout and Arctic Charr* (Swan Hill Press, 1995)

Harris, J.R., *An Angler's Entomology* (Collins, 1952)

Headley, Stan, *Trout & Salmon Flies of Scotland* (Merlin Unwin, 1997)

Kingsmill Moore, T.C., *A Man May Fish* (Herbert Jenkins, 1960)

McLaren, Charles, *The Art of Sea Trout Fishing*, rev. edn (Unwin Hyman, 1989)

Stuart, Hamish (ed. Rafael Sabatini), *The Book of the Sea Trout* (Jonathan Cape, 1952)

# Index

Note: entries in **bold** indicate photographs or illustrations within the text

**C**

caddis fly (gen. *Trichoptera*), *see* sedges
caddis larvae, 96, 109, 171–2
Caenis sp., 118, 126–9, 172–3, 188, 208, 233–4
Caithness, 37, 195, 230–5, 243
Caladail, Loch, 38, 225–6, 232
camouflage, 35
Canadian Pondweed (*Elodea canadensis*), 178, 293
Cape Wrath, 101
Cardine Bay, 238
Carnill, Bob, 207
Castle Island, 236
catch and release, 47–9, 151, 276–8
Central Fisheries Board, Ireland, 46
char, 15, 16, 76, 227–8
Chironomid sp., *see* midge
Clan Chief, 258
climate change, 282–3
clothing, 90–1
cloud, 179–80
coming short, 27–8, **28**, 77, 98, 146, 151, 194
conservation, 47–9, 151, 276–8, 294
copepods, 201–2
cow dung fly (gen. *Diptera*), 118, 123, 139, 141, 174, 180
Crane Flies (gen. *Diptera*), *see* Daddy-long-legs
Croispol, Loch, 225–6
culling, selective, 48
Currane, Lough, 272,
cyclical nature of stock recruitment, the, 282, 285–8

**D**

Dabblers, 131–2, 138, 153, 155, 158–9, 173
Dabblers, Sparse, 156, 158–9
Daddy-long-legs, 118, 123–4, 139–41, 174, 180
daphnia, 23, 34, 77–8, 172–3
dapping, 266–7
dapping flies, 157
dapping technique, 266–7
density compensation in fly lines, 81, 138
Dionard, Loch, 253, 270–1
Doobry, 40, 159, 258
drogues, 84–6, 190
dropper lengths, 69, 257
droppers, 66–8, 256–7
Druidibeg, Loch, 205
dry fly
    fishing, 86, 107, 116–29, 139–45, 147, 229, 233, 241, 268–70
    leaders, 68–9
Duchess' Loch, 101–2
Dunbar, Keith, 206, 229, 264–5, 271
Durness limestone lochs, 33, 37, 75, 225–30
dynamic process, 16–18, **19**, 201, 291

**E**

early season fly fishing, 75
Earn, River, 18
East Ollay, 248
ectotherm, 22
eels, 23–4, 201, 203–4
emergers, 120
environmentally sustainable development, 281